A
Writer's Handbook
from A to Z

DONNA GORRELL

ST. CLOUD STATE UNIVERSITY

ALLYN AND BACON

Boston   London   Toronto   Sydney   Tokyo   Singapore

Editor in Chief, Humanities: Joseph Opiela
Editorial Assistant: Brenda Conaway
Production Administrator: Rowena Dores
Editorial-Production Service: Tara L. Masih
Text Designer: Anna George
Cover Administrator: Linda Dickinson
Manufacturing Buyer: Louise Richardson
Composition Buyer: Linda Cox

Library of Congress Cataloging-in-Publication Data
Gorrell, Donna
    A writer's handbook from A to Z / Donna Gorrell.
      p. cm.
    Includes indexes.
    ISBN 0-205-13764-4
    1. English language—Rhetoric—Handbooks, manuals, etc. 2. English
language—Grammar—Handbooks, manuals, etc. I. Title.
PE1408.G6294 1994
808'.042—dc20
                                          93-32599
                                               CIP

 This book is printed on
recycled, acid-free paper.

Printed in the United States of America
10 9 8 7 6 5 4 3 2 1   98 97 96 95 94 93

Contents

Topical Guide to Alphabetical Entries   *xi*

Preface   *xvi*

PART ONE   WRITING AN ESSAY   *1*

The Rhetoric of Writing   *3*
Audience   *4*
The Role of the Writer   *5*
Subject and Purpose   *6*
   Informative purposes   6
   Persuasive purposes   7
The Process of Writing   *8*
Prewriting and Invention   *8*
   Listing or brainstorming   8
   Mapping or clustering   9
   Journalist's questions   9
   Classical probes   11
   Freewriting   12
   Imitation   12
Thesis   *13*
   Informative and persuasive theses   14
   Placement of theses   14
Development   *14*
   Narration   15
   Description   15
   Exemplification   16
   Cause and effect   16
   Classification   17
   Comparison and contrast   18
   Analogy   18

Definition 19
Process analysis 19
Organization *20*
Question and answer 20
Problem and solution 21
Emphasis 21
General to specific 21
Specific to general 21
Outlining *22*
Drafting *23*
Introductions and conclusions 23
Coherence 24
Revision *25*
Reading as if you were the reader 25
Using invention questions 26
Applying a checklist 26
Getting peer review 27
Sample student paper, draft 28
Editing *30*
Proofreading *31*
Sample student paper, final draft 31

PART TWO   THE ALPHABETICAL REFERENCE GUIDE 35

A
Abbreviations *37*
Absolute Phrases *38*
Abstract Words/Concrete Words *39*
Adjective Clauses *39*
Adjective Phrases *40*
Adjectives *40*
Adverb Clauses *42*
Adverb Phrases *42*
Adverbs *42*
Agreement of Pronouns and Antecedents *44*
Agreement of Subjects and Verbs *46*

Antecedents *52*
Apostrophes *53*
Appositive *55*
Articles *55*

B
Brackets *60*

C
Capitalization *61*
Cases *63*
Clauses *67*
Clichés *67*
Collective Nouns *68*
Colloquialisms *68*

Colons *68*
Commas *69*
Commas, Unnecessary *73*
Comma Splices *77*
Common Nouns *79*
Complements *80*
Complex Sentences *80*
Compound Antecedents *81*
Compound-Complex
  Sentences *81*
Compound Predicates *82*
Compound Sentences *83*
Compound Words *84*
Conjunctions *85*
Connectors *87*
Connotation/Denotation *88*
Contractions *88*
Coordinating Conjunctions *89*
Coordination *89*
Count Nouns *90*
Cover Letter *91*

D
Dangling Modifiers *91*
Dash *93*
Demonstrative Pronouns and
  Adjectives *94*
Determiners *95*
Diction (Word Choice) *95*
Dictionaries *96*
Direct Objects *98*
Double Negatives *99*

E
Ellipsis Dots *100*
Emphasis *101*
Euphemism *103*
Exclamation Point *103*
Exclamatory Sentences *104*
Expletives *104*

F
Facts *104*

Fallacies in Logic *105*
Figures of Speech *108*
Finite Verbs *108*
Fragments (of Sentences) *109*
Fused Sentences (Run-on
  Sentences) *112*

G
Gender *113*
Generalizations *114*
General Words/Specific
  Words *114*
Gerund Phrases *115*
Gerunds *115*

H
Helping Verbs *117*
Homonyms *119*
Hyphens *120*

I
Idioms *120*
Imperative Mood *122*
Indefinite Articles *122*
Indefinite Pronouns and
  Adjectives *122*
Independent Clauses *124*
Indicative Mood *124*
Indirect Objects *124*
Indirect Questions *124*
Indirect Quotations *125*
Infinitive Phrases *126*
Infinitives *127*
Intensifiers *128*
Interjections *129*
Interrogative Words *129*
Intransitive Verbs *129*
Inverted Sentence Order *129*
Irregular Verbs *130*
Italics (Underlining) *131*

J
Jargon *132*

L
Linking Verbs   *134*

M
Mass Nouns (Noncount
   Nouns)   *135*
Mechanics   *137*
Metaphors   *137*
Misplaced Modifiers   *138*
Misspelled Words,
   Common   *139*
Mixed Constructions   *142*
Modals   *144*
Modifiers   *144*
Mood of Verbs   *145*

N
Negative Constructions   *146*
Nominalizations   *147*
Nonrestrictive Elements   *148*
Nonsexist Language   *149*
Nonstandard Usage   *150*
Noun Clauses   *151*
Noun Phrases   *151*
Nouns   *151*
Number   *153*
Numbers   *153*

O
Object Complements   *155*
Objects   *155*

P
Parallelism   *157*
Paraphrases   *159*
Parentheses   *160*
Parenthetical Elements   *160*
Participial Phrases   *161*
Participles   *162*
Parts of Sentences   *164*
Parts of Speech   *165*
Passive Voice   *166*
Periods   *167*

Person   *169*
Personal Pronouns   *169*
Phrases   *170*
Plagiarism   *172*
Plurals   *172*
Possessive Case   *176*
Predicates   *178*
Prefixes   *178*
Prepositional Phrases   *179*
Prepositions   *180*
Pronoun Reference   *181*
Pronouns   *183*
Proper Adjectives   *187*
Proper Nouns   *186*
Punctuation   *186*

Q
Question Marks   *187*
Questions   *188*
Quotation Marks   *188*
Quotations   *190*

R
Redundancies   *191*
Reflexive Pronouns   *192*
Regular Verbs   *192*
Relative Adjectives and
   Adverbs   *192*
Relative Clauses   *193*
Relative Pronouns   *194*
Repetition   *195*
Restrictive and Nonrestrictive
   Elements   *196*
Run-on Sentences   *197*

S
Semicolons   *198*
Sentence Patterns   *199*
Sentences   *201*
Sentence Types   *203*
Sentence Variety   *205*
Shifts   *207*
Simile   *211*

Simple Sentences *211*
Singular *212*
Slang *212*
Slash *213*
Spelling *214*
Split Infinitives *217*
Standard English *217*
Subject Complements *217*
Subject of Sentence *217*
Subjunctive Mood *219*
Subordinate (Dependent)
  Clauses *219*
Subordination *221*
Suffixes *222*

T
Tag Questions *223*
Tenses of Verbs *224*
Titles *229*

Transitional Adverbs
  (Conjunctive Adverbs) *230*
Transitive Verbs *232*

U
Uncountable Nouns *232*

V
Verbal Phrases *233*
Verbals *233*
Verbs *234*
Voice (Active or Passive) *241*

W
Wordiness *243*
Word Omissions *246*

Z
ZIP Code *247*

PART THREE   WRITING A RESEARCH
PAPER *249*

The Community of Scholars *251*
Types of Research *252*
  Primary research 253
  Secondary research 253
Overview of the Research Process *254*
The Rhetoric of Research Reports *255*
  Your role as writer 255
  Your audience 256
  Your subject 257
  Your purpose 257
Selecting and Narrowing the Topic *258*
  Exploring your own interests 258
  Exploring your library 259
Phrasing Your Research Question(s) and Tentative Thesis *260*
Developing Your Bibliography *262*
Searching the Library *264*
  The reference collection 264
  Periodicals 265
  The central catalog 268

Government publications   269
Computer searches   270
Taking Notes on Your Reading   *270*
Index cards   270
Other note-taking systems   272
Quotation, paraphrase, and summary   272
Plagiarism   274
Organizing Your Notes: Thesis and Outline   *275*
Evaluating your notes and sources   276
Drafting Your Paper   *277*
Using your sources   277
Introduction, conclusion, and title   278
Coherence and clarity   279
Documenting Your Sources   *280*
Documenting with MLA (Modern Language Association)   280
*Documenting with APA (American Psychological
   Association)   283*
Revising Your Paper   *286*
Format of Your Final Draft   *289*
The End   *291*
Sample Student Research Papers (MLA and APA)   *292*
Outline of sample student paper   313

PART FOUR   SPECIALIZED WRITING   319

Abstracts and Summaries   *321*
Writing a summary or an abstract   321
Critiques   *323*
Writing a critique   323
Essay Examinations   *324*
Preparing for the essay exam   324
Writing an essay exam   326
One final point   328
Business Letters   *328*
Appearance   328
Parts of the letter   329
Envelope   331
Memorandums   *332*
Application Letters and Resumés   *334*

Index   *338*

ESL Index   *361*

Topical Guide
to Alphabetical Entries

Parts of Speech

Verbs   *234*
Nouns   *151*
Pronouns   *183*
Adjectives   *40*
Adverbs   *42*
Prepositions   *180*
Conjunctions   *85*
Interjections   *129*
Articles   *55*

Sentence Parts

Clauses   *67*
  Independent clauses   67
  Subordinate clauses   67
  Adjective clauses   39
  Adverb clauses   42
  Noun clauses   151
  Restrictive and nonrestrictive elements   196
Phrases   *170*
  Prepositional phrases   179
  Verbal phrases   233
  Participial phrases   161
  Infinitive phrases   126
  Gerund phrases   115
  Noun phrases   151
  Verbal phrases   233
  Restrictive and nonrestrictive elements   196
Modifiers   *144*
  Adjectives   40
  Adverbs   42
  Phrases   170
  Clauses   67

Dangling modifiers   91
Misplaced modifiers   138
Pronouns   *183*
   Cases   63
   Reference   181
   Agreement with antecedents   52
   Gender   113
Verbs   *234*
   Agreement with subjects   46
   Transitive   232
   Intransitive   129
   Linking   134
   Helping (auxiliary)   117
   Irregular   130
   Tenses   224
   Person   169
   Number   153
   Voice (active or passive)   241
   Mood   145
   Shifts   207
   Verbals   233

Sentence Structure

Sentences   *201*
Coordination   *89*
Subordination   *221*
Sentence Patterns   *199*
Sentence Types   *203*
Sentence Variety   *205*

Sentence Faults

Comma Splices   *77*
Fused Sentences (Run-on Sentences)   *112*
Fragments (of Sentences)   *109*
Subject-Verb Agreement Errors   *46*
Pronoun-Antecedent Agreement Errors   *44*
Faulty Predication   *178*
Shifts   *207*
Mixed Constructions   *142*
Faulty Parallelism   *158*

Punctuation

Commas   *69*
Periods   *167*
Semicolons   *198*
Colons   *68*
Apostrophes   *53*
Question Marks   *187*
Exclamation Point   *103*
Hyphens   *120*
Dash   *93*
Parentheses   *160*
Brackets   *60*
Quotation Marks   *188*
Ellipsis Dots   *100*

Mechanics

Capitalization   *61*
Abbreviations   *37*
Numbers   *153*
Italics (Underlining)   *131*
Spelling   *214*
Hyphens   *120*
Contractions   *88*
Dates   *154*
Apostrophes   *53*
Manuscript Format   *290*

Spelling

Commonly Misspelled Words   *139*
Spelling Rules   *215*
Homonyms   *119*
Plurals   *172*
Apostrophes   *53*
Compound Words   *84*
Hyphens   *120*

Style and Clarity

Diction (Word Choice)   *95*
   Abstract and concrete words   *39*

General and specific words   *114*
Connotation and denotation   *88*
Dictionaries   *96*
Idioms   *120*
Nonsexist language   *149*
Wordiness   *243*
Sentence Variety   *205*
Coordination   *89*
Subordination   *221*
Emphasis   *101*
Parallelism   *157*
Repetition   *195*
Wordiness   *243*
Coherence and Transitions   *230*
Manuscript Format   *290*

Common Errors (marked ⚠ in alphabetical entries)

Comma Omissions   *69*
With introductory elements   *70*
In compound sentences   *70*
With nonrestrictive sentence elements   *71*
In series   *71*
Unnecessary Commas   *73*
Comma Splices   *77*
Fused Sentences (Run-on Sentences)   *112*
Sentence Fragments   *109*
Faulty Pronoun Reference   *184*
Lack of Agreement between Pronouns and Antecedents   *44*
Lack of Agreement between Subjects and Verbs   *46*
Faulty Verbs   *234*
Wrong or missing verb endings   *237*
Wrong tense   *224*
Wrong Word Choice   *95*
Misused Apostrophe   *53*
In possessive nouns   *53*
In possessive pronouns   *243*
In contractions   *54*
Confusion of it's *and* its   *132*
Shifts   *207*
In verb tense   *208*
In pronouns   *207*

Wrong or Missing Preposition   *179*
Faulty Parallelism   *158*
Misspellings   *139*
(In addition, see CAUTION notes within entries.)

ESL Interests (marked ▼ in alphabetical entries)

Verbs   *234*
 Agreement of subjects and verbs   46
 Helping verbs   117
 Infinitives   127
 Participles   161
 Gerunds   115
 Irregular verbs   130
 Modals   144
 Numbers   153
 Plurals   172
 Tenses of verbs   224
 Voice (active or passive)   241
Nouns   *151*
 Count nouns   90
 Mass nouns (noncount nouns)   135
Pronouns   *183*
 Cases   63
 Agreement of pronouns and antecedents   44
 Demonstrative pronouns and adjectives   94
Articles   *55*
Idioms   *120*
Diction (Word Choice)   *95*
Prepositions   *180*
Adjectives   *40*
Conjunctions   *85*
Questions   *188*
 Indirect questions   124
 Tag questions   223
Apostrophes   *53*
(Other Constructions)
 Indirect quotations   125
 Negative constructions   146
 Mixed constructions   142
 Shifts   207
 Relative clauses   194

Preface

A Writer's Handbook from A to Z responds to requests from teachers and students for a handbook that is easy to use, in which items are arranged according to a system students know and understand. Alphabetical arrangement meets that need. As a classification system familiar to all, it turns a composition handbook into a true reference work where information is as easy to locate as in a dictionary or an encyclopedia.

In one alphabetical section, the main portion of *A Writer's Handbook from A to Z* responds to questions that ordinarily send students to handbooks: questions of grammatical usage (sentence and clause types, uses of prepositional phrases, descriptions of verbs and how they are used, and so on), punctuation (listed by type of mark, such as comma or hyphen), common sentence errors (including lack of subject-verb agreement, faulty pronoun reference, and shifts), and style (such as idioms, nonsexist language, and emphasis). In addition, all items of diction ordinarily found in a glossary are included in the alphabetical list, set in italic type to differentiate them from other entries: ***advice, advise*** thus follows **adverbs.** The discussions are nonprescriptive, concise, and oriented toward college writing. All entries are illustrated with sample sentences.

The convenience of the alphabetical arrangement is extended with cross-references and indexes. Writers might thus find a discussion of comma splices by turning directly to **comma splices** under "**C.**" Needing more information, they can follow the boldfaced cross-references to related entries, such as **commas, independent clauses,** and **compound sentences.** They can also look up *comma splices* in the extensive index and find several other entries that apply. Because of these three ways of locating information, writers can find what they need even when terminology is unfamiliar.

Special problems are marked accordingly. The ⚠ icons point to common usage errors (the most common are also listed, with page references, inside the back cover). CAUTION labels mark usage trouble spots—as, for example, the warning about over-subordination in the entry on subordination. Throughout the book, color highlighted boxes summarize useful information, providing quick and holistic access to basic concepts. Because of increasing numbers of college students who use English as a second language, entries that may be of special ESL interest are marked with ▾ icons. As part of the ⚠ icons, this ESL mark reflects an awareness that common usage errors apply also to ESL writing. In addition, an ESL index accompanies the main index.

While the alphabetical arrangement of Part Two enables writers to use the handbook as a reference tool, the book is also adaptable to classroom instruction. Using the "Topical Guide to Alphabetical Entries," teachers and students can locate selected coverage. For instance, from the listing under style and clarity can be drawn related items such as coherence, emphasis, sentence variety, and transitions—or conciseness, diction, and idioms. The cross-references lead to additional related coverage. For classes in which individual or collaborative practice of concepts is desired, a coordinated exercise book (with answers) is available at nominal cost.

Because matters of rhetoric are as likely to be covered in the classroom as at the writing table, they are set apart as separate discursive units. Part One, "Writing an Essay," addresses prewriting, drafting, and revising essays and has highlighted checklists on audience, revision, and editing that students can refer to either while writing or as part of peer review. A student paper illustrating one writer's process of composing is useful also for individual study or class discussion. Part Three, "Writing a Research Paper," takes students through the process of entering the "community of scholars," where they explore topics of interest and engage in all aspects of researched writing including the documentation of sources and the final steps of formatting the finished paper. This section has a sample student paper to illustrate MLA style and a partial paper illustrating APA style. Finally, Part Four, "Specialized Writing," provides brief coverage of abstracts and summaries, critiques, essay examinations, business letters, memorandums, and application letters and resumés. The section is illustrated with samples.

Acknowledgments

This book began with the encouragement of colleagues who, like me, were dismayed that many of their students never used their handbooks because of the difficulty locating the information they needed.

xviii *Preface*

In particular, I want to thank Elizabeth Larsen at West Chester University, who inspired me to get started; Joe Opiela at Allyn and Bacon, who thought it was a good idea; Anna George, who provided a wonderful design, and the other admirable people involved in production; my husband Ken, who solved software and hardware problems as they came up; and my colleagues and teaching assistants at St. Cloud State University, whose support I value. Reviewers are always important for keeping a book on track with coverage that is clear, succinct, yet complete. I owe a debt of gratitude to Rebecca Argall, Memphis State University; Mary Bly, University of California—Davis; Joseph Dunne, St. Louis Community College; Barbara Gaffney, University of New Orleans; Patricia Graves, Georgia State University; Ernest Johansson, Ohio University; Joyce Kinkead, Utah State University; Martha McGowan, University of Massachusetts—Lowell; Carol Pemberton, Normandale Community College; Richard Ramsey, Indiana University—Purdue University; and Cheryl Ruggiero, Virginia Polytechnic Institute.

PART ONE

Writing an Essay

Writing an Essay

The Rhetoric of Writing, *3*
Audience, *4*
The Role of the Writer, *5*
Subject and Purpose, *6*
The Process of Writing, *8*
Prewriting and Invention, *8*
Thesis, *13*
Development, *14*
Organization, *20*
Outlining, *22*
Drafting, *23*
Revision, *25*
Editing, *30*
Proofreading, *31*

People write for many reasons—to communicate, to reflect, to remember, to learn, to entertain, to show someone what they know, to practice the skills of writing, even to make money. You may write in school or on the job for one reason or for a combination of reasons. On essay examinations, you write to show a teacher that you have learned certain concepts or facts. When taking notes, you write to remember and to learn. When you write a report, you communicate information, but you also show that you have discovered and assimilated the information. In a writing class, you write mainly to acquire and practice the skills of writing; skills that enable you also to achieve other purposes for writing: you are better able to communicate, to remember, to show what you know, and—face it—eventually to make money. It's a fact of life that, in many occupations, better writers get better jobs.

This book addresses the skills of writing. The main portion of the book—"The Alphabetical Reference Guide"—explains grammar and usage. And because the entries are alphabetically arranged and extensively cross-referenced, you should be able to find the grammar terms and word usage entries you are looking for. This section deals with the essay (or "theme," or "paper")—that genre of school writing that enables you to practice a wide variety of writing skills: discovering, exploring, arranging, revising, and editing ideas. Even though you may not write another essay after leaving your writing class, the skills that you practice will help you to write better letters and memos, better reports, better essay examinations, and so on. At the end of the book are two sections that specifically address other kinds of writing: the research paper and specialized writing (resumés and application letters, memorandums and business letters, summaries and abstracts, and essay examinations).

The Rhetoric of Writing

The word *rhetoric* stands for the skills writers use for getting ideas across to an audience. (When people misuse their skills of rhetoric to convince others of untruths or to obscure the truth with empty statements, they are accused of using "*mere* rhetoric.") While grammar deals with sentence-level skills, rhetoric involves skills beyond the sentence, encompassing discovering, arranging, and revising ideas to suit an audience.

Audience

Because you write for an audience, you need rhetoric. The way you present your ideas depends on the needs, interests, and preferences of that audience. A letter to a parent requesting a loan is not quite the same as a letter making the same request of a bank or an employer. Sometimes you apply your awareness of audience quite naturally in your writing; at other times you probably need to remind yourself of it. You cannot assume, for example, that all teachers have the same expectations concerning writing: that sentence fragments are unimportant to all teachers because they weren't important to one teacher, or that you should never use the first-person pronoun *I* in an essay. If you assume a friendly audience when writing a persuasive essay, you could present insufficient evidence and reasoning to convince an opposing audience.

Awareness of audience is important wherever you are. In business it determines the differences in how you write to an employer, a client, or a colleague. Socially, it determines how you write a thank-you note to a close friend or a distant aunt. In school, the ultimate audience, as all students know, is the teacher, even though classmates and others may be intermediary audiences. Sometimes teachers assign a fictional audience to provide the opportunity for practice in various rhetorical situations. Whether your audience is fictional or real, attend closely to the teacher's specifications for your assignment: topic, length, method(s) of organization, placement of thesis, ways of achieving coherence, and so on—as well as format, such as margins and line spacing. To disregard these specifications is to disregard the expectations of your audience.

When the audience is someone you know well, you probably can get your ideas across to your reader with little thought. But when your audience is unfamiliar, turn to rhetoric to help you make decisions about how to approach your subject, what details to include and omit, how to organize your material, what level of vocabulary to use, what level of formality is appropriate, and so on. Use the following questions to assess your audience while you're still exploring your subject, while you're composing, and while you revise.

QUESTIONS ABOUT AUDIENCE

1. Who is my audience?
2. What does my audience know about my subject?

3. What does my audience know about me?
4. What is my relationship to my audience?
5. How interested is my audience in my subject?
6. How can I stimulate audience interest?
7. What is my audience's attitude toward my subject?
8. What is my audience's attitude toward me?
9. Do I want to change what my audience knows—or how it feels—about me and my subject?
10. What experiences and knowledge do I share with my audience?
11. How can I use those experiences and that knowledge to present my subject?
12. Does my audience perceive the rhetorical situation in which I am writing to be reflective, persuasive, informative, or something else?
13. What level of grammar and vocabulary will my audience expect in my writing? What style will appeal to my audience?

The Role of the Writer

Closely related to audience considerations is your role as writer of a given piece of writing. People have many legitimate roles; you are a son or daughter, a male or female, a student, a classmate, possibly a roommate, possibly a lover or spouse, perhaps a parent, probably an employee, and so on. All of your roles are truly you, yet each role differs from the others in significant ways. Your roles in writing differ too. When you write for a teacher, you are a student; when you write for a classmate, you are a peer; when you write for a high-school audience, you are Joe or Jill College. Your role as writer also is affected by your attitudes and opinions on issues: pro or con on abortion, capital punishment, and gun control, to name a few. On some subjects you are quite knowledgeable and can write as an authority, but on others you are less informed and will sound more tentative.

As your role changes, the expression of it—your voice—changes too. Like your spoken voice, your written voice adjusts to each situation. Your vocabulary, grammar, style, tone, organization, treatment of details, even your subject all influence the qualities of your written voice. An essay for a writing class, while not highly formal, does nevertheless require more formality than your everyday speech or personal writing. You avoid slang and colloquial expressions, use vocabulary befitting the situation, and edit errors carefully. To appear informed about your subject, you try to be thorough and specific. To give the impression of an orderly mind, you organize your writing logically. At the same time, you are not overly stiff and formal, because your audience doesn't want to be bored with stuffy expressions, unnecessary explanations, unremitting sentences and paragraphs, and repetitive generalizations that take the place of illustrative details.

Adjustments in role are often unconscious, especially when the writing is for a familiar audience. In school or work writing, however, you may need to consciously strike a balance between the overly familiar and the overly formal.

Subject and Purpose

The best subjects to write about are those you know well. In a course where the subject is assigned, the subject is usually based on reading assignments, class discussions, or lectures. When the subject is open, you owe it to yourself and your reader to select something you are familiar with—perhaps even expert in. See "Prewriting and Invention" for some ways of discovering and exploring subjects.

But the subject is not of first importance in writing. Writers write for a *purpose*: to persuade, to entertain, to record, to report, to inform, to explain, to instruct, to praise or censure, to summarize, to respond, to answer questions, and so on. Often these purposes are combined: as you explain, you also hope to persuade; as you respond, you also inform. Whatever your purpose is, considerations of subject, audience, and your role as writer are part of that purpose. For example, if your purpose is to give instructions on assembling a bicycle, the subject and the knowledge of the writer are givens, but at the same time you consider the reading and comprehension levels of your audience. Here is a brief discussion of some of the purposes for writing.

Informative purposes

Recording pertains to present happenings: reaction to a storm, observation of a fire, a play-by-play account of a baseball game or tennis match, and so on. The writer records what he or she perceives, often with no expression of opinions, no interpretations or judgments. *Reporting* is a step removed from the subject; it involves past happenings, such as lab experiments, library research, articles or books read, and work accomplished. Reports are usually objective, but they may include opinions, interpretations, and judgments. *Informing* generalizes; it tells an audience the way something is or how something works, and it is usually based on knowledge acquired from repeated experience or careful study of the subject. Examples include information about the benefits of exercise, the dangers of ozone depletion, and the value and benefit of organic gardening. Information uses facts, statistics, testimony, and historical evidence. *Explaining* assumes that the writer has even more familiarity with the subject, because the writer must tell not only the *what* and *how* of a subject but also the *why*. Explaining gives reasons, causes, effects. It almost always includes opinions, interpretations, and judgments. A writer might explain the resurgence of Nazism, the causes of racism, the effects of feminism, the results of an election, the consequences of a decision, and so on.

Persuasive purposes

Persuasive writing uses information (facts, statistics, testimony, and historical evidence) and factually supported opinions to bring about change in an audience. The anticipated end may be a proposed action (such as voting in a particular way or contributing to a given cause) or a new attitude (such as appreciating other cultures or accepting homosexuality). Done well, persuasion avoids **fallacies in logic** and exaggerated emotional appeals. It does not substitute personal beliefs (for example, "capital punishment is inhumane") for opinions that can be supported with facts ("capital punishment is not an effective crime deterrent"). Writers wanting to persuade others will bear in mind that their audience probably doesn't agree with them; consequently, writers will give close attention to the interests and biases of their audience, building on what interests the writer and the audience have in common and avoiding inflammatory language and unsubstantiated opinions. Persuasive writers try to appear fair by acknowledging the strengths of opposing arguments and try to appear honest, respectable, and informed.

The Process of Writing

The writing process has three major parts: prewriting, drafting, and revising. These parts don't always occur in linear order. You probably do some prewriting before you write, but you may also continue prewriting after you've begun a draft; you revise after you've completed a draft, but you may also revise while you are composing. Depending on your subject, your audience, your purpose, and your background as a writer, your writing processes may differ from one time to another—and from the writing of someone else. You have probably also discovered that not all of this writing work occurs on paper (or on-screen). Much of your prewriting probably occurs in your head, beginning when you get an assignment or have a reason for writing. For many of your short writings, for instance, you may not write an outline, but in your head you know how you will organize your ideas.

Prewriting and Invention

Before you begin to write, you may need to explore your subject to discover what and how much you can say about it. This exploration may occur both inside and outside your own knowledge. For subjects you know little about, you will need to do some research—reading, surveying, interviewing, viewing films and videos, listening to radio or tapes, and so on. Such research is often essential to academic and professional writing (see Part Three, "Writing a Research Paper"). Exploring what you already know may be facilitated with heuristics (searching questions) and other methods of invention: listing or brainstorming, mapping or clustering, journalist's questions, classical probes, freewriting, and imitation.

Listing or brainstorming

One of the simplest ways to prewrite is to list, or brainstorm, ideas. Begin with a topic and write down everything that comes to mind, whether related or not. When listing, try to work fast. And when your ideas begin to dry up, go back over the list and strike out unlikely ideas, group the remaining ideas according to similarities, and brainstorm again to fill in gaps. Or choose one item from your list and start a separate new list specific to your topic. Brainstorming works well in collaboration with one or more than one other person. You can work together on building a list or, after you have brainstormed alone for a while, ask someone else for input.

Mapping or clustering

A variation of listing is mapping, or clustering. Again, you start by jotting down everything that occurs to you on a topic. The difference is that you write the ideas in clusters and then map out related thoughts, as in Figure 1-1. The topic is in the center, double-circled; it is the starting place. From there, related thoughts are jotted down and circled, then connected to associated ideas. Mapping allows you to see how parts of your topic relate to the whole, whether you know enough about the topic, and which parts of the topic need to be expanded with more information. As with listing, you may decide to select one aspect of the topic and begin a new map.

Journalist's questions

Another variation of list making involves compiling a list of questions to assist your brainstorming. Sometimes known as the five *W*'s and an *H*, these **interrogative words** will start your journalist's questions: *who, what, where, when, why,* and *how.* Use each word as often and as many times as you can. On the topic of extrasensory perception (ESP), for example, you might start by asking questions like these:

> *What* is ESP?
> *Who* believes in ESP?
> Do I know anyone *who* has ESP?
> *When* did I first learn of ESP?
> *How* does ESP work?
> Is there any location *where* ESP is more common?
> *Why* am I interested in ESP?
> *Where* can I learn more about ESP?
> *What* are the types of ESP?

The first round of questions could go on for another page or two, or you could take the answer to one question, such as the last one, and ask further questions along that line.

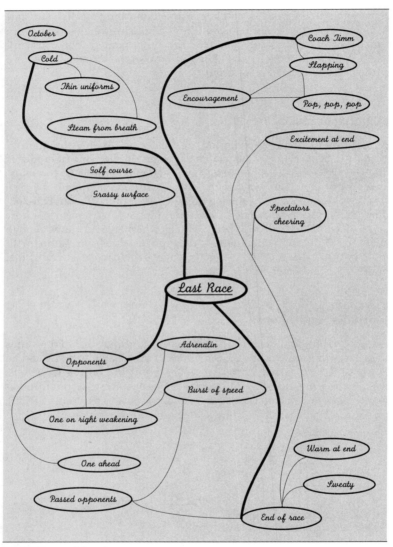

FIGURE 1-1 Mapping

What are the types of ESP?
What is telepathy?
What is clairvoyance?
What is precognition?
Do I know anyone *who* has telepathy? clairvoyance? precognition?
How do telepathy, clairvoyance, and precognition compare?

As some interrogatory words begin to dominate, a pattern of development emerges. The essay that is developing here is probably a definition, answering the *what* questions (see page 19).

Classical probes

People have a great deal more knowledge than they usually use. The classical probes tap into that knowledge with categories of questions that elicit information about specific topics. These categories—identification, comparison and contrast, classification, cause and effect, process analysis, and exemplification—are effective because they coincide with ways the mind collects and stores information. The following sample questions explore the topic of ESP:

IDENTIFICATION
What is ESP?
What does ESP look like?
What does ESP feel like?

COMPARISON AND CONTRAST
How is ESP like other things?
How is ESP different from other
    things?

CLASSIFICATION
What are ESP's parts?
How does ESP relate to other
    things?
How are ESP's parts interrelated?

CAUSES AND EFFECTS
What are ESP's causes?
What are ESP's effects?

PROCESS ANALYSIS
How does ESP operate?
How is ESP produced?

EXEMPLIFICATION
What are some examples of
    ESP?

As with other methods of exploring ideas, this one can lead to others. You can take the answer to any question and ask additional questions about that idea.

Freewriting

With freewriting, you write fast on a particular topic—without stopping, without planning, without making corrections or worrying about
what word to use or how to spell it. Like most other methods of
discovering and exploring ideas, freewriting is based on the classical
notion that people accumulate a wealth of knowledge and may need a
strategy for tapping that knowledge. It also derives from the modern
theory that people learn—generate ideas—by writing. That is, when
you freewrite you not only draw information from your memory bank
but also *do* something with that information: analyze it, compare it,
combine it with other information, actually *engender new thoughts* as
you write. Observe how an idea begins to emerge from the following
freewriting:

> *I really dont know much about esp only that my roomate thinks she
> has it. she says she has a 6th sense that tells her when something terible is
> going to happen like when her brother had a bad car accident. But I
> would like to know more about esp how it works and what it is. Is there
> really such a thing? maybe, I don't know. Do people really believe in it?
> (people other than my roomate)*

Imitation

Surprisingly, imitating the structures of other people's writing could
enable you to develop your own topics. If you study a model paragraph or essay and then write a paragraph or essay patterned on it, you
may find that while you concentrate on the form of the original you
discover ideas of your own. You find something that fits. Once you
have begun to generate ideas, you can depart from the pattern and
write an essay that contains not only your own ideas but also your own
structure. The following example of a model paragraph and an imitation shows how a new idea is generated.

MODEL: The world of Greek mythology was not a place of terror for
the human spirit. It is true that the gods were disconcertingly
incalculable. One could never tell where Zeus's thunderbolt would
strike. Nevertheless, the whole divine company, with a very few
and for the most part not important exceptions, were entrancingly
beautiful with a human beauty, and nothing humanly beautiful is
really terrifying. The early Greek mythologists transformed a world
full of fear into a world full of beauty.

–EDITH HAMILTON, *Mythology*

IMITATION: The world of parapsychology is not reality for many people. It is true that many unexplainable incidents have occurred. My roommate predicted that her brother would have an automobile accident. Nevertheless, the whole idea, with a few notable but not well-known exceptions, is obviously unsubstantiated with any scientific explanations, and what can't be explained is often not believable. Parapsychology sees a world beyond the world of the senses.

Thesis

A thesis states the main idea of an essay. But it is more than a statement of subject: it also contains an assertion about the subject and may also specify the method of development.

SUBJECT: ESP

ASSERTION: is not very believable

DEVELOPMENT: because it is unsubstantiated scientifically and because so-called psychic events often have reasonable explanations [cause-and-effect development].

THESIS: ESP is not very believable because it is unsubstantiated scientifically and because so-called psychic events often have reasonable explanations. [The essay will develop both causes for the lack of believability.]

To go from a simple statement of subject or topic (such as "This essay is about ESP") to a thesis, you may need to ask yourself a number of questions.

QUESTIONS LEADING FROM TOPIC TO THESIS
1. What interests me about X (such as ESP)?
2. What is significant about X?
3. What do I want readers to remember about X?
4. What is my angle on X?
5. What is my point about X?

Answers to such questions should lead you to an assertion (ESP *is not very believable*) and then a method of developing and organizing your essay (in this case, stating reasons).

Informative and persuasive theses

Theses may be *informative* or *persuasive*, depending on your purpose for writing. Compare these two statements on the same subject:

INFORMATIVE: The amount of teenage gambling has greatly increased in the last few years.

PERSUASIVE: The problem of increased teenage gambling requires immediate action.

You see how the assertion changes from *has greatly increased in the last few years*, a statement of information, to *requires immediate action*. Even though information is part of the persuasive thesis, the assertion itself is persuasive. Development of the *informative* thesis would give evidence of the increase in teenage gambling. The *persuasive* thesis would also require this evidence, but with a different slant—to show what immediate action is required and why.

Placement of theses

In an essay, the thesis often appears at the end of the introduction—after the subject has been introduced and before it is developed. In some essays, particularly narratives, the thesis may not occur until the end, stating the point in a final punch line. In still other essays, the thesis is unstated but is implicit throughout. In academic and business writing, however, the thesis is usually explicit to ensure that the reader does not miss the point.

Development

Knowing what you want to say beforehand and stating your assertion in your thesis makes organizing your essay easier than beginning with only a vague idea. In fact, sometimes a well-phrased thesis may be the only guide you'll need for writing a short essay, a business memo or letter, or some other uncomplicated composition with a single subject. The thesis states (1) your subject and (2) your point (assertion); it may also state or imply (3) whether your piece is informative and persuasive and (4) your method of development. The example theses on teenage gambling (see above) imply facts, statistics, and examples (exemplification); the thesis on extrasensory perception (see p. 13) implies reasons (cause and effect). These are common methods of developing ideas; others are narration, description, classification, comparison and contrast, analogy, definition, and process analysis. These methods of development have similarities to prewriting methods. If, in exploring your topic, you find that you are mainly comparing things, you will probably develop your essay through comparison; if you find you are seeking causes, your essay is likely to develop through cause and effect. These methods are used singly or in combination to develop individual paragraphs or entire essays.

Narration

Narrations tell stories, recount events, give anecdotes. They are arranged chronologically, in order of occurrence. Here is an example.

> And then she began to dance, a slow sensuous movement; the smoke of a hundred cigars clinging to her like the thinnest of veils. She seemed like a fair bird-girl girdled in veils calling to me from the angry surface of some gray and threatening sea. I was transported. Then I became aware of the clarinet playing and the big shots yelling at us. Some threatened us if we looked and others if we did not. On my right I saw one boy faint. And now a man grabbed a silver pitcher from a table and stepped close as he dashed ice water upon him and stood him up and forced two of us to support him as his head hung and moans issued from his thick bluish lips. Another boy began to plead to go home.
> —RALPH ELLISON, *Invisible Man*

Ideas developed chronologically are connected by transitional expressions such as *then, now, next,* and *finally.*

Description

Descriptions give verbal pictures of people, places, buildings, and other things. Descriptions are often arranged spatially—for example, vertically, horizontally, circularly—or according to how the writer recalls them. They are usually written from a single perspective. In the following passage, the senses of sight and smell focus the description.

> There were then approximately ten thousand apartments in New York into which no sun ray penetrated directly; such windows as they had opened only on a narrow court from which rose fetid

odors. It was seldom cleaned, though garbage and refuse often went down into it. All these dwellings were pervaded by the foul breath of poverty, that moldy, indefinable, indescribable smell which cannot be fumigated out, sickening to me but apparently unnoticed by those who lived there. When I set to work with antiseptics, their pungent sting, at least temporarily, obscured the stench.

–MARGARET SANGER, *An Autobiography*

Ideas developed spatially are often connected with place-orienting words: *over there, beside, above,* and, more specific to the piece by Margaret Sanger, such words as *apartments in New York, these dwellings, a narrow court.*

Exemplification

You can often develop your point most effectively with examples— sometimes with one or two extended examples, at other times with a series of brief illustrations.

The Puritans were a daring lot, but they had a mean streak. They hated the theater and banned Christmas. They punished people in a cruel and inhuman manner. They killed children who disobeyed their parents. When they came in contact with those whom they considered heathens or aliens, they behaved in such a bizarre and irrational manner that this chapter in the American history comes down to us as a late-movie horror film. They exterminated the Indians, who taught them how to survive in a world unknown to them, and their encounter with the calypso culture of Barbados resulted in what the tourist guide in Salem's Witches' House refers to as the Witchcraft Hysteria.

–ISHMAEL REED, *Writin' Is Fightin'*

The series of short examples in this paragraph would be balanced with longer examples in other paragraphs. You might use words and phrases such as *for example, for instance, an illustration,* and *specifically* to relate examples to the points they develop.

Cause and effect

Writers often explain with reasons, causes, and effects: why something happened, what the effects of particular actions were, what will happen if something is done or not done, and so on. In this example, specified actions result in certain effects.

You have to work with emoluments that range from nothing to three cents an hour! But once you accept the pay job in the prison's industrial sector you cannot get out without going through the bad conduct process. When workers are needed, it isn't a case of accepting a job in this area. You take the job or you're automatically refusing to work, even if you clearly stated that you would cooperate in other employment. The same atmosphere prevails on the recreation yard where any type of minor mistake could result not in merely a bad conduct report and placement in adjustment center, but death. A fistfight, a temporary, trivial loss of temper will bring a fusillade of bullets down on the darker of the two men fighting.

–GEORGE JACKSON, *Soldad Brother*

Key words in cause-and-effect development are *because, result, cause, reason, bring about, consequently,* and *thus.*

Classification

Classification groups similar things—usually for ease of comprehension and recall but often also for clarity in supporting a point. In the following example, the writer describes how color categories help people identify and talk about colors.

Charts obtainable at paint stores provide samples of hundreds of colors to help homeowners select the exact ones they want. An English speaker who glances quickly at one of these charts recognizes certain colors and can name them immediately as *yellow, green,* and so forth. Other colors require a moment of hesitation before the speaker finally decides that a particular hue falls into the category of, let us say, *green* rather than *yellow.* Still other colors demand not only considerable thought but also a hyphenated compromise, such as *greenish-yellow.* Finally, the English speaker finds himself totally unable to name many colors by any of the categories available to him; he is forced to make up his own term or to use a comparison, such as *It looks like the color of swamp water.* The ease with which verbal labels can be attached to colors is known as "codability." The color that a speaker of English unhesitatingly describes as *green* has high codability for him, and it also evokes a quick response from speakers of his language, who immediately know what hues fall into that category.

–PETER FARB, *Word Play:*
What Happens When People Talk

Key words denoting classification are *group, category, class, type, classification,* and the like.

Comparison and contrast

It is the nature of people to compare and contrast things: classes, soap operas, videos, sound systems, and so on. For this reason, comparison and contrast are useful methods of developing ideas. In this example, the key word *different* signals contrast.

> People who all believe in God can be divided according to the sort of God they believe in. There are two very different ideas on this subject. One of them is the idea that He is beyond good and evil. We humans call one thing good and another thing bad. But according to some people that is merely our human point of view. These people would say that the wiser you become the less you would want to call anything good or bad, and the more clearly you would see that everything is good in one way and bad in another, and that nothing could have been different. Consequently, these people think that long before you got anywhere near the divine point of view the distinction would have disappeared altogether. We call a cancer bad, they would say, because it kills a man; but you might just as well call a successful surgeon bad because he kills a cancer. It all depends on the point of view. The other and opposite idea is that God is quite definitely "good" or "righteous," a God who takes sides, who loves love and hates hatred, who wants us to behave in one way and not in another. The first of these views—the one that thinks God beyond good and evil—is called Pantheism. It was held by the great Prussian philosopher Hegel and, as far as I can understand them, by the Hindus. The other view is held by Jews, Mohammedans and Christians.
>
> —C. S. Lewis, *Mere Christianity*

Comparison and contrast shows similarities and differences, advantages and disadvantages. Comparisons often have such connecting words as *similarly* and *likewise*; contrasts such words as *but, although, however, on the contrary,* and *in contrast.*

Analogy

Analogy attempts to describe one thing in terms of something else— usually something unknown or abstract in terms of something known or concrete. In the analogy "The fog was like pea soup—thick and green," the intangible, *fog,* is described in terms of something experienced by the senses: *pea soup—thick and green.* In the following example, the writer uses the analogy of a ship in a dense fog to describe something even more intangible.

Have you ever been at sea in a dense fog, when it seemed as if a tangible white darkness shut you in, and the great ship, tense and anxious, groped her way toward the shore with plummet and sounding-line, and you waited with beating heart for something to happen? I was like that ship before my education began, only I was without compass or sounding-line, and had no way of knowing how near the harbour was. "Light!" was the wordless cry of my soul, and the light of love shone on me in that very hour.

–HELEN KELLER, *The Story of My Life*

Analogy uses words such as *seems, like, as,* and *as if.*

Definition

It's often necessary for writers to define terms—within a paragraph or in an entire essay. In the following paragraph, the writer defines the term *labels of primary potency,* which he uses elsewhere in the essay.

Some labels, such as "blind man," are exceedingly salient and powerful. They tend to prevent alternative classification, or even cross-classification. Ethnic labels are often of this type, particularly if they refer to some highly visible feature, e.g., Negro, Oriental. They resemble the labels that point to some outstanding incapacity—*feeble-minded, cripple, blind man.* Let us call such symbols "labels of primary potency." These symbols act like shrieking sirens, deafening us to all finer discriminations that we might otherwise perceive. Even though the blindness of one man and the darkness of pigmentation of another may be defining attributes for some purposes, they are irrelevant and "noisy" for others.

–GORDON W. ALLPORT,
The Nature of Prejudice

Defined words are indicated by **italics** or **quotation marks**.

Process analysis

Process analysis tells how something is done or has been done. Sometimes it takes the form of instructions; sometimes it is a report of procedures, as in the following example. Like narration, it is arranged chronologically.

Hunter duly trained some dogs and other animals on Pavlov's lines. They were taught that when a light came on over one of three tunnels out of their cage, that tunnel would be open; they could escape down it, and were rewarded with food if they did. But once he had fixed that conditioned reflex, Hunter added to it a deeper idea: he gave the mechanical experiment a new dimension, literally—the dimension of time. Now he no longer let the dog go to the lighted tunnel at once; instead, he put out the light, and then kept the dog waiting a little while before he let him go. In this way Hunter timed how long an animal can remember where he has last seen the signal light to his escape route.

—Jacob Bronowski, *Proceedings of the American Academy of Arts and Letters,* 1967

Key connecting terms with process report and analysis are time-related: *first, next, now, later, soon, then,* and *when.*

Organization

Your method of development helps you organize your essay. If you are writing a narrative or a process analysis, you arrange your details chronologically; with a description, your organization may be spatial. However, if you are explaining the causes of something, you have to decide how to arrange these causes into the several paragraphs you devote to them. Common methods of organization are question and answer, problem and solution, emphasis, general to specific, and specific to general. These methods can be used individually or in combination.

Question and answer

You may lead into your subject by asking questions and then develop your essay by providing answers. In this example the authors use questions as a means of exploring a feminist statement.

English is a sexist language! Angry women have often been driven to make such a statement. But is it accurate? Can we really label some languages as more sexist than others? In a recent movie, a rather obnoxious adolescent described his favorite pastime as "cruising chicks." If the adolescent had been female, she would not have had a parallel term to refer to finding boys. This asymmetry in vocabulary is a linguistic reflection of sexism in our society.

—Francine Frank and Frank Ashen, *Language and the Sexes*

Problem and solution

You may state a problem and offer a solution. In this example, an eighteenth-century satirist describes a problem for which he later offers a solution.

> It is a melancholy object to those who walk through this great town or travel in the country, when they see the streets, the roads, and cabin doors, crowded with beggars of the female sex, followed by three, four, or six children, all in rags and importuning every passenger for an alms. These mothers, instead of being able to work for their honest livelihood, are forced to employ all their time in strolling to beg sustenance for their helpless infants, who, as they grow up, either turn thieves for want of work, or leave their dear native country to fight for the Pretender in Spain, or sell themselves to the Barbadoes.
>
> –JONATHAN SWIFT, "A Modest Proposal"

Organization of this type is effective in persuasive essays, the solution being the proposed action.

Emphasis

The most emphatic positions in a piece of writing—whether it is a sentence, a paragraph, or a whole essay—are the beginning and the end. When using emphasis as a method of organization, you begin with one of your strongest points—one that will attract the interest of your audience—and end with another—perhaps the most conclusive.

General to specific

Probably most of your academic writing is organized from general to specific; that is, in your introduction you state your thesis (a generalization), which you develop with specific statements and illustrations in the remainder of the essay, ending with a fitting conclusion.

Specific to general

In specific to general organization, you accumulate illustrations and specific statements, finally arriving at a thesis or statement of topic in your conclusion. Narrative essays sometimes develop in this way, not revealing the significance of the described occurrence until the end.

Outlining

Writing plans sometimes take the form of outlines—sometimes formal but more often informal. An informal outline may be no more than a list of points a writer wants to make. A student essay about a track event might begin with an informal outline like this one:

Intro—cold
Clapping hands, running
Running opponents
Clapping, finish
No longer cold, hands still clapping

Such an outline makes little sense to anyone but the writer.

Although most short essays don't require a formal outline, there may be times when you'll need one. The careful and thoughtful planning that goes into an outline often makes the writing go more smoothly. Formal outlines are usually constructed with combinations of letters and numbers to designate sections.

I.
  A.
  B.
    1.
    2.
      a.
      b.
        (1)
        (2)
          (a)
          (b)
II.

In writing a formal outline, follow these principles:

1. An outline divides, or classifies, material with a combination of Roman numerals, capital letters, Arabic numerals, and lowercase letters.
2. Items at the same level are coordinate (parallel in importance); categories at a lower level are subordinate.
3. Items at the same level have the same type of numbering or lettering and the same indentation.
4. Because a lower-level item divides an upper-level item, all subdivisions must logically have at least two parts.

For a sample formal outline, see page 313.

Drafting

Drafting is what many people think of as writing: putting the pen to the page, the fingers to the keyboard. Drafting is working your way through a writing project, getting your ideas down and creating new ones as you go, arriving finally at your last period, when you can take a rest before you start preparing your piece for readers. Drafting is often preceded by some kind of prewriting and a plan for arranging ideas. It is usually followed by some kind of revision. You may find that when you do more prewriting you do less revising, but when you start drafting with very little idea of how your ideas will develop you need to do extensive revising. You probably also find that you continue to prewrite (using heuristics as described in "Prewriting and Invention," p. 8) while you draft and that you revise while drafting too.

As you write, remember that your first draft doesn't have to be perfect. First drafts very seldom are. The main thing is to make your point, developing your thesis as fully as you can. Faulty sentences, repetitions, misspelled words, an incomplete introduction, and lack of a title can all be addressed later. For now, keep on track with your subject, remember the needs and interests of your audience, and write as authoritatively as you can. Reread your thesis occasionally to remind yourself of where you are going. If you get stuck, take a break, and when you come back reread what you have written to get your thoughts flowing. Remember that pauses and dry periods are common to writing. Just don't procrastinate; get back to the keyboard or pen and paper.

Introductions and conclusions

Introductions tell readers what to expect of the essay. Effective introductions do five things:

1. Interest the reader
2. Present the subject
3. State the thesis
4. Establish a relationship between writer and audience
5. Set the tone

You might try some of the following ways of introducing your subject:

- Attention-getting statements
- Curiosity-arousing details
- Questions
- Quotations

- Background statements
- Challenging statements
- Statements of problems
- Statistics
- Narratives (anecdotes)
- Humor

Whatever tone you set in your introduction (objective, cynical, contentious, angry, humorous), be consistent throughout your essay. When essays begin on a serious note, for example, readers are unprepared for a late appearance of humor.

Your *conclusion* should make the same point as your introduction. Before writing it, reread the entire essay, giving particular attention to your introduction, and write something that finishes what you started. Restate your thesis, answer a question you asked, refer to an anecdote you began with, or summarize your solution to the problem you detailed. If you don't write your essay at the last minute, you can let it rest for a while, then reread it later, when a conclusion may easily occur to you. Conclusions are usually only a few sentences long and do not present new information, examples, or opinions.

Coherence

In a well-written essay, all the paragraphs relate to the main idea expressed in the thesis and are connected to one another. If all these connections are made, the essay has coherence. The primary means of making an essay coherent is to express the main idea in a thesis and then repeat its key words throughout the essay. For example, in the following thesis, the key words are *genetic engineering* and *benefits*.

Genetic engineering has a number of benefits.

With each occurrence of these key words, a connection is made to the thesis. A topic sentence, which expresses the main idea of a paragraph, works in much the same way, holding a paragraph together through the repetition of its key words. Many writers use the topic sentence not only to give coherence to a paragraph but also to connect one paragraph to the preceding one.

While the study of gene structure is valuable, perhaps more exciting is the mapping of nuclear transplantation.

The *while* clause refers to the preceding paragraph, and the remainder of the sentence announces the subject of the new paragraph, its key words being *mapping* and *nuclear transplantation*.

An effective method of achieving coherence within paragraphs is to keep your subjects as consistent as possible, beginning each sentence with a connection to the previous sentence and ending it with a new statement. To see how this method works, notice the first paragraph in this section. The second sentence begins with a reference to the first sentence (*If all these connections are made*) and ends with new information. The third sentence begins with a reference to the second sentence (*The primary means for making an essay coherent*) and ends with new information. Other connections can be made with a judicious use of **transitional adverbs** (such as *however, therefore,* and *then*). These words are effective in orienting the reader to what will follow: *however* flags a contrasting idea, and *therefore* signals result.

Revision

You may do some revising while you write your draft—changing words, reconstructing sentences, striking out repetitions, adding details, and so on. Even so, when you put down that last period on your first draft, you know you don't have a perfect paper. It needs more work. This section suggests a few procedures to follow in revision: reading as if you were the reader, using invention questions, applying a checklist, and getting peer review.

Reading as if you were the reader

Try to remove yourself from the role of writer and put yourself in the mind of someone who doesn't know your subject as you do. Does your main idea come through clearly? Do your details lend sufficient support to that central idea? Is it clear how all parts of your essay are connected to one another? Which of the following types of revision do you need to do?

> What do I need to *add?*
> What do I need to *delete?*
> What do I need to *substitute?*
> What do I need to *rearrange?*

Using invention questions

If you need to add or substitute details, use the invention questions in "Prewriting and Invention" (p. 8). The journalist's questions, the classical probes, and the questions about audience (see p. 4) are particularly helpful. If you had written about left-handedness, for example, you might ask yourself, What does my audience know about left-handedness? How will left-handed people respond to what I've written? How will right-handed people respond? Did I achieve my purpose? Or you might ask, Did I make the *effects* of left-handedness clear? Did I give enough *examples* of what it's like to be left-handed? How does being left-handed *compare* to being right-handed?

Applying a checklist

Every revision is specific to a piece of writing, so no revision checklist applies to all situations. But this revision checklist gives you general guidelines.

REVISION CHECKLIST

1. Is my *purpose* apparent throughout the essay?
2. Does my *thesis* state the point of my essay and my subject?
3. Are all *paragraphs* clearly related to my thesis?
4. Is each *paragraph* developed fully enough that my readers aren't left with unanswered questions?
5. Do I have any *paragraphs* that should be combined? Any that should be separated?
6. Are my *paragraphs* clearly connected to one another?
7. Does my *introduction* appeal to the interests of my audience, and does it prepare my audience for what I am about to say?
8. Does my *conclusion* end with the point I stated in my thesis?
9. Do I have a clear, authoritative *voice* that is appropriate for my subject, my audience, and my purpose?
10. Is there anything I should delete to avoid inappropriate *repetition or inconsistencies?*
11. Is there anything I should add to *clarify my position?*

12. Do the *grammar and usage* in my sentences clearly express my meaning?
13. Have I used *words* that convey my meaning accurately and unambiguously, without bias, pretensions, and unintended connotations?
14. Have I shown how the parts of my essay *relate* to my thesis and *connect* to one another?
15. Does my *title* both describe my subject and interest my audience?

Getting peer review

One way of learning how an audience responds to your writing is to have an audience read an early draft. You may be able to get together with a group of your classmates to share drafts and get feedback from one another. In some groups, writers read their drafts aloud; in others, students exchange papers; in still others, writers make enough copies of their drafts to distribute them to everyone in the group. You may at one time or another use all of these methods. Reading your writing aloud gives you feedback mainly on content and works well with early drafts that are still in a form too rough for an audience, whereas exchanging papers works better when you need closer attention to details. There are varying ways of getting feedback too: response sheets that you or your teacher prepare, oral commentary and discussion, or open-ended written response.

When getting feedback on your writing, you may need to moderate your sensitivity to criticism. You may feel as if your writing is an extension of yourself, as if criticism of your writing is criticism of you. To make the review easier for both you and your reviewers—and more helpful for you—tell them how you want them to read your writing, what you want them to look for. If you're concerned about focus, tell your readers to consider whether your essay concentrates on a central idea or seems to slip off at times. If you think your examples might not be concrete enough, tell your readers to give close attention to how you illustrate your points. If you want an overall assessment, ask your readers to use the revision checklist on page 26.

Sample student paper, draft

Observe how student writer Deneen Young applied revision to the following draft.

> The Last Count Down
>
> The cold October air was biting my arms, legs, and face. My uniform, ~~consisting of~~ a pair of cotton shorts and a t-shirt *-- allowed the cold to pass right through.* ~~wasn't enough to keep anyone warm in October, especially on such a chilly day.~~ The athletic socks covering my arms to my elbows made me pretend that my fingers weren't as numb as my *frozen* ~~forzen~~ toes. I didn't even notice the numbness of my nose because my concern was for my lungs, which ached from the cold, brisk air. The heavy breath *billowing* from my cold lungs, oddly ~~enough,~~ was warm enough to create steam when it escaped through my mouth.
>
> *Pop. Pop. Pop.* The loud hollow echo of Coach Timm's hands clapping together *sounded from* ~~could be heard in~~ the distance. ~~The~~ dew from the wet grass soaked my shoes, chilling ~~not only~~ my toes, *and* ~~but~~ even the balls and heels of my feet. My feet wouldn't have been so cold if I *had* ~~would have~~ worn socks inside of my spiked shoes, but socks will slow you down, *I'm told.* We kept running. Pop, pop, pop. We ran stead*ily* to the beat of those clapping hands.
>
> My legs, pounding as endlessly and quickly as my heart, were in rhythm not only

to the clapping, but also to the legs and heart of an opponent directly on my right side. I could see another opponent a few yards in front of us, she also kept our same steady pace. After completing one and a half miles, only half a mile remained in the race. | *expand!*

Pop. Pop. Pop.
ʌThe friendly and familiar clap was an inspiration to me and every one of my teammates. It ⟨could⟩ be heard throughout the golf course. ʌ It encouraged me to run | *expand!*
faster. It reminded me that I could run
Pop. Pop. Pop. ————————————— | *That sound*
better. ʌ The clapping quickened, making my | *was drawing*
arms pump faster, my legs move quicker. | *nearer and*
| *urging me*
Although my adrenalin had been pumping | *to dig deeper*
throughout the race, it seemed to pump | *for more*
faster as the sound of the clapping grew | *power.*
closer and my opponents were left farther behind. I saw the look of excitement in my coach's eyes as I passed yet another opponent. I felt that excitement as I crossed the finish line.

The blood didn't stop flowing just because I stopped running. It was rushing through my body. I finally felt warm. I ʌ*clumsily* walked over to my sweatsuit and tried to pull it onʌ *over my sweaty body.* The crowd was still cheering, but I could only hear Coach Timm. He was still clapping. Urging my teammates to run their last race of the year as their best.

Editing

Related to revising is editing, or preparing a revised draft for your audience. When writers edit, they correct spelling and punctuation and make other changes so that their writing conforms to conventional standards. When you edit, look for the kinds of errors that usually crop up in your writing. If you commonly write sentence **fragments**, look for fragments. If **pronoun reference** is a problem, make sure that every time you use a **pronoun** the **noun** it refers to is absolutely clear. If you have a problem with the forms of your **verbs**, read your essay through once looking only at verbs. You probably can't get your editing done in one pass. Most writers need to go over their writing repeatedly to make all the corrections they have to make. Refer often to your Alphabetical Reference Guide. Here is a checklist to use as a guide to editing (the references to "The Alphabetical Reference Guide" are in boldface type).

EDITING CHECKLIST

1. Does my **punctuation** follow conventional usage?
2. Should I check the **spelling** of any of my words?
3. Does every **verb** agree with its **subject**, especially in sentences where subjects and verbs are widely separated (**agreement of subject and verb**)?
4. Am I consistent in my use of verb tenses and moods? Do I use the appropriate tenses and moods for my verbs?
5. Does every **pronoun** (particularly *it, this, they, he, she*) clearly refer to a **noun** or another pronoun (**pronoun reference**)?
6. Does every **modifier** have an obvious connection to the word I want it to modify (**dangling modifier, misplaced modifier**)?
7. Do my coordinating **conjunctions** (*and, but, or, nor, for, so, yet*) connect equivalent sentence elements (**parallelisms**)?
8. Do I use **capitalization, abbreviation, numbers,** and **italics** (**underlining**) according to conventional usage?
9. Do I have any **wordiness** and unintentional **repetition**?
10. Do I use any **clichés**?

Proofreading

Proofreading is done on the final copy to make sure it conforms to conventional standards. There should be no errors in typing, spelling, or punctuation, no unintentionally omitted or repeated words, no strikeovers or smudges—in other words, the copy should be clean and ready for a reader.

> **PROOFREADING TIPS**
> 1. Look at every word and punctuation mark.
> 2. Resist the temptation to overlook the first and last words on a line.
> 3. Read aloud; doing so slows your reading.
> 4. Point at each word as you read.
> 5. Read backward from the end of the essay.
> 6. Use a spelling checker if you have it; then look for words it overlooks: misspelled **homonyms** (such as *there, their, they're* and *it's, its*) and words that may be spelled correctly but are the wrong words or wrong forms (such as *when* for *went, ran* for *run,* and *ask* for *asked*).
> 7. If you're using a word processor, give your document a careful reading on your screen before printing. To concentrate your reading, keep the line you are proofreading at the bottom of your screen, and scroll to the next line only after you've read the last word on the line you're reading. Always proofread your paper copy as well.

Sample student paper, final draft

Here is the final draft of Deneen's paper after she has edited her revised draft and proofread the final copy.

The Last Countdown

Deneen Young

The cold October air was biting my arms, legs, and face. My uniform--a pair of cotton shorts and a t-shirt--was thin clothing on such a chilly day. The athletic socks covering my arms to my elbows made me pretend that my fingers weren't as numb as my frozen toes. I didn't even notice the numbness of my nose because of my concern for my lungs, which ached from the cold, brisk air. The heavy breath billowing from my cold lungs, oddly, was warm enough to create steam when it escaped through my mouth.

Pop. Pop. Pop. The loud hollow echo of Coach Timm's hands clapping together sounded from the distance. Dew from the wet grass soaked my shoes, chilling my toes and even the balls and heels of my feet. My feet wouldn't have been so cold if I had worn socks inside my spiked shoes, but socks slow you down, I'm told. We kept running. Pop. Pop. Pop. We ran steadily to the beat of those clapping hands.

My legs, pounding as endlessly and quickly as my heart, were in rhythm not only to the clapping but also the legs and heart of an opponent directly on my right side. I could see another opponent a few yards in front of us, keeping the same steady pace. The breathing of the opponent on my right told me she was having trouble keeping our pace. She started breathing heavier, faster. Knowing that her strong, pale legs felt as much like rubber as mine did, I decided this was the

right time to make my move. It was time because of
her apparent fatigue, but it was also the right time
during the race. After one and a half miles over the
soft grassy surface, only half a mile remained in the
race.

Pop. Pop. Pop. The friendly and familiar clap
was an inspiration to me and every one of my teammates. It could be heard throughout the golf course.
It was the only sound I could hear over the cheering
of the spectators as we raced around the last corner
toward the finish line. It encouraged me to run
faster. It reminded me that I could run better.
Pop. Pop. Pop. That sound was drawing nearer and
urging me to dig deeper for more power. The clapping
quickened, making my arms pump faster, my legs move
quicker. Although my adrenalin had been pumping
throughout the race, it seemed to pump faster as the
sound of the clapping grew closer and my opponents
were left farther behind. I saw the look of excitement in my coach's eyes as I passed yet another
opponent. I felt that excitement as I crossed the
finish line.

The blood didn't stop flowing when I stopped running.
It was rushing through my body. I finally felt warm. I
clumsily walked over to my sweatsuit and tried to pull it
on over my sweaty body. The crowd was still cheering, but
I could only hear Coach Timm. He was still clapping,
urging my teammates to make their last race of the year
their best.

PART TWO

The Alphabetical Reference Guide

The Alphabetical Reference Guide

A, *37*

B, *58*

C, *61*

D, *91*

E, *100*

F, *104*

G, *113*

H, *117*

I, *120*

J, *132*

K, *133*

L, *133*

M, *135*

N, *146*

O, *154*

P, *157*

Q, *187*

R, *191*

S, *198*

T, *223*

U, *232*

V, *233*

W, *242*

Y, *247*

Z, *247*

a, an, the Words known as *noun determiners* because they precede nouns, *a* and *an* are **indefinite articles;** *the* is a **definite article.** See also **articles.**

abbreviations

> SECTION OVERVIEW
> Abbreviations acceptable in most writing
> Abbreviations acceptable after they have been explained
> Abbreviations acceptable in some situations
> Abbreviations usually unacceptable in writing for a general audience

Use abbreviations only when your reader will readily understand them. In most cases, avoid them when writing for a general audience. Abbreviations fall into four classes: those acceptable in most writing, those acceptable after they have been explained, those acceptable in some situations, and those usually unacceptable in writing intended for a general audience. Each class is illustrated below.

Abbreviations acceptable in most writing

Many common abbreviations can be used without explanation.

> Elizabeth Jackson, Ph.D., was the guest speaker at the 7:00 a.m. breakfast.

Shortened forms of names, titles, and time designations are often abbreviated.

Paul Dougherty, Jr.	Elizabeth Jackson, Ph.D.
Mr. Paul Dougherty	Dr. Elizabeth Jackson
William T. Smith	T. S. Eliot
St. Louis	Ms. Charlotte Ambrose
448 B.C. and A.D. 198	7:00 A.M. or 7:00 a.m.

Abbreviations acceptable after they have been explained

The usual practice for using most abbreviations in written texts is to write out the full name of the organization, place, or professional term on first mention and to put the abbreviation in parentheses after the full name.

> The American Society of Mechanical Engineers (ASME) will meet in St. Louis next year. This will be the first time the ASME convention has come to that city.

Abbreviate names of organizations, corporations, and countries.

AIDS [Acquired Immune Deficiency Syndrome]
C.C.A. [Circuit Court of Appeals]
U.K. [United Kingdom]
ASME [American Society of Mechanical Engineers]

When in doubt about whether to use periods in abbreviations, consult your dictionary. See also **capitalization** and **periods.**

Abbreviations acceptable in some situations

The acceptability of some abbreviations depends on the situation.

The house sparrow (i.e., English sparrow) eats seeds and insects. [parenthetical note]

IN ADDRESSES:
IL [Illinois]   ONT. [Ontario]   USA *or* U.S.A.
FOR SPECIALIZED AUDIENCES:
cal [calorie]   pmt. [payment]   kg [kilogram]
IN PARENTHETICAL NOTES:
i.e. [that is]   etc. [et cetera]   et al. [et alii]

Do not use such abbreviations in essays and other prose writing. Abbreviate *United States* as *U.S.* when used as an adjective, but spell it out as a noun (*the U.S. economy; the economy in the United States*). Usually write out geographical designations such as *street* and *Illinois.* See also **ZIP code** and "Business letters" in Part Four, "Specialized Writing."

Abbreviations usually unacceptable in writing for a general audience

Avoid the following types of abbreviations in most school and business writing:

NAMES AND TITLES: Wm. [William]   prof. [professor]
PLACES: Mass. [Massachusetts] bldg. [building]
DATES: Wed. [Wednesday]   Oct. [October]

Professor [not *Prof.*] *William* [not *Wm.*] Collins will hold his *first* [not *1st*] class outside the *science building* [not *sci. bldg.*] next *Wednesday* [not *Wed.*], *September* [not *Sept.*] 9.

absolute phrases   A group of words consisting of a **participle** plus the noun or pronoun it modifies and any modifiers, set off from its sentence with a comma or a dash. An absolute phrase itself modifies an entire sentence or clause.

A land still being reclaimed from the sea, the Netherlands fights a never-ending battle against flooding. [The participle *being reclaimed* modifies *land.* The absolute phrase modifies the entire sentence.]

The reclamation is an ongoing process of pumping water back into the sea—*a process once powered by windmills.* [The participle *powered* modifies *process.*]

Unlike **participial phrases**, an absolute is rarely a **dangling modifier** and is therefore an effective stylistic device.

abstract words/concrete words   Abstract **nouns** and other abstract words refer to intangible qualities and ideas, or things that cannot be experienced by the senses. *Responsibility, relationship, fanciful, good, integrity* are a few examples of abstract words.

Electronic games engage players in *tests* of *skill* that have *applications* for *entertainment* and *education.*

Concrete nouns and other concrete words refer to things that can be experienced with the senses: *paper, light, smoky, salty.*

The *paper* was *wrinkled* and *yellow* at the *edges.*

See also **general words/specific words**.

accept, except   *Accept* is a **verb** meaning "to receive" or "to agree to."

The committee *accepts* the conditions of the contract.

Except is a **preposition** meaning "excluding" or "other than."

Agreement has been reached on all stipulations *except* that concerning salary.

active verbs   (See **voice**)

active voice   (See **voice**)

addresses   (See "Business letters" under Part Four, "Specialized Writing")

ad hominem   (See **fallacies in logic**)

adjective clauses   A **subordinate clause** functioning as an **adjective**.

adjective phrases   **Phrases** that function as **adjectives**.

adjectives   Words that modify (describe, limit, explain, or otherwise alter) **nouns**. They usually precede their nouns but may also follow as **subject** or **object complements**.

> *Real* robots bear *little* resemblance to the *humanoid* figures of *science* fiction. [These adjectives precede their nouns.]
>
> *Industrial* robots are *essential* to production. [The adjective *industrial* precedes the noun *robots*; the adjective *essential*, following the verb *are*, serves as a complement to *robots*.]

Adjectives may be classified as descriptive (*dangerous* task, *green* carpet); limiting (*their* reports, *this* meeting, *whose* paper, *three* choices, *each* person); and proper (*English* class, *Mexican* cities, *September* rainfall, *Oldsmobile* convertible—see **capitalization**). Other words serving as adjectives are **participles** (*assembled* parts, *tiring* work); **possessive** nouns (the *world's* leader); and compound words (*present-day* robots).

> CAUTION: Do not use adjectives as **adverbs**.
>
> Many people still don't take robots *seriously* [not *serious*].
>
> Robots play an *increasingly* [not *increasing*] significant role in industrial automation.

▼ Unlike adjectives in many other languages, adjectives in English do not change form to match their nouns.

> Robots can perform *dangerous, uncomfortable, tiring,* and *monotonous* tasks. [adjectives modifying a plural noun]
>
> Robots can perform a *dangerous, uncomfortable, tiring,* and *monotonous* task. [adjectives modifying a singular noun]

The adjectives are the same for singular and plural nouns.

Coordinate and cumulative adjectives

A series of adjectives modifying a noun may be *coordinate* or *cumulative.* Coordinate adjectives modify their noun equally and are separated by **commas.** To test whether adjectives are coordinate, try reversing their order or try replacing each of the commas separating them with *and.*

> **TEST 1:**   Robots can perform *monotonous, uncomfortable, dangerous,* and *tiring* tasks.

TEST 2:   Robots can perform *dangerous* and *uncomfortable* and *tiring* and *monotonous* tasks.

When adjectives in a series cannot meet these tests, they are *cumulative*. Cumulative adjectives are not separated by commas.

The Czech writer Karel Capek coined the word *robot* in a *1921 satirical* play titled *R.U.R. (Rossum's Universal Robots)*. [The adjectives *1921* and *satirical* cannot be reversed or joined by *and*.]

▼ Usage calls for descriptive adjectives in series to appear in this order: size, shape, and color. Other descriptors always follow those denoting size and shape.

The *small square humanoid* figure is a fictive robot. [size, shape, other descriptor]

The *angular machine* tool is a real robot. [shape, other descriptor]

Comparative and superlative forms

Descriptive adjectives have comparative and superlative forms. The comparative is used to compare two things and the superlative to compare more than two things. Add *-er* to form the comparative and *-est* to form the superlative for most one-syllable and many two-syllable adjectives. For longer words use *more* and *most* (*less* and *least* for negatives).

FORMS OF ADJECTIVES

POSITIVE	COMPARATIVE	SUPERLATIVE
fine	finer	finest
blue	bluer	bluest
long	longer	longest
important	more important	most important
efficient	more efficient	most efficient
brilliant	more brilliant	most brilliant

IRREGULAR FORMS

good	better	best
bad	worse	worst
little	less, littler	least, littlest

▼   CAUTION: To avoid a double comparative or a double superlative, do not use *more* or *most* with adjectives ending in *-er* and *-est*.

Robots perform many tasks with *greater* [not *more greater*] speed than people do.

Robots are often better [not *more better*] at performing tasks.

Robots are often *more accurate* in their performance also.

But they are *less useful* in decision making.

Do not use comparative and superlative forms of absolute words such as *complete, final, illegal, unique, perfect, dead, impossible,* and *infinite.*

The purchase of the robot was *illegal* [not *most illegal*].

See also **indefinite pronouns and adjectives**.

adverb clauses   **Subordinate clauses** functioning as **adverbs.**

adverb phrases   **Phrases** functioning as **adverbs.**

adverbs   Adverbs modify **verbs, adjectives,** other adverbs, and entire **phrases** or **clauses**. Like adjectives, they describe, limit, explain, or otherwise alter the words they modify.

Plastics are made *chiefly* of polymers. [adverb modifying the verb *are made*]

A *quite* important material, celluloid, was one of the first plastics. [adverb modifying the adjective *important*]

However, celluloid has been replaced by a wide variety of newer plastics. [adverb modifying the entire sentence]

Adverbs serve five functions: they tell us how, where, how often, when, and to what degree something occurs or occurred.

TYPES OF ADVERBS		
	FUNCTION	*EXAMPLES*
manner	how	carefully, quickly, fast, well, together
place	where	here, close, upstairs, inside, near, down
frequency	how often	never, usually, again, hardly, once, often
time	when	after, already, later, first, soon, tomorrow
degree	to what degree	quite, very, completely, inadequately, too

Many adverbs are formed by adding -*ly* to adjectives: *careful, carefully; usual, usually; complete, completely.* However, not all words ending in -*ly* are adverbs: *timely* and *friendly*, for example, are adjectives. And not all adverbs end in -*ly: here, upstairs, yesterday, well* are adverbs.

CAUTION: Do not use **adjectives** where adverbs are needed.

Heat and pressure are applied *directly* [not *direct*] to the plastic powder.

Comparative and superlative forms

Like adjectives, many adverbs have comparative and superlative forms. Adverbs ending in -*ly* and some irregular adverbs use *more* and *most* (*less* and *least* for negatives); most single-syllable adverbs not ending in -*ly* take the endings -*er* and -*est: more carefully, less commonly, closer, fastest.*

FORMS OF ADVERBS		
POSITIVE	*COMPARATIVE*	*SUPERLATIVE*
soon	sooner	soonest
fast	faster	fastest
early	earlier	earliest
efficiently	more efficiently	most efficiently
often	less often	least often
IRREGULAR FORMS		
well	better	best
badly	worse	worst
little	less	least

CAUTION: To avoid a double comparative or a double superlative, do not use *more* or *most* with adverbs ending in -*er* and -*est.*

We'll get to the game *earlier* [not *more earlier*] if we drive.

Transitional adverbs

A special kind of adverb is the **transitional adverb** (or conjunctive adverb). It ordinarily modifies entire clauses and sentences, relating them to previous clauses or sentences.

For example, Plexiglas and Lucite have replaced celluloid. [*For example* modifies the entire sentence and relates this sentence to a preceding sentence.]

Plastics have a major disadvantage; *specifically*, their disposal is difficult. [The transitional adverb modifies the second clause and relates it to the preceding clause.]

Transitional adverbs are ordinarily set off with commas. See also **transitional adverbs**.

advice, advise   *Advice* is a **noun** meaning "recommendation"; *advise* is a **verb** meaning "to give a recommendation."

I *advise* you to take the *advice* of your attorney.

affect, effect   In ordinary usage, *affect* is used as a **verb**, *effect* as a **noun**. *Affect* as a verb means "to influence"; as a noun it is a specialized term referring to emotional influence.

The legislative decision *affected* everyone in the state. [verb]

Educational psychologists were studying the part *affect* plays in learning. [noun]

Effect as a noun means "result"; as a verb it means "to bring about."

The legislative decision had an *effect* throughout the state. [noun]

Environmentalists *effected* a change in how people dispose of their trash. [verb]

aggravate   A word meaning "to make worse." Do not use *aggravate* to mean "to irritate," "to annoy," or "to exasperate."

Continuing to run every day only *aggravated* her shin splint.

She was truly *annoyed* [not *aggravated*] when her car failed to start.

▲ agreement of pronouns and antecedents

> SECTION OVERVIEW
> Agreement between pronouns and collective nouns
> Agreement between pronouns and compound antecedents
> Agreement between pronouns and generic nouns
> Agreement between pronouns and indefinite pronouns and adjectives

Pronouns agree with their **antecedents** in **number** and **person**.

Conscientious objectors refuse military service on the basis of *their* conscience. [Number: the plural pronoun *their* agrees with the plural antecedent *objectors*; person: the third-person pronoun *their* agrees with the plural noun *objectors* (all nouns are third person).]

Any nation with a military draft is likely to have *its* conscientious objectors. [The third-person singular pronoun *its* agrees with the singular antecedent *nation.*]

Most pronoun and antecedent agreement errors occur in only a few situations: with collective nouns, compound antecedents, generic nouns, and indefinite pronouns and adjectives.

Agreement between pronouns and collective nouns

Collective nouns such as *committee, jury, class, audience, family,* and *team* act as singular nouns unless their context is clearly plural.

The *committee* has completed *its* work in record time. [The *committee* acts as a whole.]

The *committee* have arrived from *their* separate locations. [The *committee* acts as individuals.]

Agreement between pronouns and compound antecedents

Two or more antecedents joined by *and* to form a compound antecedent require a plural pronoun.

The United States and Britain have treated *their* conscientious objectors similarly. [The compound antecedent *The United States and Britain* takes a plural pronoun.]

When the words in a compound antecedent are joined by *or* or *nor*, the pronoun agrees with the nearer antecedent.

Neither the *United States* nor *Britain* allows *its* objectors to claim political opposition to military service. [The singular pronoun *its* agrees with the nearer singular antecedent *Britain.*]

Neither the *United States* nor most other *countries* allow *their* objectors to claim political opposition to military service. [The plural pronoun *their* agrees with the nearer antecedent *countries.*]

Agreement between pronouns and generic nouns

Generic nouns are singular nouns that often seem to have plural meanings because they represent typical individuals in a group: *a student, a person, a doctor.* Pronouns referring to these antecedents are therefore singular.

A conscientious objector must declare religious or humanitarian convictions as the basis for *his or her* resistance.

Because English has no singular third-person generic pronoun, *his or her* is used to refer to a conscientious objector of either sex. To avoid the wordy *he or she* construction, writers often choose plural nouns and use the third-person plural pronoun *they* instead.

> *Conscientious objectors* must declare religious or humanitarian convictions as the basis for *their* resistance.

See also **nonsexist language**.

Agreement between pronouns and indefinite pronouns and adjectives

Indefinite pronouns and adjectives refer to nonspecific persons or things. Though they sometimes imply plural meanings, grammatically they are singular. Pronouns referring to indefinite pronouns or the nouns' indefinite adjectives modify must therefore be singular.

> *Anyone* wanting to claim conscientious objector status must prove *he or she* holds [not *they hold*] deep ethical and religious beliefs. [The indefinite pronoun *anyone* takes the singular pronoun construction *he or she*.]

> *Each* conscientious objector must prove *he or she* holds deep ethical and religious beliefs. [The indefinite adjective *each* takes the singular pronoun construction *he or she*.]

To avoid the wordy *he or she* construction, you might change the subject to plural or recast the sentence.

> *People* wanting to claim conscientious objector status must prove *they* hold deep ethical and religious beliefs. [The subject is changed to plural.]

> *Anyone* wanting to claim conscientious objector status must prove deeply held ethical and religious beliefs. [The sentence is recast to avoid the need for a pronoun.]

See also **nonsexist language**.

agreement of subjects and verbs

> SECTION OVERVIEW
> Agreement between verbs and mass nouns and count nouns
> Agreement between verbs and collective nouns
> Agreement between verbs and compound subjects
> Agreement between verbs and indefinite pronouns and
>   adjectives

Agreement and inverted subject-verb order
Agreement and intervening words
Agreement and linking verbs
Agreement and nouns of plural form and singular meaning

Verbs agree with their **subjects** in **number** (**singular, plural**) and **person** (first, second, third). Problems arise mainly with third-person singular present-tense verbs (such as *shows, sings, drives, reads*) and **helping verbs** in the present tense (such as *does, has,* and *is*). Many times writers neglect the *-s* (*-es*) ending or do not know their irregular verb forms: *works, has worked, is working; jump, has jumped, is jumping; writes, does write, is written, has been written.* The *-s* (*-es*) form is needed with all singular nouns: *The cat jumps; The paper is written; The stereo does not work.* It is also needed with the **pronouns** *he, she,* and *it*: *She jumps; It is written; He does not work.* Further trouble can occur with *was,* the third-person singular past-tense form of the irregular verb *be: She was gone, It was written.*

CAUTION: Do not add the *-s* ending to a verb when your subject is *I, you, we,* or *they:*

I *want* [not *wants*] to know the assignment.

▼   *Agreement between verbs and mass nouns
and count nouns*

Mass nouns (or noncount nouns—things that cannot be counted, such as *advice* and *information*) are singular; their present-tense verbs therefore take an *-s* or *-es* ending.

Information is arriving from several wire services.

Pollution is evident in the skyline.

Understanding increases with knowledge.

Count nouns (such as *calendar* and *desk*) can be singular or plural and take verbs that agree accordingly.

The *calendar shows* thirty-one days for June. [singular]

Both *calendars have* errors for the month of June. [plural]

Most subject-verb agreement errors occur with collective nouns, compound subjects, indefinite pronouns and adjectives, inverted subject-verb order, intervening words, linking verbs, and nouns of plural form and singular meaning.

Agreement between verbs and collective nouns

Collective nouns such as *committee, jury, class, audience, family*, and *team* take singular verbs unless their context is clearly plural.

> The *audience was* not *pleased* at the antics of the lecturer. [The audience acts as a whole.]

> The *family have set* separate vacation itineraries. [The members of the family act as individuals.]

To avoid the awkward sound of the second example, many writers would recast the sentence.

> The *family members have set* separate vacation itineraries.

Agreement between verbs and compound subjects

Two or more subjects joined by *and* to form a **compound subject** take a plural verb.

> *Cesare Borgia* and *his sister Lucretia Borgia were* members of a Spanish-Italian Renaissance family.

When a compound subject refers to a single thing or is introduced by *each* or *every*, the verb is singular.

> The *brother* and *leader* of the family, Cesare, *was* cruel and treacherous. [*Brother* and *leader* refer to the same person; the verb is singular.]

> Every *city* and *enemy* he conquered *has attested* to that fact. [The indefinite adjective *every* makes the subject singular.]

When two or more subjects are joined by *or* or *nor* to form a compound subject, the verb agrees with the nearer subject.

> Neither *Lucretia* nor her *brothers have been treated* kindly by history. [The verb is plural, agreeing with the nearer subject *brothers.*]

Agreement between verbs and indefinite pronouns and adjectives

Indefinite pronouns and adjectives refer to nonspecific persons or things. Though they sometimes imply plural meanings, grammatically most of them are treated as singular. Verbs referring to indefinite pronouns or the nouns' indefinite adjectives modify must therefore be singular.

> *Everyone knows* of the cruelty and treachery of Cesare Borgia. [indefinite pronoun *everyone*; singular verb *knows*]
>
> *Every* schoolchild *has heard* of his cruelty and treachery. [indefinite adjective *every* modifying *schoolchild*; singular verb *has heard*]

A few indefinites take singular or plural verbs depending on the **nouns** or **prepositional phrases** that follow them.

> *Most* of the stories about Cesare Borgia *are* probably true. [The indefinite pronoun *most* is plural because of the phrase that follows it.]
>
> But there *is* only *some* truth to the stories about Lucretia Borgia. [The indefinite adjective *some* is singular because of the word that follows it.]

Agreement and inverted subject-verb order

Changes in the normal subject-verb word order of a sentence do not affect the agreement of subject and verb.

> There *is* little *truth* to the stories about Lucretia Borgia. [The singular verb *is* precedes the singular subject *truth*.]
>
> Are her crimes and vices legendary? [The plural verb *are* precedes the plural subject *her crimes and vices*.]

Agreement and intervening words

Words that come between the subject and the verb usually have no effect on the number of the verb.

> The *stories* of her treachery *are* unfounded. [plural subject, *stories;* plural verb *are*]
>
> Her legendary *treachery* in Donizetti's opera, in addition to these unfounded stories, *contributes* to the false notions of her character. [The intervening plural words do not affect the singularity of the subject, *treachery*, and the verb, *contributes*.]

Agreement and linking verbs

Verbs that link subjects and complements agree with the subject.

> The treacherous *pair* of the legend *was* Lucretia and her brother Cesare. [The singular subject *pair* takes the singular verb *was*.]
>
> *Lucretia and her brother Cesare were* the duo of legend. [The plural subject *Lucretia and her brother Cesare* takes the plural verb *were*.]

*Agreement and nouns of plural form and
singular meaning*

A few nouns in English look plural because they end with *-s* but
are singular in meaning and take a singular verb. Also measurements
and numbers that appear plural but refer to units are treated as singular because they function as a singular subject.

> The opportunistic *politics* of her villainous brother *was* not charac-
> teristic of Lucretia. [The singular subject *politics* takes the singular
> verb *was.*]

> Lucretia's *thirty-nine years was* not a short lifetime by Borgia
> standards. [The subject *thirty-nine years* is a singular unit that takes
> the singular verb *was.*]

See also **noun phrases**.

ain't   Nonstandard for *am not, are not (aren't), is not (isn't).*

> I'm the last person arriving, *am I not* [not *ain't I* or *aren't I*]?

> He *isn't* [not *ain't*] going to come at all.

all ready, already   *All ready* means "completely prepared"; *already* means "previously" or "by now."

> The plaintiff was *all ready* to sign the final papers.

> The attorneys had *already* signed them.

all together, altogether   *All together* means "gathered in one
place" or "in unison." *Altogether* means "entirely."

> The committee members are *all together* in the conference room.

> The building is *altogether* [entirely] too shabby to renovate.

allude, refer, elude   *Allude* means "to refer indirectly" to something. *Refer* means "to refer directly."

> The reporter *alluded* to improprieties in the courthouse.

> In writing his story, the reporter *referred* twice to U.S. census
> figures.

Elude means "to evade" or "to escape."

> The meaning of the report *eluded* the staff.

allusion, illusion   An *allusion* is an indirect reference to something. An *illusion* is a false perception.

Your *allusion* to "Goldilocks" makes me wonder if you ever read the story.

Optical *illusions* have always mystified me.

alot, a lot   *A lot* is commonly misspelled as one word: *alot.* It should be written as two words: *a lot.* In most school and business writing, substitute more formal terms such as *many, a great deal,* and *extensively.*

> *Many* [instead of *a lot of*] people have been arrested for driving while intoxicated.
>
> Students Against Drunk Driving have campaigned *extensively* [instead of *a lot*] against driving while intoxicated.

already   (See **all ready**)

alright, all right   *All right* is the correct spelling.

> The meeting time is *all right* [not *alright*] with me.

altogether   (See **all together**)

among, between   In formal usage, *among* indicates a relationship with more than two people or things; *between* relates or compares two things.

> *Among* the four unattractive options, the first was least desirable.
>
> The choice was *between* good and evil.

amount, number   In formal usage, *amount* means an uncountable quantity of something (**mass noun**); *number* means a countable quantity (**count noun**).

> The *amount* of paperwork is staggering.
>
> The *number* of people who can do it is limited.

an   (See **articles**)

and/or   A compound widely used in legal writing to mean "one or the other or both." The term gives a bureaucratic quality to general writing.

ante-, anti-   Prefixes meaning "before" (*ante-*) and "against" (*anti-*): *antedate, anteroom; antihero, antihistamine.*

antecedents   In grammar, the words to which **pronouns** refer.

The Russian-American novelist *Vladimir Nabokov* is internationally recognized for *his* lepidoptery. [*Vladimir Nabokov* is the antecedent of *his*.]

Pronouns must agree with their antecedents in **number** and **gender** (see **agreement of pronouns and antecedents**).

CAUTION: The antecedent of a pronoun must be a **noun** or another **pronoun**, not an **adjective**, a **possessive case** noun, a **clause**, or a **phrase**.

FAULTY: In Nabokov's novel *Lolita, he* tells the story of a middle-aged man's infatuation with a twelve-year-old girl. [The possessive noun *Nabokov's* cannot function as the antecedent of *he*.]

REVISED: In *his* novel *Lolita, Nabokov* tells the story of a middle-aged man's infatuation with a twelve-year-old girl. [*Nabokov* is the antecedent of *his*.]

See also **pronoun reference**.

anxious, eager   In formal usage, *anxious* cannot be substituted for *eager. Eager* carries a sense of happy expectations; *anxious* means "worried" or "uneasy."

I was *anxious* about finishing my paper on time.

I was *eager* [not *anxious*] to see if I won the contest.

▼ *Anxious* is usually followed by *about, eager* usually by *to*.

any body, anybody; any one, anyone   *Anybody* and *anyone* are **indefinite pronouns.** In the phrases *any body* and *any one, any* is an **indefinite adjective** modifying *body* and *one*.

Anyone who has not seen *any one* of those movies is fortunate.

Does *anybody* know of *any body* of water not polluted in some way?

anyplace, anywhere   *Anyplace* is a colloquial term for *anywhere.* Avoid it in writing.

anyway, anyways   *Anyways* is nonstandard for *anyway*.

⚠ apostrophes

> SECTION OVERVIEW
> Apostrophes in possessive case of nouns
> Apostrophes to form contractions
> Apostrophes in special uses

Punctuation that performs three primary functions: marks possessive case of **nouns,** forms **contractions,** and performs special uses.

Apostrophes in possessive case of nouns

Ownership or connection is indicated by adding an apostrophe to English nouns.

> Sigmund *Freud's* early work was poorly received by other psychiatrists.

> His later *work's* influence has been significant.

To make nouns possessive, follow one of the following methods.

MAKING NOUNS POSSESSIVE

For singular nouns, add -*'s: patient* + *'s* = *patient's; Marx* + *'s* = *Marx's.*

For plural nouns ending in -*s,* add *': psychiatrists* + *'* = *psychiatrists'.*

For plural nouns not ending in -*s,* add -*'s: women* + *'s* = *women's.*

COMPOUND WORDS.   With compound words (such as *mother-in-law, attorney-at-law, everybody else*), add the apostrophe to the last word of the compound.

> I borrowed my *sister-in-law's* car.

> *Everybody else's* vote was counted.

JOINT POSSESSION.   When you want to show joint possession by two or more persons, places, or things, add the apostrophe only to the last word.

> *Boyle and Johnson's* book was a huge success. [The two people are connected to one book.]

When you want to show that two or more persons, places, or things hold individual possession, add apostrophes to each person, place, or thing.

Boyle's and Johnson's books were both huge successes. [Each person is connected to a book.]

CAUTION: Do not use apostrophes to make nouns plural.

The *Lewises* [not *Lewis's*] collaborated on writing their book.

The paper *supplies* [not *supply's*] will not last a month.

Do not use apostrophes with possessive **personal** and **relative pronouns**.

The book owes *its* [not *it's*] theoretical foundations to Freud, *whose* [not *who's*] influence has spread to many disciplines.

See also *it's, its* and **who's, whose**.

Apostrophes to form contractions

Apostrophes stand in place of omitted letters in contractions.

doesn't	does not
I'd	I would
isn't	is not
it's	it is *or* it has
let's	let us
we'll	we will
who's	who is *or* who has
you've	you have

Because contractions reflect a casual, conversational style, they are used sparingly in formal writing.

CAUTION: Do not confuse the contracted *it is* (*it's*) and *who is* (*who's*) with the possessive pronouns *its* and *whose*. (See also *it's, its* and **who's, whose**.)

Apostrophes in special uses

Apostrophes mark plurals of letters, words used as words, and sometimes numbers.

There were more *A's* than *B's* on the anthropology test.

The *6's* and *7's* outrank the *4's. or* The *6s* and *7s* outrank the *4s.*

The sentence was strung together with five *and's.*

In current usage, the plural for years in decades or centuries is usually formed without an apostrophe.

The *1990s* are a time for change.

In informal writing or quoted dialogue, the apostrophe can mark the omission of letters or numbers.

The class of *'92* will have a reunion party next summer.

"You're really *jinglin'* tonight," he quipped.

appositive   A noun, **phrase**, or **clause** that renames a **noun** or **noun phrase**.

Scotland, *a political division of the United Kingdom of Great Britain and Ireland*, is bounded by England to the south. [phrase as appositive]

The three divisions of Great Britain—*England, Scotland, and Wales*—share one Parliament. [nouns as appositive]

Scotland includes three island groups: *the Orkneys, the Shetlands, and the Hebrides.* [nouns as appositive]

The fact *that the official church of Scotland is Presbyterian* has influenced Scotland's history. [clause as appositive]

Nonrestrictive appositives are set off with **commas, dashes,** or **colons.** **Restrictive** appositives, such as in the last example, are not separated from other words in the sentence by punctuation.

CAUTION: Appositives punctuated as sentences are sentence **fragments.**

FAULTY: In 1707 Scotland was united with England and Wales. Two other parts of the United Kingdom of Great Britain.

REVISED: In 1707 Scotland was united with England and Wales, two other parts of the United Kingdom of Great Britain.

appropriate language   (See **diction**)

articles   The articles are *a, an,* and *the.* They are often called *determiners* because they signal that a noun follows: *a car, an automobile, the convertible.* Do not use *an* when *a* is called for. Usage depends on *sound.* Use *a* before words beginning with a consonant sound, *an* before those beginning with a vowel sound: *a paper, a yellow book, a usual occurrence, a happy child; an unusual event, an hour, an exception, an ice storm.* With abbreviations, use *a* before initial letters with a consonant sound, *an* before initial letters with a vowel sound: *a*

U.S. ambassador, *an* MTV video. With acronyms, read the abbreviations as words: *a* SALT agreement, *a* UNICEF contribution, *an* OPEC decision. Do not omit articles when usage calls for them.

FAULTY: Place paper in tray before turning on machine.

REVISED: Place the paper in the tray before turning on the machine.

▼ Articles can be troublesome for ESL speakers. A brief summary of usage follows.

1. *A* and *an* are **indefinite articles;** use them to precede nouns that represent things not already identified. *The* is a **definite article;** use it when the noun it precedes is specific or known to the reader.

   An infectious disease discovered in recent years has been termed Legionnaire's disease. [*An* signals one disease among many.]

   The disease struck over 180 people attending *the* 1976 American Legion Convention in Philadelphia. [*The* signals an identified disease and a specific convention.]

2. Use *a* and *an* with singular **count nouns**: *a computer, an Apple computer, a paper, an astronomy paper.*

3. Do not use *a* and *an* with plural nouns: computers (not *a computers*), Apple computers (not *an Apple computers*).

4. Do not use *a* and *an* with **mass** (noncount) **nouns**: *information* (not *an information*), *homework* (not *a homework*). Many nouns are either mass or countable depending on their meaning.

   We put *gas* in the car just yesterday. [mass noun]

   The leaking *gases* are very volatile. [count noun]

5. Use *the* before singular or plural specific count nouns and before specific mass nouns.

   The women in the car were injured only slightly. [specific count noun]

   The information we needed arrived too late. [specific mass noun]

   Do not use *the* with plural nouns or mass nouns that are nonspecific or refer generally to all members of a group.

   We will receive *information* later in the day. [nonspecific information]

   Women still encounter a "glass ceiling" in many fields. [women in general]

6. Ordinarily, no article is used with place names: *Asia, Italy, Lake Huron, Sacramento, Greenland.* But collective and plural place names take *the: the United States, the People's Republic of China, the Great Lakes, the Himalayas.* Usually, *the* precedes bodies of water, land masses, and regions: *the Atlantic Ocean, the Caribbean Sea, the Mississippi River, the Painted Desert, the South Pole, the Southwest.*

as   Because of its numerous meanings, *as* is often ambiguous. For clearer writing, substitute one of its synonyms (*since, because, for, that, at that time, when, while*) whenever possible.

> *Because* [not *As*] they regarded him as a security risk, the Atomic Energy Commission suspended J. Robert Oppenheimer from its advisory committee.
>
> *While* [not *As*] he was directing the Los Alamos laboratory, the first atomic bomb was built.
>
> He was not convinced *that* [not *as*] the hydrogen bomb should be developed.

as, as if, like   In formal usage, *as* is a **preposition** or a subordinating **conjunction**, *as if* is a conjunction, and *like* is a preposition. Prepositions precede **objects**; conjunctions introduce **clauses.**

> *As* a child, Charles Dickens lived in poverty. [preposition]
>
> His novels portray London *as* [not *like*] it was in the mid-nineteenth century. [clause]
>
> His descriptions make readers feel *as if* [not *like*] they are stepping into the past. [conjunction]
>
> Stories *like* those told in his novels live on for generations. [preposition]

As prepositions, *like* and *as* express different meanings. *As* suggests that its object (*child* in the first sentence) is the same as the noun the prepositional phrase modifies (*Charles Dickens*), whereas *like* suggests resemblance (stories told in Dickens's novels are only representative of *Stories* named in the last sentence).

assure, ensure, insure   Use *assure* to mean "make confident"; *ensure* to mean "make certain"; and *insure* to mean "make certain" in a commercial sense.

> The pilot *assured* us that the trip would not be rough.

We checked the weather report to *ensure* that we would not encounter turbulence.

To be doubly careful, we *insured* our lives against unexpected events.

as to   Replace with *about*.

We were concerned *about* [not *as to*] your decision.

at, where   Avoid using *at* after *where*.

Where do you suppose he is? [not *Where do you suppose he is at?*]

at this point in time   (See **wordiness**)

auxiliary verbs   (See **helping verbs** and **verbs**)

awful, awfully   An adjective and an adverb commonly used in conversation. Avoid them in formal speech or writing.

awhile, a while   *Awhile* is an **adverb** meaning "for a short time." *A while* is a noun phrase that means "a period of time"; it can follow a preposition. Do not use *awhile* after a preposition.

We can stay only for *a while*. [noun phrase acting as the object of the preposition *for*]

We can stay *awhile*. [adverb modifying *can stay*]

B

---

bad, badly   *Bad* is an **adjective**, *badly* an **adverb**. After a **linking verb,** use *bad* as a complement to modify a **subject.**

Wilson felt *bad* when he missed the freethrow. [*Bad* describes the subject *Wilson*.]

Use *badly* to modify **verbs.**

Wilson tossed the ball *badly*. [*Badly* describes the verb *tossed*.]

bandwagon   (See **fallacies in logic**)

be   *Be* (with its forms *am, is, are, was, were, being, been*) is the most common **verb** in English. It is not only a **helping verb** in numerous compound verb forms (or **verb phrases**) but also a **linking verb** that connects **subject complements** to their **subjects.**

> Aspirin *is* still the best medicine for cold relief. [The linking verb *is* connects the noun complement *medicine* to the subject *Aspirin.*]
>
> Cough syrup can *be* taken for coughs. [The helping verb *be* with *can* and *taken* creates the **passive voice.**]
>
> A congressional panel *is* charging that people buy cold medicines that don't work. [The helping verb *is* with *charging* creates a progressive verb form (see **verbs** and **tenses of verbs**).]
>
> Decongestants *are* more effective than antihistamines, the panel claims. [The linking verb *are* connects the adjective complement *effective* to the subject *decongestants.*]

Besides being the most common English verb, *be* is also the most irregular. Here are its forms:

	I	HE, SHE, IT, AND SINGULAR NOUNS	WE, YOU, THEY, AND PLURAL NOUNS	PARTICIPLES
PRESENT:	am	is	are	being
PAST:	was	was	were	been

FORMS OF *BE*

See further discussions at **agreement of subjects and verbs** and other entries marked here with boldface type.

because of   (See *due to*)

begging the question   (See **fallacies in logic**)

being as, being that   Avoid these nonstandard phrases in writing. Use *because* instead.

> *Because* [not *being that* or *being as*] the crowd was so noisy, Wilson missed his freethrow.

beside, besides   *Beside* means "next to"; *besides* means "except" or "in addition to."

If you place the negative criticisms *beside* the lukewarm reviews, you find a quite negative reception of the book.

Besides the two negative criticisms, the book received three lukewarm reviews.

between   (See ***among***)

between you and me   *Between you and me* is the correct form. The preposition *between* must be followed by the objective **case** of the first-person **pronoun:** *me. Between you and I* and *between you and myself* are incorrect.

Between you and me [not *Between you and I*], the book should never have been published in the first place.

See **case** and **pronouns**.

brackets   Use brackets within quotations to enclose your comments or changes.

"Pleonasm," says H. W. Fowler, "is the using of more words [such as *if and when*] than are required to give the sense intended."

Use the word *sic* (meaning "so" or "thus") in brackets to indicate that you have quoted an error in the original.

The newspaper heading read "DNR to investigate Albany cougar sitings [*sic*]."

Do not use brackets when **parentheses** are called for or parentheses when brackets are needed.

bring, take   Use *bring* to indicate movement toward a person, place, or thing, *take* to indicate movement away from a person, place, or thing.

The stereotypical view of the suburban male is of one who *brings* home the bacon and *takes* out the garbage.

but, yet   Use *but* or *yet* as appropriate to indicate contrasting **coordination;** do not use *but* and *yet* together.

The author of the article claims ownership of the material, *yet* [not *but yet*] some of the data was copyrighted fifteen years ago.

See also **conjunctions**.

C

can, may In formal usage, *can* expresses the capacity or ability to do something, *may* the permission for, or possibility of, doing something.

> Scientists *may* learn more about the universe if they *can* devise a way of seeing to its outer reaches.

can't hardly, can't scarcely **Double negative** phrases for *can hardly* and *can scarcely.*

> I *can hardly* [not *can't hardly*] believe all the changes computers have made in our lives.

can't help but A redundant phrase for *can't help.*

> I *can't help* wondering [not *can't help but wonder*] what life would be like without computers.

capitalization Capitalization is a way of marking words and letters. Most writers agree on the following practices:

1. Always capitalize the first word of a sentence and the pronoun *I.*
2. In titles of works, capitalize the first and last words and all words except internal **conjunctions, prepositions, articles,** and the **infinitive** marker *to: The Heat of the Day, A Tale of Two Cities.*
3. Capitalize abbreviations for government agencies and other organizations or acronyms: UNESCO, EPA, MDOT, IBM, FFA, NEA, MTV, CD-ROM. The use of periods in abbreviations varies; for specific usages, consult your dictionary. See also **Periods.**
4. Capitalize all proper names, including those for people, places, institutions, historical periods or events, races and nationalities, geographical regions, and trade names.
5. Do not capitalize seasons or compass directions. Capitalize references to family relationships and honorary titles when they are part of proper names (*Aunt Michele, Mayor Ross*). Do not capitalize such references when they are preceded by an **article,** an **adjective,** or a possessive **pronoun** (*my aunt, the mayor*).

CAPITALIZATION		
	CAPITALIZE	*DON'T CAPITALIZE*
ABBREVIATIONS:	CIA, M.D., NBC, B.C.	i.e., etc., pp., rpm
PEOPLE:	Michael Smith	teacher
PLACES:	the Lincoln Memorial	a historical shrine
INSTITUTIONS:	Cornell University	a university
HISTORICAL PERIODS:	the Middle Ages	the twentieth century
HISTORICAL EVENTS:	the Civil War	a civil war
NATIONALITIES:	Chicano, Hmong	—
RACES:	Caucasian, African-American	white, black
REGIONS:	the Midwest, the South	a southern city
TRADE NAMES:	Packard-Bell	a computer
COURSES:	Biology 101	biology
LANGUAGES:	English, Swahili	—
DAYS, MONTHS, SEASONS:	Tuesday, April	summer, spring
COMPASS DIRECTIONS:	—	south, northwest
FAMILY RELATIONSHIPS:	Dad, Grandmother	my dad, an uncle
TITLES:	Professor Smith	a professor
HOLIDAYS:	Fourth of July, Labor Day	—

Quoted and parenthetical material

Capitalize the first letter of introduced **quotations.**

Under the heading *comptroller, cont-,* H. W. Fowler says, "*The* first spelling is not merely archaic, but erroneous."

Do not capitalize the first letter of quotations that are worked into your own sentence and that cannot stand alone as sentences.

According to H. W. Fowler, the word *comptroller* "*is* not merely archaic, but erroneous."

Capitalize the first letter of a sentence enclosed in parentheses when the parenthetical text does not belong within another sentence.

The correct term, says Fowler, is *controller.* (*Some* statutes erroneously stipulate the archaic term.)

The correct term, says Fowler, is *controller* (*though* some statutes erroneously stipulate the archaic term).

cases

SECTION OVERVIEW
Case forms of personal and relative pronouns
Nominative case
Objective case
Possessive case
Pronouns with *and* or *or*
Pronouns after *as* or *than*
Pronouns as subject complements
Pronouns as appositives
Pronouns in relative clauses
Interrogative pronouns
Pronouns and parenthetical insertions

Case is a grammatical term for the way **nouns** and **pronouns** show their relationships to other parts of a sentence. English nouns have only two cases: the regular form (the one listed in the dictionary, such as *week*) and the **possessive case,** used to show ownership or connection, such as *week's* (see **apostrophes**). English pronouns, however, have retained their case forms. Shown below are the case forms of English personal and relative pronouns.

CASE FORMS OF PERSONAL AND RELATIVE PRONOUNS			
	NOMINATIVE	*OBJECTIVE*	*POSSESSIVE*
PERSONAL:	I	me	my, mine
	you	you	your, yours
	he	him	his
	she	her	her, hers
	it	it	its
	we	us	our, ours
	they	them	their, theirs
RELATIVE:	who	whom	whose
	whoever	whomever	whosoever
	which	which	
	that	that	

Nominative case

Use the *nominative* case for **subjects** and **pronouns, complements, and appositives** referring to subjects.

SUBJECT: College students need to start early if *they* want to find a job when they graduate. [*They* is the subject of the verb *want*.]

SUBJECT COMPLEMENT: The aggressive job-seekers know *who* they are and what they want. [*Who* complements the first *they*.]

APPOSITIVE: *We* students must begin networking early. [*We* and *students* are in apposition to, or rename, one another.]

Objective case

Use the *objective* case for **objects, appositives** of objects, and subjects of **infinitives.**

DIRECT OBJECT: Placement personnel will assist *us* in our job search.

INDIRECT OBJECT: No one will give *us* a job on a silver platter.

OBJECT OF A PREPOSITION: It's up to *us* to work at job hunting. [*Us* is the object of the preposition *to*.]

APPOSITIVE: Finding a job will take time for *us* graduating students. [*Us* and *students* are in apposition to, or rename, one another and serve as an object of the preposition *for*.]

SUBJECT OF INFINITIVE: At the same time, placement personnel will help *us* to locate job openings. [*Us* is the subject of *to locate*.]

Possessive case

Use the *possessive* case to show ownership and connection.

This *year's* job market may be a little tighter than last *year's*. [The possessive indicates the job markets of this year and of last year.]

A job *candidate's* resumé initiates *his or her* application process.

Unlike possessive nouns, possessive pronouns are not formed with apostrophes. Do not confuse them with **contractions** such as ***it's*** (meaning *it is* or *it has*) and ***who's*** (meaning *who is* or *who has*).

Except for their possessive forms (explained under **apostrophes**), nouns rarely present problems in case. Pronouns, however, are a different matter. The most common problems come up with *and* or *or,* after *as* or *than,* when pronouns act as subject complements, when pronouns act as appositives, with pronouns in relative clauses, with interrogative pronouns, and with parenthetical insertions.

Pronouns *with* **and** *or* **or**

The case of a pronoun joined to a noun or another pronoun by *and* or *or* is the same as it would be if the pronoun appeared alone. Test the case by removing the other half of the compound.

> If *he* ~~and an employer~~ are/is already acquainted, a candidate may have an inside track to a job. [Faulty: *If him ~~and an employer~~ are/is already acquainted. . . .*]
>
> Networking gives *him* ~~and the potential employer~~ useful information ~~about one another~~. [Faulty: *Networking gives he ~~and the potential employer~~. . . .*]

Pronouns after *as* or *than*

In comparisons using *as* or *than*, the pronoun is almost always a subject and therefore should take the nominative case.

> An employer knows her employment needs better than *we* [not *us*]. [*We* is the subject of the unstated verb *do*. Many writers would include the verb: *An employer knows her employment needs better than we do.*]

Occasionally, meaning calls for a pronoun in the objective case after *as* or *than*: *An employer knows her employment needs better than us* means "An employer knows her employment needs better than she knows us." For clarity's sake, complete the thought by stating the implied words.

Pronouns as subject complements

Because **subject complements** rename subjects, they take the same case as subjects, the nominative.

> Many job applicants think, It could have been *I* who was offered that job. [*I* complements *It*, an **expletive** standing for the real subject of the sentence, the clause *who was offered that job.*]

In informal usage, people commonly use phrases such as "It's me" and "It was them" instead of "It's I" and "It was they."

Pronouns as appositives

Appositive pronouns take the subjective or objective case depending on how the words they name function within the sentence.

> *We* applicants should learn how to take advantage of an employer's own referral system. [*We* and *applicants* are in apposition to one another and function as the subject of *should learn.*]

Knowing the referral system gives *us applicants* an edge in the employment market. [*Us* and *applicants* are in apposition to one another and function as the indirect **object** of *gives*.]

Pronouns in relative clauses

The case of **relative pronouns** is determined by their function within the **relative clause** and is not influenced by the function of the relative clause within the sentence.

Applicants often wonder *whom* an employer finally hired. [*Whom* is the direct object of *hired*. The relative clause *whom an employer finally hired* is the direct object of *wonder*.]

Applicants often wonder *who* finally got the job. [*Who* is the subject of *got*. The relative clause *who finally got the job* is the direct object of *wonder*.]

Interrogative pronouns

Because of the inverted word order of **questions**, the case of interrogative **pronouns** is sometimes troublesome. To determine the case of the pronoun, you may find it helpful to recast the sentence in normal word order and replace the interrogative word with another pronoun in the correct case.

Who knows the best way to begin the application process? [*She* knows. *Who* is the subject of *knows*.]

To *whom* should we send our resumés? [We should send our resumés to *him*. *Whom* is the object of the preposition *To*.]

Whom did the employer finally hire? [The employer finally hired *him*. *Whom* is the direct object of *did hire*.]

Pronouns and parenthetical elements

The case of pronouns is not affected by parenthetical elements in a sentence; that is, words that intervene between the pronoun and the verb or the subject and verb and the pronoun.

Who do you think will get the job? [*Who will get the job?*]

Whom do you suspect the firm will hire? [*Whom will the firm hire?*]

center around   A common but illogical expression; substitute *center on*.

The report *centers on* [not *centers around*] the correlation between overweight and heart disease.

clauses   A clause is a group of words that contains a **subject** and a **verb**. Some clauses may stand alone as sentences.

subject   verb
who   have high blood pressure

subject   verb
You   should limit your alcohol intake to one drink per day.

subject   verb
if you   want to avoid high blood pressure

Independent clauses may function as **simple sentences.**

> Too much alcohol commonly leads to high blood pressure. [*Alcohol* is the subject, *leads* the verb.]

A sentence that contains two independent clauses is a **compound sentence.**

> High blood pressure is a major health concern, but people can sometimes lower their blood pressure with a change in lifestyle.

Subordinate clauses must be connected to independent clauses; they cannot stand alone as sentences.

> People *who have high blood pressure* should limit their alcoholic drinks to one a day. [In the subordinate clause, *who* is the subject and *have* is the verb.]
> *If you drink and want to avoid high blood pressure*, limit your drinks to one a day. [In the subordinate clause, *you* is the subject and *drink* and *want* are the verbs.]

A sentence containing an independent clause and a subordinate clause (such as each of the last two examples) is a **complex sentence**. One that has more than one independent clause and at least one subordinate clause is a **compound-complex sentence**. Subordinate clauses written as sentences are **fragments;** for example, *If you drink and want to avoid high blood pressure* is not a sentence. See also **semicolons, periods,** and **commas**.

clichés   Clichés are once-colorful statements that have lost their color through overuse. Examples are *last but not least, powers that be, leave no stone unturned, tip of the iceberg, from the frying pan into the* *fire, crystal clear.* While they may still convey the intended idea, they are often considered evidence of lazy thinking on the part of the writer.

collective nouns   Collective nouns name groups, for example, *family, committee, team, staff.* Their intended meaning is usually singular; that is, when the group acts as a whole, a singular verb is used.

The *committee has agreed* to delay hiring a replacement.

When the sentence means that members of the group are acting individually, however, the verb and any related pronouns are plural.

The *team are arriving* from *their* separate home cities.

See also **agreement of subjects and verbs, agreement of pronouns and antecedents,** and **nouns.**

colloquialisms   Colloquial language is a conversational style appropriate in everyday speech and some personal writing but not in academic, professional, and other formal writing. Words such as *kids, great* (as in *a great movie*), *flunk, pretty* (as in *pretty good*), and *figured out* are best avoided except in casual circumstances or when you want to give the impression of informality.

colons   The colon is commonly used to introduce an explanatory element or elements, often in the form of a list.

Be watchful for the early signs of stress: disorganization, escape fantasies, indecision, and depression.

The part of a sentence that precedes a colon is usually an **independent clause.** Colons also link related numbers: *10:45 a.m., Luke 2:20, 7:3* (ratio). In business letters, a colon follows a salutation.

Dear Mr. Johnson:

Inappropriate interruptions of colons

Do not interrupt your sentences with colons that separate **subjects** and **verbs** or **prepositions** and their **objects.**

The early signs of stress are [not *are:*] disorganization, escape fantasies, indecision, and depression.

If you can't reduce stress, seek help from a professional, such as [not *such as:*] your medical doctor, a counselor, or a therapist.

An exception is the colon that introduces a quotation that appears either within a sentence or set off as an indented block.

> Concerning stress, doctors advise a change in lifestyle: "If and when you recognize any of these symptoms of stress, know that it's time to slow down and start taking care of yourself—before bigger problems arise."

Confusing colons with semicolons

Writers correctly use a colon between two independent clauses (instead of a **semicolon**) if the second clause explains the first.

> Be sensitive to how your body reacts to the stress in your life: be watchful for headaches, tense muscles, and unreasonable irritability.

But never use a *semicolon* where a *colon* is called for. Colons are often followed by phrases; a phrase after a semicolon would be a **fragment.**

> Look for physical symptoms of stress: [not *stress;*] headaches, tense muscles, and unreasonable irritability.

Inappropriate resumptions after colons

Only a list or an explanatory phrase or clause should follow a colon. Do not resume the first part of your sentence after text set off by a colon.

> FAULTY: One of the symptoms of stress is disorganization: losing things, forgetting where you put things, and making mistakes, but you should look at this factor only in combination with others.

> REVISED: One of the symptoms of stress is disorganization: losing things, forgetting where you put things, and making mistakes. But you should look at this factor only in combination with others.

commands   (See **imperative mood**)

 commas

> SECTION OVERVIEW
> Commas with compound sentences
> Commas with introductory sentence elements
> Commas with nonrestrictive and parenthetical elements
> Commas in series
> Commas with coordinate adjectives
> Commas with quotations
> Commas with addresses and dates
> Commas for clarity

Commas, like all punctuation, are signals to readers about how to read words; a faulty signal may result in a misreading. Notice how the second sentence below reads more clearly than the first.

Those who can travel to Switzerland.

Those who can, travel to Switzerland.

Since the whole point of writing is to communicate an idea, it makes sense to use all the tools at your disposal.

Commas with compound sentences

A comma joins two **independent clauses** connected with a coordinating **conjunction.**

Switzerland has many different regions, and each has a strong regional pride.

Sometimes, when the clauses are very short or begin with **imperative** verbs, writers omit the conjunction.

Look beneath the surface and you will find many languages in Switzerland. [*Look* is an imperative verb with *you* as the understood subject.]

Commas with introductory sentence elements

Commas set off a variety of introductory sentence elements: **clauses**, **phrases**, and, occasionally, single words.

SUBORDINATE CLAUSE: *Although Switzerland has four major languages*, in practice there are many sublanguages.

PHRASE: *As just one example*, Romansh is divided into several dialects depending on the region where its speakers live.

WORD: *Further*, there are innumerable versions of the other major languages.

Short introductory phrases are not always set off.

On the surface you might find only four languages.

However, introductory subordinate clauses and **verbal phrases** are almost always followed by commas.

ADVERBIAL CLAUSE: *When the Swiss Germans read and write*, they use a language different from the one they use for speaking.

INFINITIVE PHRASE: *Not to be outdone*, French and Italian have numerous dialects too.

Commas with nonrestrictive and parenthetical elements

If **nonrestrictive elements, transitional adverbs,** or a few other types of parenthetical elements interrupt the flow of a sentence, they are enclosed with two commas. If they come at the end of a sentence, they are set off with one comma.

NONRESTRICTIVE CLAUSE: The word *Helvetia, which is the Latin name for Switzerland,* appears on all Swiss stamps and coins.

NONRESTRICTIVE PHRASE: Switzerland, *a peaceful nation,* has strong internal pride.

NONRESTRICTIVE VERBAL PHRASE: Switzerland's strong internal pride, *coupled with a collective national pride,* makes for Helvetian unity.

TRANSITIONAL ADVERB: The Swiss are, *nevertheless,* at odds with one another occasionally.

DIRECT ADDRESS: You can see, *reader,* that Switzerland is more than chocolate and pocket knives.

Commas in series

Commas separate items in a series.

WORDS: *Chocolate, pocket knives, watches, and cheese* are the products most commonly associated with Switzerland.

PHRASES: Switzerland also is known for its *mountain summits, deep blue lakes, quiet villages, and modern cities.*

CLAUSES: *The Jura Mountains line the northwest, the spectacular Alps grace the south, and the hilly Swiss Plateau occupies the space between the two ranges.*

While usage varies about including a comma before the last item in a series, ambiguity sometimes results when it is omitted. It is good practice, therefore, to include a comma before the last item in a series.

Important sources of income in Switzerland are tourism, technology, international banking, and manufacturing. [Without the last comma, a reader might wonder if *international* modifies *manufacturing* as well as *banking.*]

Commas with coordinate adjectives

Commas separate coordinate **adjectives,** or adjectives that modify a noun equally.

Most of the country's population resides in the *narrow, hilly* Swiss Plateau.

When you're not sure about using a comma between adjectives, try inserting *and* between the two adjectives to test whether they are truly coordinate (*narrow and hilly*). Or reverse the order of the adjectives (*hilly, narrow*). Do not use a comma between cumulative adjectives or between the last adjective and the noun being modified.

> The *two massive mountain* ranges occupy about 70 percent of the country's area. [There are no commas between the adjectives because they cannot be read as *two and massive and mountain*, or *massive two mountain*. There is no comma before *ranges*, the noun they modify.]

Commas with quotations

Commas usually separate quoted sentences from the words that identify them.

> According to the *World Almanac*, "Switzerland is a leading world banking center; stability of the currency brings funds from many quarters."
>
> "Switzerland," says the *World Almanac*, "is a leading world banking center."

But don't use commas to set off a **quotation** that follows the **relative pronoun** *that* or other words used to integrate the quotation into your sentence.

> The *Almanac* further says that voters have [not *have,*] "rejected a proposal that would have opened bank records to authorities investigating domestic and foreign tax evasion."

Commas, like **periods**, precede final quotation marks.

> Switzerland maintains a state of "armed neutrality," which to some people might seem a contradiction in terms.

Commas with addresses and dates

Use a comma to separate city and state in an address, but do not set off the **ZIP code** with a comma.

> *Lakewood, California 90712*   or   *Lakewood, CA 90712*

In a sentence, enclose a state or country name with two commas.

> Send the letter to the *Lakewood, California,* address.

Be consistent in how you treat dates.

June 3, 1947   or   *3 June 1947*

Place a comma after the year when a complete date falls in the middle of a sentence.

> Whether the incident happened on *June 3, 1947,* or at a later date is still being debated.

When stating only the month and year, omit the commas: *June 1947.*

Commas for clarity

Commas are sometimes needed for clarity, even when none of the preceding rules apply. Consider these sentences:

> Once Switzerland was part of the Roman Empire.
> For the Romans had conquered the region in 58 B.C.

In their present form, these sentences lack clarity. Commas clear up their meaning.

> Once, Switzerland was part of the Roman Empire.
> For, the Romans had conquered the region in 58 B.C.

See also **commas, unnecessary**.

 commas, unnecessary

> SECTION OVERVIEW
> Unnecessary commas between subjects and verbs or between prepositions and objects
> Unnecessary commas with compound elements
> Unnecessary commas with restrictive elements
> Unnecessary commas before the first or after the last item in a series
> Unnecessary commas with adjectives that are not coordinate
> Unnecessary commas before adverb clauses and phrases
> Other misuses of commas

Unnecessary commas give readers faulty signals. Avoid using commas in the following situations.

Unnecessary commas between subjects and verbs or between prepositions and objects

Unless a **parenthetical element** follows your **subject** (in which case you would enclose it with two commas), do not place a comma after your subject. Because commas have essentially two functions, to separate (one comma) and to enclose (two commas), a comma after your subject separates it from your verb, giving a faulty signal to your readers.

> The rehabilitation of injured athletes⬛has contributed major advances to sports medicine. [*Rehabilitation*, with its modifier *of injured athletes*, is the subject of the sentence and should not be separated from its verb *has contributed*.]

> What athletes need to understand⬛is that rehabilitation after injury may reach a plateau where there is no apparent improvement. [The subject is the **noun clause** *What athletes need to understand*; it should not be separated from its verb *is*.]

It is likewise illogical to separate a **preposition** from its **object.**

> Rehabilitation is often accompanied by setbacks such as⬛additional pain and inflammation. [The preposition *such as* is illogically separated from its objects *pain* and *inflammation*.]

> Many athletes continue to play *despite⬛continued pain from injuries*. [The preposition *despite* is illogically separated from its object *pain*.]

Unnecessary commas with compound elements

Use commas before **coordinating conjunctions** (*and, but, or, nor, for, so, yet*) in only two situations: when the conjunction joins two **independent clauses** or is the last item in a series (see **commas**). Avoid other uses.

> Injuries are common⬛and probably inevitable for professional athletes. [*And* joins the **adjectives** *common* and *inevitable*.]

> Injuries can cause athletes to miss games⬛and can even end their careers. [*And* joins the **verbs** *can cause* and *can end*.]

> Professional sports always have younger performers who are still healthy⬛and who are ready to replace injured players. [*And* joins two **subordinate clauses**: *who are still healthy* and *who are ready to replace injured players*.]

Unnecessary commas with restrictive elements

Unlike **nonrestrictive elements**, **restrictive elements** are essential to the meaning of a sentence and therefore are not set off with commas.

> Professional athletes, who are injured, often face emotional trauma because of their diminished performance. [The relative clause *who*

are injured is essential for identifying what types of professional athletes are being discussed.]

Psychiatrist▪Jerry May▪says that loss of self-esteem is common to injured athletes. [The appositive *Jerry May* is essential for identifying a particular psychiatrist.]

Unnecessary commas before the first or after the last item in a series

Each item in a series is set off with a comma, but the series itself is not separated from the rest of the sentence (see **commas**).

Psychological trauma of athletes' injuries may include▪denial, anger, and depression. [The series *denial, anger, and depression* should not be preceded by a comma.]

Denial, anger, and depression▪are part of the psychological trauma that injured athletes may face. [The series *Denial, anger, and depression* should not be separated from the verb *are* by a comma.]

Unnecessary commas with cumulative adjectives

Adjectives that cannot be joined by *and* are cumulative, not coordinate, and should not be separated by commas (see **commas**).

Injured athletes generally are treated by top▪orthopedic surgeons. [*Top* and *orthopedic* cannot be joined by *and;* the adjectives are cumulative.]

Unnecessary commas between adjectives and nouns

Do not use a comma between an adjective and the **noun** it modifies.

But even highly skilled, fully equipped▪treatment usually does not speed recovery.

Unnecessary commas before adverb clauses and phrases

Adverb **clauses** and **phrases** that come at the end of sentences are ordinarily not set off with commas.

Physical injuries can give athletes negative emotions▪*whenever they have to sit out a game.*

Many doctors prescribe psychological rehabilitation▪*even for temporary disabilities.*

Adverb clauses beginning with *because* are usually not set off with commas, except when the *because* clause is not essential to the meaning of the main clause.

Doctors advise psychological rehabilitation for disabled athletes *because negative emotions can hinder physical recovery.* [There is no comma; the *because* clause is essential to the meaning of the sentence.]

Patients are encouraged to express their fears about surgery and recovery, *because doing so builds trust and confidence.* [There is a comma; the *because* clause is not essential to the meaning of the main clause.]

Other misuses of commas

AFTER A COORDINATING CONJUNCTION.   Ordinarily, do not use a comma after *and, but, or, nor, for, so,* or *yet.*

But▪the advantages of rehabilitation offset any setbacks.

BEFORE A PARENTHESIS.   Parenthetical remarks logically belong to the text that precedes them, not what follows, and therefore should be followed by any comma that may be necessary to the sentence as a whole (the **parentheses** themselves do not require commas).

FAULTY: When patients reach plateaus▪(where little improvement can be seen) recovery may seem to be too far off.

REVISED: When patients reach plateaus (where little improvement can be seen), recovery may seem to be too far off. [The comma follows the parentheses.]

BEFORE *THAT*.   In almost all cases, *that* introduces an essential or **restrictive** element and therefore is not separated from the rest of the sentence with a comma.

Patients need to accept the fact▪that pain accompanies rehabilitation.

Physical therapists say▪that there are always ups and downs in recovery.

WITH A QUESTION MARK.   Since question marks and exclamation points are marks of end punctuation, they are generally not followed by commas.

"How long am I going to be unable to play?▪" is the usual question of injured athletes. [The question mark ends the quotation; the comma is unnecessary.]

comma splices

> SECTION OVERVIEW
> Replace the comma with a semicolon or a period
> Add a coordinating conjunction
> Make one clause subordinate

A comma splice is a punctuation error in which a writer uses a **comma** to separate two **independent clauses.**

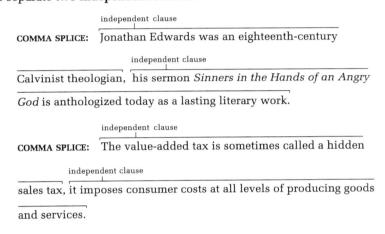

independent clause

COMMA SPLICE: Jonathan Edwards was an eighteenth-century

independent clause

Calvinist theologian, his sermon *Sinners in the Hands of an Angry*

God is anthologized today as a lasting literary work.

independent clause

COMMA SPLICE: The value-added tax is sometimes called a hidden

independent clause

sales tax, it imposes consumer costs at all levels of producing goods

and services.

Since the clauses in these **compound sentences** are independent, the commas are insufficient punctuation. The error can be corrected in one of three ways: by replacing the comma with a **semicolon** or a **period,** by adding a coordinating **conjunction,** or by subordinating one of the clauses.

Replace the comma with a semicolon or a period

Using a semicolon in place of a comma corrects the comma splice without changing the meaning.

> Jonathan Edwards was an eighteenth-century Calvinist theologian; his sermon *Sinners in the Hands of an Angry God* is anthologized today as a lasting literary work.

Use a period to separate two clauses and create two sentences when you want to treat the ideas separately.

The value-added tax is sometimes called a hidden sales tax. It imposes consumer costs at all levels of producing goods and services.

Add a coordinating conjunction

Adding a coordinating conjunction (*and, but, or, nor, for, so, yet*) allows you to show how two clauses are related (for example, use *but* for contrast, *or* for alternative, *and* for addition).

Jonathan Edwards was an eighteenth-century Calvinist theologian, *and* his sermon *Sinners in the Hands of an Angry God* is anthologized today as a lasting literary work. [a **compound sentence**]

The value-added tax is sometimes called a hidden sales tax, *for* it imposes consumer costs at all levels of producing goods and services. [a **compound sentence**]

CAUTION: Do not treat **transitional adverbs** (such as *however, moreover, nevertheless, then*) as coordinating conjunctions. If you use them to relate the ideas of two independent clauses, you need a semicolon or a period between the clauses.

Jonathan Edwards was an eighteenth-century Calvinist theologian; *indeed*, his sermon *Sinners in the Hands of an Angry God* is anthologized as a lasting literary work.

The value-added tax is sometimes called a hidden sales tax; *in fact*, it imposes costs at all levels of producing goods and services.

Make one clause subordinate

You can use **subordination** to make one clause dependent on an independent clause, thus creating a **complex sentence.**

Jonathan Edwards was an eighteenth-century Calvinist theologian *whose sermon "Sinners in the Hands of an Angry God" is anthologized today as a lasting literary work.*

"Sinners in the Hands of an Angry God," *a sermon by the eighteenth-century Calvinist theologian Jonathan Edwards*, is anthologized today as a lasting literary work.

The value-added tax is sometimes called a hidden sales tax *because it imposes costs at all levels of producing goods and services.*

The value-added tax is sometimes called a hidden sales tax *as a result of the consumer costs it imposes at all levels of producing goods and services.*

When subordinating one clause, keep your main idea in an independent clause (see **subordination**).

SUMMARY OF WAYS TO AVOID COMMA SPLICES

Separate independent clauses with a semicolon.

INDEPENDENT CLAUSE **;** *INDEPENDENT CLAUSE*

Separate independent clauses with a semicolon and a transitional adverb.

INDEPENDENT CLAUSE **;** however, *INDEPENDENT CLAUSE*

Create two separate sentences.

INDEPENDENT CLAUSE **.** *INDEPENDENT CLAUSE*

Add a coordinating conjunction between independent clauses.

INDEPENDENT CLAUSE **,** and *INDEPENDENT CLAUSE*

Make one clause subordinate to the independent clause.

INDEPENDENT CLAUSE since (when, etc.) *DEPENDENT CLAUSE*

Since (when, etc.) *DEPENDENT CLAUSE* **,** *INDEPENDENT CLAUSE*

INDEPEND- **,** who (which, etc.) *-ENT CLAUSE*

See also **fused sentences.**

common nouns   Common **nouns** do not name specific persons, places, and things. Unlike **proper nouns**, they are not capitalized. Names of the seasons (*spring, summer*) are common nouns, but names of the days of the week (*Tuesday*) and months (*July*) are proper nouns. Names of compass directions (*southeast*) are common nouns, but names of regions (*the Southeast*) are proper nouns. Words denoting family relationships are common nouns (*my mother, an uncle*), but names of specific relatives (*Mom, Uncle Bob*) are proper nouns. (See also **capitalization.**)

comparative forms   (See **adjectives** and **adverbs**)

complement, compliment   A *complement* is something that adds to or completes something else.

> The findings of Ortiz's research are a *complement* to those of Boone.

A *compliment* expresses courtesy or praise:

> Boone paid Ortiz a *compliment* on the quality of his research.

Both words can function also as verbs:

> The findings of Ortiz's research *complement* those of Boone.
>
> Boone *complimented* Ortiz on the quality of his research.

complements   A complement renames or describes a **subject** or an **object**. A **subject complement** follows a **linking verb** and renames or describes the subject.

> The Mongols are an Asiatic *people* numbering nearly 3 million. [The noun *people* renames the subject *Mongols*.]
>
> The Mongols are *nomadic* and *pastoral*. [The adjectives *nomadic* and *pastoral* describe the subject *Mongols*.]

Pronouns that are subject complements take the nominative **case.**

> It was *they* who swept Europe and Asia in the thirteenth century.

An **object complement** renames or describes the **direct object.**

> In the thirteenth century, Genghis Khan made the feuding tribes a united *nation*. [The noun *nation* renames the direct object *tribes*.]
>
> The merging of their traditional shamanism with Buddhism made the Montel religion primarily *Lamaist*. [The adjective *Lamaist* describes the direct object *religion*.]

complex sentences   A complex **sentence** combines an **independent clause** with one or more **subordinate clauses**. The subordinate clauses may occur at the beginning of the sentence, at the end, or somewhere within the sentence. Ordinarily the independent clause carries the main idea while the subordinate clauses contribute related ideas.

> Because lie detectors are not infallible, test results are usually not admissible in court. [The subordinate **adverb clause**, *Because lie detectors are not infallible*, is related causally to the independent clause.]

Another controversial use of lie detectors is to screen people who apply for jobs. [The subordinate **adjective clause** *who apply for jobs* modifies *people.*]

A lie detector tells whether or not a subject is telling the truth. [The subordinate **noun clause** *whether or not the subject is telling the truth* functions as the direct **object** of the verb *tells.*]

Complex sentences are a useful stylistic option in combination with **simple sentences** and **compound sentences**.

compound antecedents　Compound **antecedents** of **pronouns** are treated as singular or plural depending on the **coordinating conjunction** that joins them and sometimes the number of the last antecedent. If the antecedents are joined by *and*, the pronoun referring to them is plural.

John Heyl Vincent and *Lewis Miller* proposed the Chautauqua movement in 1873 when *they* attended the Methodist Episcopal camp meeting in Chautauqua, New York. [The two antecedents *John Heyl* and *Lewis Miller* require the plural pronoun *they.*]

When compound antecedents are joined by *or* or *nor*, the pronoun agrees with the nearer antecedent.

Authors or sometimes an *explorer* would share *his* experiences in these eight-week summer programs. [The pronoun *his* agrees with the singular *explorer.*]

See also **agreement of pronouns and antecedents.**

compound-complex sentences　A compound-complex sentence contains two or more **independent clauses** and one or more **subordinate clauses**. It enables writers to connect several related ideas and show the relationships among those ideas.

independent clause

Among the plants in the wide-ranging nightshade family are

independent clause

belladonna, tomato, and petunia, but the name *nightshade* is

subordinate clause

restricted to the genus *Solanum*, which is characterized by star-

shaped flowers and orange berries.

[The two independent clauses are connected with the contrasting coordinating **conjunction** *but*; the relative **pronoun** *which* begins the subordinate clause that modifies *Solanum*.]

"Boxcar" sentences

CAUTION: Writers sometimes get carried away with their ability to put together clauses and phrases, creating sentences that go on for many lines. Even though the sentences may be grammatically correct and their ideas related, inordinately long sentences make reading difficult. Be kind to your reader. If you find that you are writing a number of long sentences, or if you have a sentence that runs more than four or five lines, try to separate out some of the clauses.

Illogical connections

CAUTION: Sometimes writers get lost in the complexity of their sentences, writing clauses or phrases that go off on illogical tangents that have little connection with the main idea. Check all your compound-complex sentences for logic and **coherence**. Use **parentheses** with caution; they usually interrupt the flow of thought and may in fact contain information sufficiently unrelated as to be omitted entirely.

Faulty punctuation

CAUTION: Check your compound-complex sentences especially carefully for faulty punctuation. Look for **comma splices** and **fused sentences**, and see that you have used **commas** correctly. Odd as it may seem, a writer drafting long sentences also risks producing **fragments** by beginning a statement, interrupting it with a *who* or *which* clause, going on to another clause or two, and never completing the first idea. The whole long thing becomes a sentence fragment, as in this example:

> FRAGMENT: Many plants in the nightshade family, which includes several drug plants such as belladonna, Jimson weed, and tobacco, plus some important food plants—for example, potato, tomato, and eggplant—and ornamentals such as the petunia. [The idea beginning with *Many plants in the nightshade family* is never completed.]

compound predicates   A compound **predicate** has two or more verbs connected by a **coordinating conjunction**.

> Nikita Khrushchev *joined* the Communist party in 1918 and *became* a member of its Central Committee in 1934. [The subject *Nikita Khrushchev* has two verbs, *joined* and *became*, connected with the coordinating conjunction *and*.]

Unnecessary comma

CAUTION: Do not place a comma before or after a coordinating conjunction linking the second verb to the first in a compound predicate.

FAULTY: Nikita Khrushchev *joined* the Communist party in 1918, and *became* a member of its Central Committee in 1934.

Sentence fragment

CAUTION: Do not put a period before the coordinating conjunction linking the second verb to the first in a compound predicate, or you will create a **fragment.**

FAULTY: Nikita Khrushchev *joined* the Communist party in 1918. And *became* a member of its Central Committee in 1934.

compound sentences   A compound sentence contains two or more **independent clauses** joined by a comma and a **coordinating conjunction** (*and, but, or, nor, for, so, yet*) or a **semicolon.** This type of sentence is effective for relating two ideas of equal importance.

Ralph Lauren was first known for his men's fashions, but now he has gained fame for his tailored women's clothing.

Designer Bill Blass began his own company in 1970; he immediately became known for both men's and women's wear.

Be sure that the independent clauses are related. In the following example, the reader might be perplexed about the connection between the two clauses.

The Italian fashion designer Emilio Pucci began his career in 1947; among his creations are car roofs.

You can relate the second clause to the first with a semicolon and a transitional adverb.

Christian Dior designed the long-skirted "New Look" of 1947; however, he soon replaced it with the sack dress of the 1950s.

Unequal coordination

CAUTION: When you write a compound sentence, be sure that the independent clauses are of equal importance. If you want to place less emphasis on one clause, use **subordination**, creating a **complex sentence.**

Comma splices

CAUTION: Be wary of **comma splices** or **fused sentences**. Punctuate your compound sentences with a semicolon or with a comma and a coordinating conjunction between the clauses.

compound words   A compound word is two or more words used as a single word. It may be hyphenated, written closed up as one word, or remain two separate words with a single meaning: *best-selling, low-grade, well-constructed, parents-in-law; textbook, oneself; quantum mechanics, post office.*

Hyphenation

To know whether to hyphenate a compound word, refer to your dictionary. However, you can be guided by a few generalizations.

COMPOUND ADJECTIVES.   Hyphenate two or more words functioning as a single adjective before a noun: a *well-designed* room, a *self-serving* lawyer. However, when the adjective follows the noun it modifies, omit the hyphen.

The room was *well designed.*

The lawyer they hired was *self serving.*

FRACTIONS AND NUMBERS.   Hyphenate fractions, compound numbers, and ordinals from twenty-one to ninety-nine: *one-fifth, forty-nine, thirty-fifth.*

PREFIXES AND SUFFIXES.   Most prefixes do not take hyphens: *postwar, semitrailer, antihistamine, nonsmoking.* But prefixes followed by capital letters are hyphenated: *anti-American, non-European, neo-Nazi.* Compounds with *ex* meaning "former" are also hyphenated: *ex-husband.* A number of nouns, adjectives, and adverbs act as prefixes, and compound adjectives made up of these words often take hyphens: *self-starter, decision-maker.* Because many compounds are written as one word (*bedroom, newsstand*) and some remain separate words (*night blindness, pile driver*), be sure to check your dictionary.

Suffixes usually do not take hyphens. Exceptions are *-elect* and those suffixes that might cause confusion without the hyphen: *senator-elect, thrill-less.*

COINED COMPOUNDS.   In moderation, you may want to coin your own compound adjectives to precede nouns: *a never-mind-I'm-going-to-do-it-anyway question.*

Plurals

Plurals of most compound words are formed by adding -*s* at the end of the word: *streambeds, post offices, spoonfuls, groomsmen, triggerfish.* When the first word is the main word, it receives the -*s* ending: *brothers-in-law, attorneys-at-law.*

Possessives

The **possessive case** of compound words is formed in the usual way, by adding -*'s* or *'* to the end of the word: *ex-husband's car, pile driver's job, brother-in-law's house, attorney-at-law's office.* (See also **apostrophes.**)

comprise, compose   *Comprise* means "include"; *compose* means "constitute" or "make up [the parts of]." The whole *comprises* the parts; the parts *compose* the whole (or the whole *is composed* of the parts).

> Wherever the game of baseball is played, the equipment *comprises* cowhide-covered hard balls, wooden bats, and padded gloves.

> Wherever the game of baseball is played, the equipment *is composed* of cowhide-covered hard balls, wooden bats, and padded gloves.

conciseness   (See **wordiness**)

concrete words   (See **abstract words**)

conjunctions

> SECTION OVERVIEW
> Coordinating conjunctions
> Correlative conjunctions
> Subordinating conjunctions

Conjunctions connect sentence parts: words, **phrases**, or **clauses**. On occasion, they may also relate a sentence or sentences to preceding ones.

> Tokyo is a bustling city, the administrative, financial, *and* cultural center of Japan. *But* it also comprises farms and mountain villages.

Coordinating conjunctions

And, but, or, nor, for, so, and *yet* connect two or more grammatically equivalent elements.

WORDS: Tokyo is the administrative, financial, *and* cultural center of Japan.

PHRASES: Tokyo has the world's first public monorail line, linking the city with other urban centers *and* making it the envy of other cities.

SUBORDINATE CLAUSES: Tokyo is a world economic center that rivals New York and London *but* that maintains its own integrity.

INDEPENDENT CLAUSES: The city has not submitted to natural disasters, *nor* has it yielded to the destruction of World War II.

COORDINATING CONJUNCTIONS		
CONTRAST:	but	yet
ALTERNATIVES:	or	nor
RESULT:	so	for
ADDITION:	and	

Correlative conjunctions

Like coordinating conjunctions, correlative conjunctions join equivalent grammatical structures, but they are always used in pairs: *both . . . and, either . . . or, neither . . . nor, not only . . . but (also),* and *whether . . . or.* In using correlative conjunctions, be careful that the parts they connect are grammatically equivalent.

Tokyo has been destroyed *not only* by the bombs of World War II *but also* by devastating earthquakes. [*Not only . . . but also* connect two **prepositional phrases.**]

Neither the earthquake of 1923 *nor* the bombs of World War II destroyed all of the city's famous landmarks. [*Neither . . . nor* connect two **noun phrases.**]

See also **parallelism.**

Subordinating conjunctions

Subordinating conjunctions stand at the beginning of **subordinate clauses**, connecting and relating **subordinate clauses** to other words or clauses. All adverb clauses and some noun clauses are introduced by subordinating conjunctions.

Because Tokyo has rebuilt after numerous disasters, it is one of the world's most modern cities. [The adverb clause beginning with *Because* is related causally to the independent clause.]

It is Tokyo's good fortune *that* many of its famed landmarks have not been destroyed. [The noun clause beginning with *that* serves as an **appositive** renaming *fortune*.]

Here is a list of subordinating conjunctions organized according to the relations these conjunctions set up.

SUBORDINATING CONJUNCTIONS	
TIME:	after, as, as soon as, before, since, until, when, whenever, while
PLACE:	where, wherever
CAUSE:	as, because, in order that, since, that
MANNER:	as, as if, as though
CONDITION:	if, in case, on condition that, provided that, unless
RESULT:	so that, that
CONCESSION:	although, even if, even though, though
COMPARISON:	as, than

▼   CAUTION: Avoid duplicating subordinating and coordinating conjunctions.

FAULTY: *Although* the Japanese capital city was once called Edo, *but* the emperor renamed it Tokyo in 1868 when he regained power. [The two conjunctions give conflicting signals: *although* introduces a subordinate clause, and *but* appears to connect grammatically equivalent elements.]

REVISED: *Although* the Japanese capital city was once called Edo, the emperor renamed it Tokyo in 1868 when he regained power. [**complex sentence**]

REVISED: The Japanese capital city was once called Edo, but the emperor renamed it Tokyo in 1868 when he regained power. [**compound sentence**]

See also **transitional adverbs** for words that have a relational, not connecting, function.

conjunctive adverbs   (See **transitional adverbs**)

connectors   Words or phrases that relate words, phrases, clauses, or sentences. See **conjunctions**, **prepositions**, and **transitional adverbs.**

connotation/denotation   A word has two kinds of meaning. Its denotation is its literal, dictionary meaning, and its connotation is its implied, often emotional meaning. Words such as *angel soft, silky smooth,* and *dreamlike* all have favorable connotations, whereas *spongy soft, slippery smooth,* and *nightmarish* bring about decidedly unpleasant reactions. A *notorious* lawyer is much less likely to be consulted than a *famous* one. When you write, it is important that your words carry the connotations you intend. The usage notes in a good **dictionary** can assist you with word choice.

conscience, conscious   *Conscience,* a noun, means "a sense of right and wrong"; *conscious,* an adjective, means "aware" or "capable of thought."

The looters appeared to have no *conscience.*

They were *conscious* that the police were on strike.

consensus of opinion   A redundant phrase for *consensus,* which by itself means "a general agreement."

consequently, subsequently   *Consequently* means "as a result"; *subsequently* means "following close after."

Forensic medicine has advanced over the years; *consequently,* checking fingerprints has been supplanted by DNA testing and other technological advances.

DNA was discovered in 1953; *subsequently,* forensic and genetic medicine have greatly advanced.

continual, continuous   Both adjectives mean "occurring over a long period of time," but *continual* is usually restricted to intermittent action, whereas *continuous* refers to uninterrupted action.

The *continual* call of the wren made them wonder why they installed the bird house.

The wren's visits to and from the tiny bird house seemed *continuous.*

contractions   A contraction is a shortened form of a word or words in which the omitted letters are replaced by an **apostrophe.**

can't for *cannot*	*won't* for *will not*
isn't for *is not*	*who's* for *who is* or *who has*
it's for *it is* or *it has*	*aren't* for *are not*

First person

CAUTION: The phrase *am not* does not have an acceptable contracted form. Do not use *aren't* with *I* (not *aren't I right?*). Don't use *ain't.*

Confusion with possessive pronouns

CAUTION: Writers often mistake the possessive pronouns *its* and *whose* for *it's* and *who's,* the contracted forms for *it is* and *who is.* Remember, the possessives do not have apostrophes. See **apostrophes, it's, its,** and **who's, whose.**

Informality

CAUTION: Contractions are often too informal for some academic and professional writing. Avoid using them unless you know they are acceptable.

coordinate adjectives   (See **adjectives** and **commas**)

coordinating conjunctions   A **coordinating conjunction** connects two or more grammatically equivalent elements. There are only seven: *and, but, or, nor, for, so, yet.* (See also **conjunctions.**)

coordination   When two or more equivalent grammatical elements are connected, they are coordinate. By means of coordinating **conjunctions** (*and, but, or, nor, for, so,* and *yet*) or correlative conjunctions (such as *both . . . and, neither . . . nor*), you can join **clauses, phrases,** or single words to similar clauses, phrases, or single words.

INDEPENDENT CLAUSES: The Magna Carta has been viewed by some as a democratic document, but others see it only as a guarantee of feudal rights.

SUBORDINATE CLAUSES: It only implied *that subjects were protected by law* and *that they were entitled to trial by jury.*

VERBAL PHRASES: Its purpose was *to guarantee baronial privileges* and *to ensure feudal rights.*

PREPOSITIONAL PHRASES: The document was signed at Runnymede in 1215 by *King John* and by *the English barons.*

ADJECTIVES: Whatever its original purpose, the Magna Carta is a *significant* and *influential* document.

Coordinate elements are sometimes separated by punctuation.

The Magna Carta has been viewed by some as a democratic document; others see it only as a guarantee of feudal rights. [semicolon to separate independent clauses]

Whatever its original purpose, the Magna Carta is a significant, influential document. [comma to separate coordinate adjectives]

Coordination allows writers to connect related ideas and sometimes to reduce wordiness. Overuse of coordination, however, can work against good writing, creating sentences that lack emphasis, variety, and shades of meaning. In combination with **subordination,** coordination is a useful tool. See also **commas, comma splices, compound sentences, compound predicates,** and **compound words.**

correlative conjunctions   Conjunctions that are used in pairs to join equivalent grammatical structures: *both . . . and, either . . . or, neither . . . nor, not only . . . but also, whether . . . or.* (See also **conjunctions.**)

could of   Nonstandard usage for *could have.* (See also **of, have.**)

▼ **count nouns**   Count nouns stand for things that can be counted. Unlike **mass** (noncount) **nouns,** count nouns can be both **singular** and **plural** and require corresponding **verb** forms: *a printer works, printers work; the cloud is moving, clouds are moving; an administrator tries, administrators try; a passport is needed, passports are needed; any wish helps, wishes help.*

CAUTION: Singular count nouns are preceded by *a, an, the,* or some other **determiner:** *a book, an object, the coat, any hour, that dictionary, this window.* (See also **articles.**) Plural count nouns take *the* when their identity is known to the reader: *the new kittens, the boys down the street.* They take other determiners when appropriate, and, for indefinite uses, can take no article: *new kittens, erasers, tables.*

	ARTICLES WITH COUNT NOUNS			
	IDENTITY KNOWN	*IDENTITY UNKNOWN*	*OTHER DETERMINER*	*NO ARTICLE NEEDED*
SINGULAR:	the book	a book	any book	—
	the object	an object	that object	—
	the window	a window	any window	—
PLURAL:	the books	books	those books	books
	the objects	objects	several objects	objects
	the windows	windows	some windows	windows

See also **plural** for formation of plural count nouns.

couple of   Colloquial for "two" or "few."

cover letter   A letter of transmittal accompanying a **resumé** or some other document. See "Application letter" and "Business letter" in Part Four, "Specialized Writing."

criteria, criterion   *Criteria* is plural, *criterion* singular.

> Employers have several *criteria* for selecting potential employees; the first *criterion* is a carefully constructed resumé.

cumulative adjectives   (See **adjectives** and **commas**.)

D

▲ **dangling modifiers**   Dangling modifiers are ambiguous **phrases** that may appear to modify sentence elements other than the **nouns** or **pronouns** they were meant to modify. They are usually **verbal phrases (participial phrases, gerund phrases, infinitive phrases)** but may also be **prepositional phrases** and elliptical **subordinate clauses**.

> *Situated in the South China Sea*, tourists will enjoy a trip to Singapore. [The **participial phrase** appears to modify *tourists*, not the intended *Singapore*.]
>
> *As an introduction to Asia*, the overseas traveler would do well to stop at Singapore. [The **prepositional phrase** appears to modify *traveler*, not the intended *Singapore*.]
>
> *Comprising Singapore Island and about 60 small islands*, elements of China, Malaysia, and India make up the Republic of Singapore. [The **participial phrase** appears to modify *elements*, not the intended *Republic of Singapore*.]
>
> *When in Singapore*, the tropical heat and humidity may be a discomfort to some people. [The elliptical **subordinate clause**, short for *When they are in Singapore*, seems to modify *heat and humidity* rather than the intended *people*.]
>
> *To see Singapore at its best*, a walking tour is advisable. [The **infinitive phrase** seems to modify *tour*; the word it is intended to modify (*tourists*) is unexpressed.]

Dangling modifiers usually occur at the beginning of sentences, where they appear to modify the next occurring noun, usually the **subject**.

One way you can correct them, then, is to recast the sentence so that the word you intended to modify is the subject.

> *As an introduction to Asia,* Singapore is a good stop for overseas travelers. [The prepositional phrase correctly modifies *Singapore.*]
>
> *Comprising Singapore Island and about 60 small islands,* the Republic of Singapore has elements of China, Malaysia, and India. [The participal phrase correctly modifies *Republic of Singapore.*]
>
> *When in Singapore,* some people may find the tropical heat and humidity uncomfortable. [The elliptical subordinate clause correctly modifies *people.*]
>
> *To see Singapore at its best,* tourists should take a walking tour of the city. [The infinitive phrase modifies *tourists.*]

Another way to correct these sentence errors is to convert the dangling phrase into a clause that contains the noun or pronoun you intended to modify.

> *When you are in Singapore,* you may find the tropical heat and humidity uncomfortable.
>
> Tourists *who want to see Singapore at its best* should take a walking tour of the city.

Verbal phrases and implied subjects

Participial phrases, gerund phrases, and often infinitive phrases have implied subjects that, normally, are the same as the subject of the sentence.

> Fringed by mangrove swamps, Singapore has a tropical rain-forest climate. [The subject of the sentence, *Singapore,* is the implied subject of *Fringed.*]

Dangling modifiers occur when writers lose track of the implied subject of their verbal phrase or when for other reasons the implied subject differs from the subject of their sentence.

> CAUTION: Passive **voice** can lead to dangling modifiers because the doer of the action is not the subject of the sentence.

> *To accommodate the tropical heat,* loose-fitting cotton clothing should be worn. [The infinitive phrase seems to modify *clothing;* the doer of *should be worn* is not named.]

An appropriate revision strategy is to change the passive voice to active voice, making the subject of the sentence the doer of the action.

To accommodate the tropical heat, tourists should wear loose-fitting cotton clothing. [*Tourists* is the subject of the sentence and the implied subject of *to accommodate*.]

(See also **misplaced modifiers.**)

dash The dash (two unspaced hyphens on the keyboard) separates sentence elements with greater emphasis than a **comma** and less formality than a **colon.**

The Himalayan Mountains range through Pakistan, India, Tibet, Nepal, Sikkim, and Bhutan—six countries. [The dash gives greater emphasis and clarity than a comma.]

The southern Himalayas have three zones—the Great Himalayas, the Lesser Himalayas, and the Outer Himalayas. [The dash is less formal than a colon; in most academic and professional writing, the colon would be preferable.]

The dash also sets off nonrestrictive elements that have internal commas:

The Great Himalayas—which contain the highest peaks in the world, including Mt. Everest—have elevations up to 29,028 feet.

CAUTION: Don't forget the second dash for interruptions within a sentence. Like commas that set off **nonrestrictive** elements in the middle of a sentence, dashes are used in pairs—at the beginning of the interruption and at the end.

Use dashes sparingly. Overuse gives the impression that the writer is careless or uninformed about punctuation, and it leads to less effective writing.

data In formal usage *data* is plural for *datum* and takes a plural verb and plural pronouns.

These data have influenced our decision.

However, if you are using the word *data* to refer to a single collection, the singular verb may be acceptable.

The *data is classified* under convention expenses.

Be aware, however, that many readers would not accept *data* as a singular noun.

dates (See **numbers**)

days of the week   (See **capitalization**)

definite articles   (See **articles**)

demonstrative adjectives   (See **demonstrative pronouns and adjectives**)

▼ **demonstrative pronouns and adjectives**   Demonstrative pronouns and adjectives—*this, that, these*, and *those*—point out specific persons, places, or things. *These* is the plural of *this*, and *those* is the plural of *that*. Demonstrative *pronouns* stand in for or call attention to the person, place, or thing they refer to.

> *This* is the book I told you about.
> *That* is not a reasonable opinion.
> *These* are the books I want you to read.
> *Those* are unreasonable opinions.

Demonstrative *adjectives* modify the person or thing they point to.

> *This article* was published posthumously.
> *These articles* were published posthumously.
> For *that reason*, the conclusion is incomplete.
> For *those reasons*, the editor added a concluding sentence.

Clarity

CAUTION: When the person, place, or thing the pronoun points out is not named in the predicate (as it is in each of the pronoun example sentences), clarity is more certain with a demonstrative *adjective* than with a pronoun. You thus specify the reference: *This article was published posthumously* instead of *This was published posthumously*.

Agreement

CAUTION: Demonstrative adjectives used with *kind, type*, and *sort* should agree with their nouns in **number**: *this kind, those kinds; this type, these types; that sort, those sorts*.

denotation   (See **connotation**)

dependent clauses   (See **clauses** and **subordination**)

determiners   A determiner precedes a noun and acts as a signal that a noun follows. The most common determiners are the **articles,** *a*, *an*, and *the*. Other determiners include the **possessive adjectives** *my*, *your*, *his*, *her*, *its*, *our*, and *their* and the **indefinite adjectives**, such as *some*, *any*, *all*, *each*, *either*, *every*, and *no*. See **Articles.**

⚠ diction (word choice)   Diction in writing generally refers to choice of words. In choosing words, you consider level, situation, and accuracy.

Level

Words that are appropriate in casual conversation may be out of place in academic and professional writing. Words that your dictionary labels **slang, colloquial, informal,** and **nonstandard** are inappropriate for most formal writing; words labeled *nonstandard* (such as *hisself, ain't,* and *gots*) are never appropriate among educated people.

Situation

JARGON.   Words that are appropriate in some surroundings may be vague or pretentious in others. Each field of work has its own technical vocabulary, or **jargon.** Words such as *PIFs* for computer specialists, *caesura* for poets, *quark* for physicists, and *ontology* for philosophers allow people within a field to communicate clearly with one another, whereas other readers outside the field might be mystified or even annoyed at encountering such words. When writing for a nontechnical audience, define your technical terms when they first occur.

OTHER LIMITED USAGE.   **Euphemisms** (such as *passed away* for *died*) as indirect substitutes for blunt or offensive words have limited uses, depending mainly on your audience and the occasion for your writing. Also generally avoid regional words and expressions when you write; the Milwaukee *bubbler* (a local word for *drinking fountain*) is a case in point. Words that exclude or stereotype women were once considered acceptable but are now regarded as sexist (such as *mankind, little woman, fireman,* and *lady detective*); avoid them. (See also **nonsexist language.**)

Accuracy

Accuracy is always the primary determiner of word choice. To call someone *notorious*, for example, implies unfavorable fame, as opposed to *famous* or *widely known*, words that have a more positive connotation. And to say someone is *disinterested* means that person is unbiased; however, calling a person *uninterested* implies indifference. Use your dictionary to look up any meanings you are unsure of, paying particular attention to usage notes. Use a thesaurus only in combination with a dictionary. See **connotation/denotation.** See also **abstract words/concrete words, clichés, figures of speech, idioms,** and **wordiness.**

▼ **dictionaries**

> SECTION OVERVIEW
> Using a dictionary
> Spelling, syllabication, and pronunciation
> Parts of speech and usage
> Meaning
> Idioms
> Synonyms
> Usage notes
> Etymology

A dictionary is a major tool for a writer. It gives not only the meanings of words but also their spelling, syllabication, pronunciation, parts of speech, and usage. Many dictionaries also include synonyms, usage notes, idioms, and the etymology, or origins, of words. Some have supplemental lists of colleges and universities, biographical entries, and geographical entries. A recent hardcover dictionary—such as *The American Heritage, Webster's New Collegiate,* or *Webster's New World*—is a good investment because of the completeness of its coverage. If you need a more comprehensive dictionary, go to your library and use an unabridged dictionary: *The Oxford English Dictionary, The Random House Dictionary of the English Language,* or *Webster's Third New International Dictionary of the English Language.*

Using a dictionary

To make their entries as concise as possible, dictionaries use many abbreviations, which are usually defined somewhere in the front part of the book. Your dictionary can be most helpful to you if you know how to use it. Browse around to learn what information it offers you.

Spelling, syllabication, and pronunciation

Dictionaries separate multisyllabic words into syllables, usually by central dots: *po•lite, in•clude, be•gin•ning.* This feature is useful if you need to divide words at the end of a line; it also helps you visualize spelling.

A guide to pronouncing the word follows; for a key to the pronunciation symbols, check at the bottom of the page or at the front of the book.

Parts of speech and usage

An abbreviation denoting the part of speech of the word follows the pronunciation guide: for example, *v.* for verb, *n.* for noun, and *adv.* for adverb. All words that are not part of standard usage are then labeled—for example, *nonstandard, informal, regional*, and *archaic*. These labels are defined in the front part of your dictionary and can assist you in choosing the appropriate word.

Meaning

Learn how your dictionary arranges its meanings. Some begin with the most common meanings and proceed to the more specialized ones; others arrange meanings historically, beginning with the oldest. Read the entire meaning entry to make sure you fully understand the meaning of the word.

Idioms

Some dictionaries define idioms (for example, *beg the question* and *get nowhere*) in their meaning entries. Look up an idiom by finding the entry for the first word (for example, *beg* and *get*).

Synonyms

Your dictionary may include synonyms for some words, allowing you to compare several related words. The following synonym entry for *polite* comes from *The American Heritage Dictionary: Second College Edition:*

> Synonyms: polite, civil, courteous, genteel. These all describe social behavior as being proper or commendatory. *Polite* means duly respectful or indulgent with other people according to social norms. *Civil,* suggesting only the barest agreeability or tact in manners, means friendly in a reserved, correct sense. *Courteous* is similar to *polite* but implies a more voluntary, generous consideration which is of a helpful nature. *Genteel* refers to the quality of good taste or propriety in a cultured person. It can suggest fine sensibilities and respectability but now usually suggests overrefinement to the point of artificiality.

Notes such as this can aid writers in choosing the precise word they need for a particular context.

Usage notes

Helpful also are the usage notes that accompany some words. Under *include, The American Heritage Dictionary: Second College Edition* has this usage note:

> Usage: *Include* is used most appropriately before an incomplete list of components: *The ingredients of the cake include butter and egg yolk.* If all the components are named, it is generally clearer to write: *The ingredients are. . . .*

Etymology

Most dictionaries trace a word's history from its earliest record, using abbreviations such as *ME* for Middle English and *Gk.* for Greek. Etymologies can sometimes help you understand a word.

different from, different than   In formal usage, *different from* is preferred to *different than.*

> The literary definition of *romantic* is *different from* the popular idea.

But *different than* is generally accepted when it precedes a **clause** or when *from* would lead to a wordier construction.

> Reading romantic poetry of the nineteenth century was *different than I expected it to be.* [*From* would require a wordier construction: Reading romantic poetry of the nineteenth century was *different from the way I expected it to be.*]

differ from, differ with   To *differ from* means "to be unlike"; to *differ with* means "to disagree."

> The opinion you expressed in your letter *differs from* the one you've stated today.

> You seem to *differ with* every other expert in the field.

direct objects   **Nouns, pronouns,** or noun **phrases** or **clauses** that receive the action of transitive **verbs.** (See also **objects.**)

disinterested, uninterested   *Disinterested* means "impartial." *Uninterested* means "indifferent" or "without an interest."

The manager was *disinterested* in the outcome of the negotiations after having been offered a position elsewhere.

We were concerned about Lambert after he became *uninterested* in any social interactions.

division of words   (See **hyphens**)

don't, doesn't   *Don't* is a **contraction** for *do not*. Avoid using it in place of *doesn't*, a contraction for *does not*.

She *doesn't* [not *don't*] want to leave her job at Duchamp Inc.

double comparatives   (See **adjectives** and **adverbs**)

double negatives   A double **negative** is two negative words used to express one negative thought.

FAULTY: Politicians are *not* doing *nothing* to reduce taxes and tuition.

REVISED: Politicians are doing *nothing* to reduce taxes and tuition.

REVISED: Politicians are *not* doing anything to reduce taxes and tuition.

The words *barely, hardly*, and *scarcely* are regarded as negative and should not be used with another negative word.

FAULTY: We *can't hardly* make the tuition payments now.

REVISED: We *can hardly* make the tuition payments now.

Another double negative that is common in speech but unacceptable in formal writing is the phrase *couldn't* (or *can't*) *help but*.

FAULTY: We *couldn't help but* wonder what would happen next. [*Couldn't* and *but* have negative meanings.]

REVISED: We *couldn't help* wondering what would happen next.

double superlatives   (See **adjectives** and **adverbs**)

due to, because of   Do not use *due to* as a prepositional phrase meaning "because of."

Wilson missed the freethrow *because of* [not *due to*] a distraction from the fans.

Due to is appropriate after linking verbs.

Wilson's mistake was *due to* crowd noise.

E

effect   (See ***affect***)

either/or fallacy   (See **fallacies in logic**)

elicit, illicit   *Elicit* is a verb meaning "to bring out" or "to call forth." *Illicit* is an adjective meaning "unlawful."

> Hopkins claimed that the video would *elicit* behavior that most people would regard as *illicit*.

ellipsis dots   Ellipsis dots are three spaced periods that indicate an omission in quoted material.

> ORIGINAL: Modern English has lost most of the inflections that were common in Old English. In Old English, words such as *ecg, lond,* and *waeter* could, because of their forms, only be nouns. Verbs had different endings. But the modern words that derived from them— *edge, land,* and *water*—could be either nouns or verbs, depending on context.

> QUOTATION WITH ELLIPSIS: "Modern English has lost most of the inflections that were common in Old English. In Old English, words such as *ecg, lond*, and *waeter* could . . . only be nouns. . . . But the modern words that derived from them—*edge, land,* and *water*— could be either nouns or verbs, depending on context."

Notice that an ellipsis at the end of a sentence begins with the sentence period and ends with the ellipses before the next sentence begins.

elude   (See ***allude, refer, elude***)

emigrate from, immigrate to, migrate   *Emigrate from* means "to leave one country or region to settle in another." *Immigrate to* means "to enter and settle in another country or region." *Migrate* means "to move from one place to another" and can be followed by either *from* or *to;* it implies less permanence than *emigrate* and *immigrate.*

> When Israel became a state in 1948, Jewish people *emigrated* from Europe, North America, Asia, and North Africa.

> When they *immigrated to* Israel, many of them settled on collective farms known as *kibbutzim.*

> Jews continue to *migrate* to Israel.

emphasis

SECTION OVERVIEW
Subordination for emphasis
Varied sentence length for emphasis
Repetition for emphasis
Transitional phrases for emphasis
Emphasis and sentence position
Active verbs for emphasis

You can achieve emphasis in your sentences through several means: **subordination,** sentence length, **repetition,** transitional **phrases,** sentence position, and active **verbs.** Overuse of any of these devices, however, is counterproductive. In most cases, avoid resorting to **exclamation points, italics (underlining), capitalization,** and **intensifiers** such as *very.*

Subordination for emphasis

By placing less important information in **phrases** or **subordinate clauses,** you emphasize the information in the **independent clause.**

In the United States, *8,000 children are killed annually* in preventable accidents.

Parents can prevent many of children's accidental deaths, which in the United States alone are 8,000 annually.

In the first sentence, the number of children killed is emphasized; in the second sentence the prevention of accidents is stressed.

Varied sentence length for emphasis

A short sentence in the midst of longer ones is emphatic:

In the United States each year, 8,000 children are killed and some 50,000 are disabled permanently by preventable accidents. *Precautions are needed.*

Avoid such short sentences unless you want to draw attention to them.

Repetition for emphasis

Like short sentences, repetition draws attention to itself and is therefore a writer's tool for achieving emphasis.

Home *injuries* are a major cause of infant mortality, and many of these *injuries* are preventable. [repetition of the keyword *injuries*]

Reserve repetition for important words.

Transitional phrases for emphasis

Phrases such as *most importantly, foremost, indeed, certainly,* and *moreover* emphasize the text that follows.

Most importantly, these accidents can easily be prevented.

Emphasis and sentence position

Take advantage of the fact that the most emphatic sentence positions are at the beginning and, even more, at the end.

Most of these household accidents can be prevented *easily*.

Active verbs for emphasis

Use strong, active verbs to achieve emphasis.

Cover electrical outlets, and *latch* the doors of cabinets where you *store* toxic and caustic cleaning products. [This active sentence has more emphasis than the passive voice sentence *Electrical outlets should be covered and the doors latched on cabinets where toxic and caustic cleaning products are stored.*]

(See also **voice.**)

empty phrases   (See **wordiness**)

end punctuation   (See **exclamation point, period,** and **question mark**)

ensure   (See ***assure***)

enthused   Colloquial for *enthusiastic.*

City dwellers are often *enthusiastic* (not *enthused*) about opportunities to visit the country, and rural folk feel likewise about visiting the city.

especially, specially   *Especially* means "particularly" or "exceptionally." *Specially* means "for a specific reason."

Selkirk was trained for the job *especially* well.

Selkirk was *specially* trained for his new job.

et al., etc.   *Et al.* is an abbreviation for the Latin *et alii*, meaning "and others" (meaning other people); *etc.* is an abbreviation for the

Latin *et cetera*, meaning "and other things" or "and so forth." *Et al.* is used primarily for bibliographic entries referring to multiple authors. *Etc.* is generally avoided in academic and professional writing, being reserved mainly for parenthetical notations. Do not use *and* with *etc.*, and do not use *etc.* in lists introduced by phrases such as *for example* and *such as*; both usages are redundant.

euphemism   A euphemism is an inoffensive term substituted for one that is potentially offensive or blunt. People sometimes use euphemisms out of consideration for their audience, as when referring to death, sex, and bodily functions. However, substitutes are often used to conceal meaning as, for example, in governmental press releases, where words such as *taxes, retreat,* and *prison* are replaced with *revenue enhancement, strategic withdrawal,* and *correctional therapeutic community.* There is very seldom any need for euphemisms in academic and professional writing.

every day, everyday   *Every day* is an **indefinite adjective** (*every*) modifying a **noun** (*day*); *everyday* is an idiomatic **adjective** meaning "casual" or "appropriate for ordinary days."

He wore his *everyday* clothes *every day*, even on Sunday.

every one, everyone   *Every one* is an **indefinite adjective** (*every*) modifying a **pronoun** (*one*); *everyone* is an **indefinite pronoun**.

Everyone has collected *every one* of the pledges.

Both are **singular** grammatically.

except   (See *accept*)

exclamation point   The exclamation point is a mark of end punctuation that shows strong feeling such as fear, surprise, anger, or excitement. It can follow statements, **interjections**, and commands.

"Quick! Close the window!" Clara yelled.

"Yow-w-w!" screamed the cat.

Note that the exclamation points are inside the end quotation marks and are not followed by a comma. Since writers have other means of achieving **emphasis**, exclamation points are generally avoided in academic and professional writing. (See also **exclamatory sentences.**)

exclamatory sentences   Exclamatory sentences show strong feeling such as fear, surprise, anger, or excitement. They often begin with **imperative** verbs and frequently are sentence **fragments**. They end with **exclamation points.**

> Stop the car!
>
> Sit down! Now!
>
> Hurray! We won!

Exclamatory sentences are rarely needed in academic and professional writing. (See also **interjections.**)

expletives   The word *expletive* grammatically means "a word that stands in place of a word or phrase that comes later." *It* and *there* are the most common expletives.

> *It* doesn't matter what you think. [*It* stands in place of the **subordinate clause** *what you think*, which is the true **subject** of the sentence.]
>
> *There* are several ways you can look at a situation like that. [*There* stands in place of *ways*, the true subject of the sentence.]

explicit, implicit   *Explicit* means "clearly stated"; *implicit* means "implied" or "not directly expressed."

> The instructions in the message were *explicit*, but the purpose for carrying them out was only *implicit*.

F

---

facts   Facts are verifiable examples, testimony, statistics, and historical evidence that support arguments and develop essays. As support for reasoned opinions, facts are necessary components of academic and professional writing.

Examples

An example illustrates or explains a point by presenting a specific and representative instance. It may be drawn from the writer's experience, reading, or observation. A single example is usually less effective than several examples, a combination of an example with other types of facts or reasoning, or a combination of one extended example and several briefer ones.

Testimony

Testimony is an expert opinion by an authority on a subject, usually in the form of a **quotation** or **paraphrase.** The source of the opinion is always cited, lending weight to the writer's argument and giving due credit to the authority (see Part Three, "Writing a Research Paper").

Statistics

Statistics are numbers that have undergone mathematical analysis and often appear as secondary sources of information. In contrast to examples, which present individual instances, statistics can show a broader picture. Since statistics published in secondary sources have been interpreted and perhaps even manipulated, use them carefully and knowledgeably. Always verify and cite the source of your statistics.

Historical evidence

Events known to have happened are useful in developing essays. Like other facts, they must be verifiable and as correct as the record allows. Sources for verifying historical evidence are printed matter such as books, magazines, journals, and newspapers; television and radio; and your own experiences and observations.

fallacies in logic

> SECTION OVERVIEW
> Broad generalization
> Oversimplification
> Begging the question
> Either-or reasoning
> Post hoc cause
> False analogy
> Ad hominem
> Bandwagon
> Non sequitur

Fallacies in logic involve unsound or incomplete reasoning; these errors weaken an argument. The following fallacies are the most common.

Broad generalization

A generalization is an inference or an application drawn from specific **facts** and is thus necessary in developing ideas. Generalizations become fallacies when they make claims beyond what the evidence will support.

Legalizing drugs would reduce the amount of crime.

Oversimplification

Clarification and simplification help readers understand difficult issues, but concealing or ignoring aspects of a complex issue to make it seem simpler than it is is a fallacy in logic.

Prohibiting drugs makes people want them more.

Begging the question

Arguments based on unproven opinions "beg the question."

The prohibition on drugs should be lifted because the decadent morality spawned by the prohibition on alcohol decreased when that prohibition was lifted. [The statement is based on the unproven assumption that "decadent morality" decreased when prohibition was repealed in 1933.]

Either-or reasoning

Most arguments are not limited to only two positions, only one of which is right. Reducing an argument in this way is a fallacy.

If we don't legalize drugs, street crime, death, and disease will increase. [The argument overlooks other ways of preventing the increase of "street crime, death, and disease" and assumes that legalizing drugs will automatically prevent that increase.]

Post hoc cause

It is a causal fallacy to assume that an earlier event caused a later one simply by preceding it.

The repeal of Prohibition in 1933 cemented national pride during World War II.

False analogy

Analogies, or comparisons of the shared features of two otherwise unlike things, are useful in developing ideas. However, extending analogies beyond their shared features is evidence of unsound reasoning.

Like the legalizing of alcohol consumption in 1933, legalizing the use of narcotics would decrease crime and disease. [Although

alcohol prohibition and the illegality of narcotics have some
similarities, one can't assume that legalizing one would have the
same effects as legalizing the other. See also "Begging the question"
above.]

Ad hominem

It is fallacious to attack the person instead of the issue at hand on
the assumption that discrediting the person who holds an opposing
opinion will weaken his or her argument.

As someone who has used crack cocaine yourself, how can you be
credible in arguing for its legalization?

Bandwagon

The bandwagon appeal suggests that "everybody is doing it" and
you would be foolish if you didn't join the crowd.

The latest polls suggest a massive trend toward voting no on the
legalization referendum.

Non sequitur

Latin for "it does not follow," this fallacy involves a conclusion
that is logically unrelated to the ideas that have preceded it.

Anyone who votes for John Boardman deserves to lose his or her
job.

false analogy   (See **fallacies in logic**)

farther, further   Both words are comparative forms of *far*, but,
strictly, *farther* refers to distance, *further* to degree, quantity, or time.

Which is *farther* from Columbus: Cincinnati or Cleveland?

By the end of the year, Jenkins was *further* into writing his novel
than he expected to be.

faulty predication   (See **mixed constructions**)

fewer, less   Strictly, *fewer* refers to items that can be counted (see
count nouns), and *less* refers to the amount of things that cannot be
counted (see **mass nouns**).

Although the theater company has presented *fewer* plays this year,
it has not received any *less* income than in previous years.

figures of speech   A figure of speech compares two unlike things in an imaginative way, usually for the purpose of making an abstract thing more concrete. Common figures of speech include similes, metaphors, and personification.

SIMILE.   A simile is an explicit comparison using *like* or *as*: The prairie was once as wide as the sea.

METAPHOR.   A metaphor is an implied comparison: The prairie was a sea of grass.

PERSONIFICATION.   In personification, a nonhuman thing or an idea is given human qualities: The wind speaks softly in the prairie.

> CAUTION: To avoid ludicrous images, do not mix images in your figures of speech.
>
> MIXED: The sea of grass marched to the drumbeat of the wind.
>
> REVISED: The sea of grass swirled with the currents of the wind.

finalize   Many writers and readers object to this word, which is a verb formed from the adjective *final* and means "to put into final form" or "to complete."

finite verbs   A finite **verb** can function as part of a **predicate** in making an assertion. As opposed to a nonfinite verb, or **verbal** (such as an **infinitive,** a **gerund,** or a **participle**), it is capable of changing form to show **person, number,** and **tense.**

> PERSON: He *files* the letter away. We *file* the letter away.
>
> NUMBER: She *files* the letter away. They *file* the letter away.
>
> TENSE: He *files* the letter away. He *filed* the letter away. He *will file* the letter away.

firstly, secondly, thirdly   Write *first, second, third.* The *-ly* is unnecessary. And don't write *second* or *third* unless you have a *first.*

foreign words   (See **italics**)

former, latter   Avoid using these terms to refer to items previously mentioned, because *former* and *latter* require readers to look back to identify the reference. Instead, repeat the words referred to.

> Louis Pasteur is known for pasteurization and a rabies vaccine. Though he was responsible for discovering *the rabies vaccine*

[not *the latter*], he only developed *pasteurization* [not *the former*].

⚠ fragments (of sentences)

SECTION OVERVIEW
Phrase fragments
Subordinate clause fragments
Identifying fragments
Correcting fragments
Acceptable fragments

Sentence fragments are errors that involve **phrases** or **subordinate clauses** that are treated as sentences: they begin with a capital letter and end with a period. Only **independent clauses** can be written as sentences.

Phrase fragments

The most common phrase fragments are **verbal phrases** and **prepositional phrases.** They lack a **subject** and a **verb.**

The DuSable Museum of African-American History was established in Chicago in 1961. *By a group of black Chicagoans who were disturbed about the neglect of black history in American schools.* [The prepositional phrase fragment has an embedded **relative clause.**]

The museum, named after Jean Baptiste Pointe DuSable, a Haitian fur trader and one of the area's first settlers. [The **participial phrase,** beginning with *named* and ending at the period, modifies *museum*, which appears to be a sentence subject but is not followed by a verb.]

Subordinate clause fragments

Subordinate clause fragments have a subject and a verb but begin with a **subordinating conjunction** or a **relative pronoun,** so they are not sentences. Grammatically and contextually they are dependent on an independent clause.

Because the museum is housed in a building once used by the Chicago Parks Administration and located in Washington Park on Chicago's south side. [This subordinate clause, introduced by the subordinating conjunction *Because,* is a fragment.]

Inside, the building holds over 10,000 artifacts. *Which schoolchildren from Illinois and nearby states come to view.* [This subordinate clause, introduced by the relative pronoun *Which,* is a fragment]

Identifying fragments

Fragments are often difficult to identify because they are almost always in the company of related sentences. As you read what you have written, you unconsciously connect fragments to the sentences they go with. Also, you probably look more at the length of your sentences than at their completeness. In fact, one reason fragments occur is that writers think their sentences are getting too long and, in breaking them apart, unknowingly make fragments of portions of them.

To identify your fragments, you must find a way of reading separately each group of words you've written as a sentence. A trick that works well with word processing is to enter a "return" after each period. With all your "sentences" lined up in a list rather than in paragraphs, you are more likely to read each one separately. After you've identified and revised your fragments, remove the returns and reformat the sentences into paragraphs. Another trick used by some writers is to read a piece of writing from the end, moving backward from period to period. Here again, you are less likely to unconsciously connect fragments to sentences.

If you write fragments, learn what kinds of fragments you habitually create, and then look for them as you revise. Read your piece of writing at least once just for fragments.

Correcting fragments

Once a fragment is identified, it is usually easy to correct: add it to the sentence it belongs with contextually, or expand it to create a separate sentence.

The DuSable Museum of African-American History was established in Chicago in 1961 *by a group of black Chicagoans who were disturbed about the neglect of black history in American schools.* [The prepositional phrase has been connected to the preceding sentence.]

The museum was named after Jean Baptiste Pointe DuSable, a Haitian fur trader and one of the area's first settlers. [The participial phrase has been expanded into a sentence with the addition of the verb *was.*]

The museum is housed in a building once used by the Chicago Parks Administration and located in Washington Park on Chicago's south side. [The subordinating conjunction *because* has been removed to create an independent clause.]

Inside, the building holds over 10,000 artifacts, *which schoolchildren from Illinois and nearby states come to view.* [The subordinate clause has been attached to the preceding sentence.]

Incomplete thoughts

Occasionally, fragments are not easily corrected because the thought is incomplete. When a part of the thought is missing, readers cannot make sense of the fragment.

An addition named for Harold Washington, Chicago's late mayor, on the back lawn of the museum.

Readers don't know what the writer means to say about the addition to the museum. Only the writer can correct the fragment.

An addition named for Harold Washington, Chicago's late mayor, is being constructed on the back lawn of the museum.

Acceptable fragments

You probably encounter fragments every day. Titles are often fragments, as are answers to **questions** and expressions of strong emotion (**interjections** and **exclamatory sentences**).

TITLES: "A New Country and a New Way of Life," *The New York Times*

ANSWER: "Have you read the newspaper?" "No."

EXCLAMATION: "What a great movie!"

Advertising often depends on fragments.

World class adventure, world class luxury.

Three reasons to own the new Bose Acoustic Wave Music System.

Sound. Size. Simplicity.

Common as they are in everyday life, fragments are usually unacceptable in academic and professional writing. Only in rare cases will you need to use intentional fragments for effective expression of your thoughts in school or business.

fun   *Fun* is a noun. As an adjective it is **colloquial** and should be avoided in business and professional writing.

COLLOQUIAL: We had a *fun* time at the picnic.

REVISED: We had *fun* at the picnic.

further   (See **farther**)

⚠ fused sentences (run-on sentences)

> SECTION OVERVIEW
> Correcting fused sentences
> Identifying fused sentences

A fused sentence (sometimes called a *run-on sentence*) is a sentence fault in which a writer has omitted punctuation between two **independent clauses.**

> FUSED SENTENCE: Spain's government is a constitutional monarchy the reigning king is Juan Carlos I.

This sentence has two independent clauses: *Spain's government is a constitutional monarchy* and *the reigning king is Juan Carlos I.* It is a fused sentence because it has no punctuation to signal the reader that a second independent clause is coming.

Correcting fused sentences

A fused sentence can be corrected by adding a **semicolon** or a **comma** plus a **coordinating conjunction.** Or, by adding a period at the end of each clause, you can make two sentences.

> Spain's government is a constitutional monarchy; the reigning king is Juan Carlos I. [semicolon added]
>
> Spain's government is a constitutional monarchy, and the reigning king is Juan Carlos I. [comma and coordinating conjunction added]
>
> Spain's government is a constitutional monarchy. The reigning king is Juan Carlos I. [two sentences]

Fused sentences can also be corrected by changing one of the independent clauses to a **subordinate clause** or a **phrase.**

> Spain's government is a constitutional monarchy, *which is ruled by King Juan Carlos I.* [**subordinate clause**]
>
> *A constitutional monarchy,* Spain is ruled by King Juan Carlos I. [an **appositive** phrase]

When making one clause subordinate, put your main idea in the independent clause.

Identifying fused sentences

Fused sentences are difficult for their writers to identify because the ideas are usually closely related and most writers are not in the habit of examining their sentences for **subjects** and **verbs.** If your writing sometimes contains fused sentences, try reading aloud what you have written and listening carefully to the pitch of your voice. You will probably find that it drops at every period. If it were to drop after *monarchy* in the example sentence above, that would be your cue to examine the sentence to see if indeed the sentence has two independent clauses. Another method of identifying fused sentences is to examine each sentence for subjects and verbs. If you find more than one pair, look for **subordinating conjunctions** or **relative pronouns** at the beginning of the clauses. If there is no subordinating word, add a period between the two clauses and read each clause aloud, questioning whether each is complete. (See also **comma splices** and **subordination.**)

future perfect tense   (See **tenses of verbs**)

future tense   (See **tenses of verbs**)

G

---

gender   Gender, in a grammatical sense, refers to the classification of **nouns** and **pronouns** as masculine, feminine, neuter (no gender), or common (either gender).

	GENDER OF NOUNS AND PRONOUNS	
	NOUNS	*PRONOUNS*
MASCULINE:	man, boy, father, rooster, John	he
FEMININE:	woman, girl, mother, hen, Jane	she
NEUTER:	car, tree, school, love, headache	it, they
COMMON:	person, child, parent, dog, student	they, every-one

Pronouns agree with the gender of their **antecedents.**

Jimmy Carter served *his* presidency from 1977 to 1981. [The masculine pronoun *his* agrees with its antecedent, *Jimmy Carter.*]

*Agreement between pronouns and antecedents
of common gender*

Although *he, him,* and *his* were once thought to function as
common-gender pronouns, English does not have a singular pronoun
to refer to nouns of either masculine or feminine gender (such as
person, child, and *student*), to most **indefinite pronouns** (such as
everyone and *somebody*), and to nouns modified by **indefinite adjectives**
(such as *every person* and *each* student). Sometimes the plural
pronoun *they* is used in a singular sense, but such usage is not widely
accepted in formal writing.

> COLLOQUIAL: If a student wants to register early, *they* should fill out
> an early-registration form.

> COLLOQUIAL: If anyone wants to register early, *they* should fill out
> an early-registration form.

Many writers use plural nouns when both genders are intended.

> If *students* want to register early, *they* should fill out early-registration
> forms.

> If any *students* want to register early, *they* should fill out early-
> registration forms.

They also recast sentences to avoid using pronouns.

> Students who want to register early should fill out early-registration
> forms.

(See also **indefinite pronouns and adjectives** and **nonsexist language**.)

generalizations   Inferences drawn from evidence. See "Broad generalization"
under **fallacies in logic**.

general words/specific words   General words name groups or
classes of things; specific words name items within groups or classes.
Privacy Act of 1974 is more specific than *U.S. law*; *Girolamo Savonarola*
is more specific than *religious reformer*; and *Italian religious reformer
Girolamo Savonarola* is more specific than *reformer*. Specific words
are often more desirable than general ones, because they enable readers
to grasp the writer's idea more clearly. General words are needed,
however, to convey broad concepts.

> Savonarola's *attacks* on *the moral laxity* of *the pope's court*
> eventually led to his *execution*. [This sentence makes a general
> statement about Savonarola that would be obscured by more

specific words. Details could be given in preceding or following sentences.]

generic nouns   (See **nonsexist language**)

gerund phrases   A gerund phrase is a **verbal phrase** that functions as a **noun**. It is made up of a **gerund** and its **modifiers** or **complements**.

> *Establishing women's right to vote* was one of the planks in the platform of the first U.S. Progressive party. [The gerund phrase is the **subject** of the sentence; the object of the phrase is *right*.]

> By *drawing more votes than the incumbent Republican president, William H. Taft,* the first Progressive party helped the Democratic candidate, Woodrow Wilson, to be elected. [The gerund phrase serves as the object of the **preposition** *by;* it has its own object, *votes,* and a modifying elliptical **subordinate clause** *than the incumbent Republican president, William H. Taft (did)*.]

> CAUTION: Do not punctuate a gerund phrase as a sentence; the result is a **fragment.**

> FAULTY: The first Progressive party unseated the incumbent president, William H. Taft, and elected the Democratic candidate, Woodrow Wilson. By supporting a third candidate, former President Theodore Roosevelt. [The gerund phrase introduced by the preposition *By* is a fragment.]

> REVISED: The first Progressive party unseated the incumbent president, William H. Taft, and elected the Democratic candidate, Woodrow Wilson, by supporting a third candidate, former President Theodore Roosevelt.

A gerund phrase introduced with a preposition cannot function as the subject of a sentence. The result is a fragment.

> FAULTY: By the Progressive party drawing more votes than the incumbent, President William H. Taft, caused the election of the Democratic candidate, Woodrow Wilson. [The verb *caused* has no subject.]

> REVISED: By drawing more votes than the incumbent, President William H. Taft, the first Progressive party caused the election of the Democratic candidate, Woodrow Wilson.

gerunds   A gerund is the *-ing* form of a **verb** and is used as a **noun.**

> *Writing* seems easier with my word processor. [gerund as **subject**]

> As a result, I actually enjoy *writing*. [gerund as direct **object**]

Pronouns and nouns preceding gerunds are usually in the possessive **case.**

> *My writing* has improved since I got my word processor.
>
> *My teacher's reading* has become easier too.
>
> I appreciate *her reading* my earlier drafts.
>
> Other teachers have approved of *my using* the word processor to write papers.

Gerunds can also serve as the objects of verbs. See **verbs,** "Verbs followed by infinitives and gerunds." (See also **gerund phrases** and **verbals.**)

get   Avoid overusing this common verb. Many of its uses are **colloquial** and should be avoided in writing, for example, *get away with* and *get back at.* Also, avoid using *get* in place of *become* (as in *He got lost*), *get to* in place of *begin* (as in *She gets to listening to her radio every evening*), and *got to, has to,* or *has got to* in place of *must* (as in *We've got to be back by noon*). Consult your dictionary for the many acceptable uses for *get.*

▼ *Get* has many acceptable idiomatic uses, some of them informal and slang. Consult your dictionary.

good and   **Colloquial** for "very." Avoid the term in academic and professional writing.

> The roast beef was *quite* [not *good and*] done.

good, well   *Good* is an **adjective;** *well* is nearly always an **adverb.**

> Your chicken barley soup smells *good.* [The adjective *good* follows the **linking verb** *smells* and modifies *soup.*]
> You have followed my recipe *well.* [*Well* is an adverb modifying the verb *have followed.*]

As an adjective *well* is used to refer to health.

> You will feel *well* after eating the soup. [*Well* is an adjective following the linking verb *feel* and modifying the subject *you.*]

H

half a, a half, a half a   Use either *half a* or *a half*; *a half a* is redundant.

> My father's great-grandfather was hanged for stealing a horse *a half-century* [or *half a century*] before my ancestors emigrated from Germany.

hanged, hung   Both are past-tense forms of *hang. Hanged* usually refers to executions, *hung* to other uses.

> We discovered a relative in our distant past who was *hanged* for horse thievery.
>
> Just for fun, we *hung* the certificate in our family room.

hardly   (See **can't hardly**)

has got to, has to   (See **get**)

hasty generalizations   (See **fallacies in logic**)

he/she, his/her   *He/she* and *his/her* are awkward replacements for *he* and *his* to mean both male and female. Even worse is the unpronounceable *s/he*. Find other ways to avoid using male **pronouns** in a generic sense: use *he or she* occasionally and discriminately, convert to the **plural** *they,* or recast the sentence to eliminate pronouns. See **nonsexist language.**

▼ helping verbs   Helping, or auxiliary, verbs combine with main **verbs** to indicate **tense** (or time), **mood,** and **voice.** The most common helping verbs are forms of *be, have,* and *do,* plus the **modals:** *can, could, may, might, must, ought, shall, should, will,* and *would.* The modals have only one form, but *be, have,* and *do* take various forms to show tense, number, and person.

Be

Am, is, are, was, and *were* are the past and present forms of *be.* (See chart and discussion at **be.**) These forms of *be* combined with the *-ing* (present **participle**) form of a verb create the progressive **tense** of that verb.

I *was writing* my paper at the computer when the electricity went off.

Forms of *be* combined with the past participle of a verb create the **passive voice.**

As a result, the paper *was* not *written.*

Do

Do (*does, did*) is used for **questions,** negations, and **emphasis.**

Do you *know* what time the paper is due? [question]
Cheryl *doesn*'t *know* when it's due either. [negations]
I *did know,* but I've forgotten. [emphasis]

(See also ***don't, doesn't.***)

Use *do* (*does, did*) for asking questions when a form of *be* is not implied in the answer.

Did you *find* enough information? (I *found* enough information.)
Are you going to look further? (I *am* going to look further.)

Have

Have (*has, had*) combined with the past participle of a verb forms the perfect tenses.

I *have completed* my research on Italian fascism. [present perfect]
My classmate *will have helped* me locate some sources. [future perfect]
Before beginning my research, I *had studied* only German fascism. [past perfect]

Modals

Modals alter the meaning of a verb.

I *can* write the paper now.
I *should* write the paper now.
I *must* write the paper now.
I *will* write the paper now.
I *could* write the paper now.
I *may* write the paper now.

Modals do not change forms to agree with their subjects in person, number, or tense (although *could, would,* and *might* are sometimes used as past forms of *can, will,* and *may*). For example, *I can write, you can write, she can write, we can write, they can write; you could write, you could have written.*

herself   (See **reflexive pronouns**)

himself   (See **reflexive pronouns**)

his/her   (See **he/she**)

hisself   Nonstandard for *himself.*

holidays   (See **capitalization**)

homonyms   Homonyms are words that have similar sounds but different meanings. Usually the words are spelled differently too. Here are a few common homonyms:

accept, except	maybe, may be
affect, effect	of, 've (contraction for *have*)
already, all ready	passed, past
cite, sight, site	than, then
forth, fourth	their, there, they're
it's, its	to, too, two
know, no	whose, who's
lead, led	your, you're

Now in the age of spell-checkers on word-processing programs, homonyms are probably the most troublesome words to spell correctly. If you write *accept* for *except*, your computer will not flag an error; however, your reader will be left trying to puzzle out your meaning. Therefore you yourself need to carefully proofread what you've written. Use your dictionary to check the meanings of any sound-alike words you are unsure of.

A number of other words are not exactly homonyms but are similarly confused.

breath, breathe	lightning, lightening, lighting
choose, chose	loose, lose
clothes, cloths	precede, proceed
dominant, dominate	quite, quiet, quit

Other errors your computer won't flag are an -*s* or an -*ed* omitted from the end of a verb and an apostrophe or an -*s* omitted from a noun.

(See also **spelling.**)

hopefully   Many people object to the use of *hopefully* to mean anything but "in a hopeful manner," as it does in this sentence:

They proceeded down the the river *hopefully* but warily.

It's best, then, to avoid the word when your meaning is "it is to be hoped" or "I hope."

AVOID: *Hopefully*, they had no mishaps.
REVISED: *We hope* they had no mishaps.

hours and minutes   (See **colon** and **numbers**)

hung   (See **hanged**)

hyphens   Hyphens have three main uses: to divide words at the ends of lines, to form **compound words,** and to connect spelled-out **numbers.** Do not use them interchangeably with **dashes.**

DIVIDING WORDS.   Always divide words between syllables. Check your dictionary each time you are unsure about syllable breaks.

| maga- | remain- | tour- |
| zine | ing | ism |

Don't divide one-syllable words (such as *states*) or proper nouns and adjectives (such as Spanish). Don't separate only one or two letters: not *particular-ly* or *in-deed.*

FORMING COMPOUND WORDS.   See **compound words.**

CONNECTING SPELLED-OUT NUMBERS.   Hyphenate fractions, compound numbers, and ordinals from twenty-one to ninety-nine: *one-fifth, thirty-six, forty-fifth.*

I

idea, ideal   An *idea* is a thought, image, or conception; an *ideal* is a model of perfection or excellence.

The *ideal* essay is one that develops an *idea* fully and thoughtfully.

▼ idioms   Idioms are word groups that have meanings beyond the literal meanings of the individual words. Idioms develop within a language and even within a region, and newcomers to the language or region often have trouble understanding and using them. A **dictionary** can help. At the end of the entry for *take*, for example, the *American Heritage Dictionary* defines forty-three idioms, among them *on the take, take advantage of, take issue,* and *take it on the chin.* Refer to your dictionary any time a group of words doesn't make sense to you in a particular context.

Preposition use is determined mainly by idiom. Idiom, for instance, decides the difference in meaning and use between *charge <u>with</u>* and *charge <u>for</u>*, between *compare <u>to</u>* and *compare <u>with</u>*, and between *wait <u>at</u>, wait <u>for</u>,* and *wait <u>on</u>.* Again, a dictionary can help. Under *compare*, the *American Heritage Dictionary* has this usage note:

> *Compare* usually takes *to* when it denotes the act of stating or representing that two things are similar: *He compared her to a summer's day. He compared the ships to tiny shells.* It usually takes *with* when it denotes the act of examining the ways in which two things are similar: *The paper compared the president's budget with the congressional version. The police compared the forged will with the original.* When *compared* means "worthy of comparison," *with* is used: *The reproduction can't be compared with the original.*

ESL speakers and writers find bilingual and English dictionaries helpful for learning the idioms of English as a second language. However, the best way to learn idioms is through daily immersion in the language—by listening and speaking, by reading and writing. Whether you speak English as a first or second language, you can assist your memory for idioms by beginning a list of the English idioms you find difficult. Jot down the idiom, its meaning, and a sentence that illustrates its use; for example:

for the time being	"temporarily"
	You can borrow my textbook *for the time being.*
up against	"confronted with"
	When she entered the race, she had no idea what kind of competition she was *up against.*

illicit   (See **elicit**)

illusion   (See **allusion**)

immigrate to   (See **emigrate from**)

impact   *Impact* is both a noun and a verb referring to a forceful collision or the effect of one thing on another. Many people object to its use as a verb with the preposition *on*, as in *We have no doubt that the election will* impact on *the local economy*. A preferred phrasing is *We have no doubt that the election will* have an impact on *the local economy*.

imperative mood   The imperative **mood of verbs** shows that the speaker is making a request or a command.

>Go home. Stop shouting. Be on time. Don't forget to fill the gas tank.

A sentence in the imperative mood typically begins with the **verb** (in its **infinitive** form).

imply, infer   *Imply* means "to suggest"; *infer* means "to draw a conclusion." The terms are not interchangeable.

>The article *implied* that rural children do not have adequate health care and educational opportunities.

>We have *inferred* from the report that rural America requires special attention.

incomplete sentences   (See **fragments of sentences**)

indefinite adjectives   (See **indefinite pronouns and adjectives**)

indefinite articles   The noun **determiners** *a* and *an*, used in reference to persons, places, or things in general. (See also **articles.**)

indefinite pronouns and adjectives   Indefinite **pronouns** and **adjectives**, like the indefinite **articles** *a* and *an*, represent persons or things in general. Unlike other pronouns, the indefinites do not take their meaning from **antecedents**. Indefinite *pronouns* stand alone to represent nonspecific persons or things.

>Has *anybody* ever found the fountain of youth?

>*Some* of us might like to locate it.

Indefinite *adjectives* modify **common nouns.**

>*Any person* who finds that fountain will probably not share it.

>*Few people* are unselfish enough to share such a treasure.

COMMON INDEFINITE PRONOUNS AND ADJECTIVES			
all	each	few	one
any	either	neither	several
anybody	every	nobody	some
anyone	everybody	none	somebody
anything	everyone	no one	someone
both	everything	nothing	something

▲ *Agreement*

Most indefinite pronouns and adjectives are grammatically singular and therefore take singular verbs and **personal pronouns** for which they or their nouns are the antecedents.

> Ironically, *everyone knows* where *he or she* can find the fountain of youth. [*Everyone* takes the singular verb *knows* and the singular personal pronouns *he or she.*]
>
> *Each* person *wants* a nostrum that is easy for *him or her* to swallow. [The indefinite adjective *each* modifies *person* and takes the singular verb *wants* and the singular personal pronouns *him or her.*]

Because the repetition of *he or she* and *him or her* gets tiresome, many writers shift to plural constructions.

> *All* of us *want* something easier than exercising, reducing fat consumption, quitting smoking, and wearing *our* seat belts.

A few of the indefinites are singular or plural depending on their meaning, and some are only plural.

SINGULAR AND PLURAL INDEFINITES	
SINGULAR OR PLURAL	*PLURAL ONLY*
all the water, *all* the books	*both* houses
any teacher, *any* papers	*few* stories
none of the soup, *none* of the members	*several* tickets
some literature, *some* reports	

(See also **agreement of pronouns and antecedents, agreement of subjects and verbs,** and **nonsexist language.**)

Possessives

One-word indefinites form the possessive like singular nouns, by adding -'s to the end of the word: *anyone's, somebody's.* Indefinites of more than one word take the -'s on the last word: *each person's, every committee's, either programmer's, anybody else's.* (See also **apostrophes.**)

independent clauses   An independent **clause** expresses a complete thought and may function as a **simple sentence** and as part of a **compound sentence,** a **complex sentence,** or a **compound-complex sentence.** Like other clauses, it contains a **subject** and a **verb,** as well as any **modifiers** and **complements.**

AS A SIMPLE SENTENCE: No one can precisely define intuition.

IN A COMPOUND SENTENCE: We can't define intuition, but psychologists recognize it as a type of cognitive activity.

IN A COMPLEX SENTENCE: Although some people are more intuitive than others, *most of us can develop our intuitive abilities.*

IN A COMPOUND-COMPLEX SENTENCE: *Intuition depends on previous knowledge,* to which the brain applies an unconscious logical reasoning; *the effect is a fresh insight.*

An independent clause may be introduced by a **coordinating conjunction** (*and, but, or, nor, for, so, yet*) or a **transitional adverb** (such as *however, therefore,* and *then*), but not by a **subordinating conjunction** (such as *because, after, since,* or *when*) or a **relative pronoun** (*who, which, that*).

indicative mood   Speakers and writers use the indicative **mood of verbs** to state a fact or ask a question.

Do you *remember* what Archimedes discovered in his bathtub?

You surely *know* it was there that he *found* his Principle of Specific Gravity.

The indicative mood is the most commonly used, as compared to the other moods, **imperative** and **subjunctive.**

indirect objects   Indirect objects answer the question *to or for whom* or *to or for what* after transitive verbs. (See **objects**)

▼ **indirect questions**   An indirect question reports a **question** in the form of a statement instead of directly asking a question. It is usually introduced by an **interrogative pronoun,** an **adjective,** or an **adverb** or by a **subordinating conjunction** and ends with a **period,** not a **question mark.**

> Scientists still question *why dinosaurs died out after having survived ice ages and continental drifts.* [The indirect question is a **noun clause** introduced by the interrogative adverb *why.*]

The direct question would read:

> Scientists still question, "Why did dinosaurs die out after having survived ice ages and continental drifts?"

CAUTION: In writing indirect questions, do not use the verb first as you do in direct questions.

> **FAULTY:**   Scientists sometimes ask *does humankind really rule the earth.*
>
> **REVISED:**   Scientists sometimes ask *whether humankind really rules the earth.* [The indirect question is introduced by the subordinating conjunction *whether*; it follows normal subject-verb word order.]

▼ **indirect quotations**   An indirect **quotation** reports a statement made by another person but in the words of the speaker or writer, not the words of the person quoted.

> Cruz said *that he wanted to research the Children's Crusade.*

The sentence written with a direct quotation would read:

> Cruz said, *"I want to research the Children's Crusade."*

The direct quotation reports Cruz's exact words: *I* refers to *Cruz,* and the verb *want* is present tense.

An indirect quotation is written from the perspective of the person reporting it. In the example, *he* refers to *Cruz,* the quoted speaker, and the verb *wanted* is past tense. The statement is introduced by *that,* although the conjunction is sometimes understood but unstated.

> Cruz said [*that*] *he wanted to research the Children's Crusade.*

WRITING INDIRECT QUOTATIONS

1. Use third-person pronouns: *he, she, it, they.*
2. Introduce the statement with a phrase such as *she said that, he stated that,* or *they reported that.*
3. Change present-tense verbs to past. Instead of *I know* or *we understand,* write *he knew* or *they understood.* (See also **tense.**)

---

infer   (See **imply**)

infinitive phrases   An infinitive **phrase** is a **verbal phrase** consisting of an **infinitive** and its **modifiers** and **complements.**

How would you like *to count all the insects in the world?* [the infinitive *to count* with its direct **object** *insects* and its modifiers]

The figure would be too large for *anyone to comprehend.* [the infinitive *to comprehend* with its **subject** *anyone*]

Infinitive phrases can function as **nouns, adjectives,** and **adverbs.**

Scientists try *to count insects in only a limited space, such as a few acres.* [infinitive phrase as noun, functioning as the direct object of *try*]

It is not unusual *to find 2,000 insects per square yard.* [infinitive phrase as noun, functioning as delayed subject after the **expletive** *it*]

The numbers of insects are too big *to be counted in anyone's lifetime.* [infinitive phrase as adverb modifying the **complement** *too big*]

The time *to count individual species in only a square yard* is more than most of us would care to spend. [infinitive phrase as adjective modifying *time*]

Sentence fragment

CAUTION: An infinitive phrase written as a sentence is a **fragment.**

FAULTY: Insects have lived successfully on earth far longer than people. A feat *to make us wonder who really rules the earth.*

REVISED: Insects have lived successfully on earth far longer than people, a feat to make us wonder who really rules the earth.

Dangling modifier

CAUTION: An infinitive phrase can be a **dangling modifier** when the implied subject of the infinitive phrase is not the same as the subject of the sentence.

> FAULTY: *To suggest how large the insect population is*, about 1 million species have been identified. [The implied subject of *to suggest (scientists)* differs from the subject of the sentence, *species*.]
>
> REVISED: To suggest how large the insect population is, *scientists* have identified about 1 million species. [The independent clause is recast to active **voice;** *scientists* is now the subject of the sentence as well as the implied subject of the infinitive.]

To avoid sentence errors of this type, examine especially those infinitive phrases that occur at the beginning of your sentences.

infinitives   An infinitive is a **verbal** that can function as a **noun,** an **adjective,** or an **adverb.** The infinitive is the base form of a **verb,** often preceded by its marker, *to.*

> If you're a smoker, quitting smoking is the best way *to start* cancer prevention. [infinitive as adjective modifying *way*]
>
> Self-control in one's habits, it is said, helps *prevent* cancer. [infinitive as noun, direct object of *helps*; omitted *to*]
>
> Smokers ought *to worry* about their health. [infinitive as adverb modifying *ought*]

Infinitives sometimes have a stated subject.

> Nicotine patches might help *them to quit*. [*Them* is the subject of *to quit*.]
>
> For *us nonsmokers to be* intolerant of smokers is unfair. [*Us nonsmokers* is the subject of the infinitive *to be*.]

Subjects of infinitives are in the objective **case.** Infinitives sometimes serve as objects of verbs. (See **verbs,** "Verbs followed by infinitives and gerunds.")

▼   *Sequence of tenses*

Infinitives indicate **tense** relative to the tense of the **finite** verb.

> I want *to take* the book. [present action]
>
> I wanted *to take* the book. [past action]
>
> I will want *to take* the book. [future action]

I am sorry *to have taken* the book. [The book was taken in the past (indicated by the perfect infinitive *to have taken*); the writer is sorry in the present.]

I was sorry *to have taken* the book. [The book was taken in the past; the writer was sorry in the past.]

I will be sorry *to have taken* the book. [The writer took the book in the past and is not yet sorry.]

I would like *to take* the book. [Future; the book has not been taken; the writer wants to take it.]

I would have liked *to take* the book. [Past; the book was not taken; the writer wanted to take it.]

I would like *to have taken* the book. [The book was not taken; the writer regrets (present) not taking it.]

Use the combination of a finite verb and an infinitive that states what you mean to say.

CAUTION: A split infinitive is an **adverb** or adverbial **phrase** separating *to* and the verb form.

FAULTY: Harold has wanted *to* once and for all *quit* smoking. [The infinitive *to quit* is split by the adverbial phrase *once and for all*.]

Many people object to split infinitives because they unnecessarily interrupt a grammatical unit. Usually the modifier can be moved to another part of the sentence.

REVISED: Harold has wanted *to quit* smoking *once and for all*.

However, when moving the modifier creates ambiguity or awkwardness, an interruption of the infinitive may be preferable (especially if the modifier is a single word).

AWKWARD: Harold has wanted *to quit* smoking finally.

REVISED: Harold has wanted *to* finally *quit* smoking.

insure   (See **assure**)

intensifiers   Intensifiers are **adverbs** that emphasize the words they modify: *very* happy, *quite* unusual, *rather* discouraging. Use them sparingly, because often they lessen rather than increase emphasis.

That's a *very good* draft of your paper.

Instead of intensifying a general modifier (*good*), you might substitute a more specific modifier.

That's a *well-organized* draft of your paper.

Avoid using intensifiers with words that cannot logically be intensified, such as *unique, perfect, impossible, final,* and *complete.*

The report you requested is *complete* (not *quite complete*).

intensive pronouns   (See **reflexive pronouns**)

interjections   Interjections are words that express strong or sudden emotion. They usually function outside sentences and are often punctuated with **exclamation points.**

Ouch! I stubbed my toe again.

Wonderful! I knew you could do it.

O Lord, how great thou art! [Always capitalize *O*, but capitalize *oh* only when it begins a sentence.]

interrogative sentences   (See **questions**)

interrogative words   **Questions** that require other than a yes or no answer are introduced by words called *interrogatives*. They may be interrogative **pronouns** (*who, which, what, whoever, whatever*), **adjectives** (*what, which, whose, whatever, whichever*), and **adverbs** (*when, where, why, how*).

Who actually saw the accident happen? [pronoun]

Whose story are we to believe? [adjective]

Where did the accident happen? [adverb]

intransitive verbs   Verbs that do not take objects. (See also **verbs**)

inverted sentence order   Normal sentence order is a **subject** followed by its **verb.** With inverted order, the verb precedes the subject. Common occasions for inverted order are **questions** and sentences beginning with the **expletives** *it* and *there.*

How *will you get* to the bus? [The **helping verb** *will* precedes the subject *you* and the main verb *get.*]

There *will be several cars* taking people to the bus. [The verb *will be* precedes the subject *cars.*]

CAUTION: Your normal sense of verbs agreeing with subjects can be disrupted when a verb precedes its subject. In revision, check for **agreement of subjects and verbs** at all occasions of inverted order.

There *were* [not *was*] three cars waiting for us.

irregardless, regardless   *Irregardless* is nonstandard for *regardless*.

▼ **irregular verbs**   Regular **verbs** form the past **tense** and past participle by taking -*d* or -*ed* endings: *want, wanted, have wanted.* Irregular verbs form the past tense and past participle differently—usually internally but sometimes with no change to the base form or the past-tense form.

SOME COMMON IRREGULAR VERBS

BASE FORM	PAST TENSE	PAST PARTICIPLE
be	was	been
begin	began	begun
break	broke	broken
bring	brought	brought
buy	bought	bought
choose	chose	chosen
come	came	come
cut	cut	cut
do	did	done
drink	drank	drunk
drive	drove	driven
eat	ate	eaten
fall	fell	fallen
get	got	got *or* gotten
give	gave	given
grow	grew	grown
have	had	had
know	knew	known
lay	laid	laid
lead	led	led
lie	lay	lain
pay	paid	paid
rise	rose	risen
run	ran	run
say	said	said
see	saw	seen

BASE FORM	PAST TENSE	PAST PARTICIPLE
set	set	set
sit	sat	sat
speak	spoke	spoken
stand	stood	stood
steal	stole	stolen
swim	swam	swum
take	took	taken
tear	tore	torn
throw	threw	thrown
wear	wore	worn
write	wrote	written

Your dictionary lists the forms of irregular verbs.

is when, is where   (See **mixed constructions**)

italics (underlining)   Italics is a style of type that slants to the right. It is used for setting some words apart from others. In typing or handwriting, underlining serves the same purpose.

Italicize or underline titles of works
published independently

Italicize or underline titles of works published independently, such as books, plays, long poems, newspapers, magazines, journals, movies, television and radio programs, and long musical works.

Amusing Ourselves to Death: Public Discourse in the Age of Show Business [book title; note that a subtitle is also italicized and set off with a colon]

The Canadian Business Review [journal]

The Wall Street Journal [newspaper]

Northern Exposure [television series]

The Phantom of the Opera [musical play]

Italicize or underline names of ships, aircraft,
spacecraft, and trains

U.S.S. *Nimitz* [ship]

Challenger [spacecraft]

Garden State Special [train]

Italicize or underline letters, words, and phrases used as terms

Oddly enough, *saturnism* means "lead poisoning." [The word *saturnism* used as a term is italicized; **quotation marks** are used to set off the meaning of words.]

The word looked strange with three *l*'s in it. [See also **apostrophes**.]

Italicize or underline foreign words and phrases

Unfortunately, the author resorted to a *deus ex machina* ending.

Many foreign words and abbreviations commonly used in English (such as *cliché, e.g., etc., laissez-faire,* and *versus*) are no longer italicized. Refer to your dictionary.

Italicize or underline for emphasis

For emphasis, italicize or underline sparingly.

There were *forty* people at the meeting, not *fourteen* as I thought.

▲ *it's, its* *It's* is a **contraction** of *it is* or *it has; its* is a possessive **pronoun.**

It's [It is] the cockroach, with *its* flat, leathery body, that will survive any conflagration military strategists can dream up.

It's [It has] already been around for millions of years, laying *its* eggs and making more cockroaches.

If you have trouble remembering which one to use, use only one, the possessive *its,* and write out the contraction: *it is* or *it has.* (See also **apostrophes.**)

J

---

jargon Jargon is specialized or technical language used by a particular occupational group. Although important for communication within the group, in other contexts it may be meaningless. When you are writing for computer experts, for example, it may be appropriate for you to use terms such as *byte, integer array,* and *unsave,* but in other contexts you should either avoid the terms or define them at first use. (See also **diction** and **wordiness.**)

K

---

kind of, sort of   Use *kind of* and *sort of* only to refer to types of things.

What *kind of* books do you like to read?

Except in informal speech, avoid using them to mean "somewhat."

INFORMAL: He seemed *kind of* eager to leave.

Avoid using the plural adjectives *these* and *those* with the singular *kind* and *sort.*

FAULTY: Do you ever read *these kind of* books?
REVISED: Do you ever read *this kind of* books?
REVISED: Do you ever read *these kinds of* books?
REVISED: Do you ever read books of *this kind?*

L

---

latter   (See *former*)

lay, lie   *Lay* means "to put" and takes a direct **object.** Except for an occasional misspelling of its past form, it is almost always used correctly.

Lay your plans on the table before you begin. [present tense; *plans* is the direct object]

Have you *laid* your plans on the table yet? [present perfect tense *Have . . . laid;* note the irregular spelling (not *layed*)]

Lie means "to recline" and does not take a direct object.

The blueprints can *lie* on the table while you work. [present tense; *lie* is followed by the **prepositional phrase** *on the table*]

The blueprints *have lain* on the table all day. [present perfect tense]

Following his error in judgment, he decided *to lie* low for a while. [infinitive]

One of the reasons *lie* causes confusion for writers is that its past tense form is the same as the base form of the verb *lay.*

PRESENT	PAST	PAST PARTICIPLE	PRESENT PARTICIPLE
lay	laid	laid	laying
lie	lay	lain	lying

The following sentence uses *lie* in the past tense.

The blueprints *lay* on the table while I worked.

leave, let   *Leave* means "to exit"; *let* means "to allow." Do not use *leave* when *let* is called for.

We can *let* (not *leave*) him try it himself.

lend, loan   In formal usage, use *lend* as a verb and *loan* as a noun.

Do you have a pen you can *lend* me? [*lend* as a verb]
I can't pay my fees until my *loan* comes through. [*loan* as a noun]

less   (See *fewer*)

let   (See *leave*)

lie   (See *lay*)

like   (See *as*)

linking verbs   Linking **verbs** connect **subjects** with **subject complements.** Some common verbs are **be,** *seem, become, appear, grow, remain, turn, look, feel, sound, taste,* and *smell.*

Solar power *could become* the energy of choice. [*Could become* links the subject *power* and the subject complement *energy.*]

Solar power now *is* cost-effective and environmentally benign. [*Is* links the subject *power* with the **adjectives** *cost-effective* and *benign*, the subject complements.]

Most linking verbs can function also as **transitive verbs** and **intransitive verbs.**

Using wind farms as a source of energy *sounds* promising. [linking verb]

The American Wind Energy Association *has sounded* a call for turning wind energy into electrical power. [transitive verb, with *call* as direct **object**]

The call for environmentally friendly sources of power *has sounded*. [intransitive verb]

A verb performs a *linking* function only when it is followed by a subject complement. (See also **agreement of subjects and verbs.**)

literally   Use this **adverb** to mean "actually." Avoid using it to mean "in a manner of speaking."

> She was *nearly* [not *literally*] out of her mind with anticipation.
> The force of the wind *literally* moved the house from its foundation.

loan   (See **lend**)

loose, lose   *Loose* is an adjective meaning "not fastened"; *lose* is a verb meaning "to be deprived of," "to mislay," or to "fail to win," among other meanings.

> If the boat comes *loose* from its mooring, we might *lose* the boat in the storm.

lots, lots of   Both *lots* and *lots of* are **colloquial** terms meaning "very many" or "much." Avoid using them in academic and professional writing.

> I have already completed *much* [not *lots of*] research.

(See also **a lot.**)

M

---

man, mankind   Many readers object to the use of *man* and *mankind* in the sense of "all human beings" because they believe these words fail to acknowledge women. Substitute other, more generic words such as *humanity, the human race, all human beings,* and *humankind* (all of which derive from the Latin *humanus*, meaning "human" or "civilized" rather than from the Old English *man*). See also **nonsexist language.**

▼ *mass nouns (noncount nouns)*   Mass, or noncount, nouns stand for things that cannot be counted, such as *anger, cereal, courage, employment, flour, food, health, honesty, intelligence, love, meat, oil, pasta, physics, pollution, scenery, soap, transportation, water, weather,* and *work*. In contrast to **count nouns**, mass nouns have the following characteristics:

1. They do not take the plural form by adding an *-s* and cannot be used with numbers.

   FAULTY: I took *two transportations.*

   REVISED: I took *two modes of transportation.*

   To designate amounts, add a count noun: *pieces* of furniture, *gallons* of water.

2. They are more likely to follow the definite **article**, *the*, than the indefinite articles, *a* and *an*.

   Listen to *the music.*

   The furniture was delivered yesterday.

3. Like count nouns, they can follow *any, some,* and *rest.*

   FAULTY: Simon has *an information* for you.

   REVISED: Simon has *some information* for you.

4. Whereas *many* is used before count nouns, *much* is used before mass nouns.

   How *much news* do you have for me?

   We wish you *much happiness.*

5. Whereas *a few* is used before plural count nouns, *a little* is used before mass nouns.

   FAULTY: Liu has only *a few luggages.*

   REVISED: Liu has only *a little luggage.*

Some mass nouns can function also as count nouns, though the meaning is altered to indicate several varieties of something.

   MASS NOUN: Eat some *fruit* for breakfast.

   COUNT NOUN: I just love the summer *fruits.*

Recognizing mass nouns is not easy for someone using English as a second language. Remember that most of them fall into these general categories:

   Abstractions: information, news
   States of being or actions: health, homework
   Gases: oxygen, nitrogen
   Emotions: love, fear
   Fields of study: history, anthropology
   Gerunds: swimming, talking, running
   A body of similar items: poetry, literature

Languages: English, German, Chinese
Food and beverages: water, tea, coffee, chicken, bread
Natural phenomena: rain, weather
Solids and liquids: steel, lumber, oil, gasoline
Substances composed of many particles: sugar, salt, sand, rice, flour

may   (See *can, may*)

maybe, may be   *Maybe* is an **adverb** meaning "perhaps."

Maybe touchtone registration for classes will be easier than the old way.

May be (two words) is a **verb phrase** indicating permission or possibility.

We *may be* able to register in minutes instead of hours.

mechanics   *Mechanics* refers to the use of **capitalization, italics** (underlining), **abbreviations, numbers,** and **hyphens.**

media   *Media* is the plural of *medium*, meaning mass communications such as television, radio, newspapers, and magazines. Use a plural **verb** with *media.*

The *media are* often charged with creating news instead of simply reporting it.

metaphors   A metaphor is a **figure of speech** that implies a comparison between two things.

There is a garden in her face,
Where roses and white lilies grow.
                                        –THOMAS CAMPION, 1617

An occasional metaphor is useful for describing things or qualities of things that are difficult to describe. The apparatus for moving a cursor and drawing lines on a computer screen, for example, has been labeled a "mouse." Be careful, however, not to "mix" your metaphors, using more than one metaphor in a possibly ludicrous combination.

In the *autumn of his life*, he had to *swim against the current.*

Some metaphors have been used so much that they have lost their effectiveness and become **clichés.**

She's just *a shadow of her former self.*

See also **simile.**

might of   Do not use *of* in place of *have* (as in I *might of* caused an accident). See **of, have.**

migrate   (See **emigrate from**)

⚠ misplaced modifiers

> SECTION OVERVIEW
> Misplaced words
> Misplaced phrases
> Misplaced clauses

A misplaced **modifier** appears to modify the wrong word.

> FAULTY: She *only* has fifteen dollars in her checking account. [*Only* appears to modify *has* rather than the intended *fifteen*.]
>
> REVISED: She has *only* fifteen dollars in her checking account.

When the modifier could reasonably modify either of two sentence elements, it is sometimes called a *squinting modifier.*

> FAULTY: People who exercise *frequently* are healthy. [*Frequently* "squints"; it could reasonably modify *exercise* or *are healthy.*]
>
> REVISED: People who *frequently* exercise are healthy.
>
> REVISED: People who exercise are *frequently* healthy.

A misplaced modifier can be a word, a **phrase,** or a **clause.**

Misplaced words

Misplaced modifiers are often **adverbs.** Adverbs that modify **verbs** can often function in various positions in the sentence, but those that modify **adjectives** and other **adverbs** must immediately precede those words. In the example sentence *She has only fifteen dollars in her checking account, only* modifies the adjective *fifteen* and cannot be moved to another location in the sentence. In the following example, *certainly* modifies the verb *does want* and can function in more than one location in the sentence.

> She *certainly* doesn't want to overdraw her account.
>
> *Certainly*, she doesn't want to overdraw her account.

When using limiting words such as *almost, even, exactly, hardly, just, merely, nearly, only, scarcely,* and *simply,* place them in front of the words they modify. Notice how the meaning changes in the following sentences depending on the placement of *just:*

She *just* had opened the account to pay her school expenses. [She had recently opened the account.]

She had *just* opened the account to pay her school expenses. [Ambiguous: she had recently opened the account, or she had done nothing to the account but open it.]

She had opened the account *just* to pay her school expenses. [The reason she opened the account was to pay her school expenses.]

She had opened the account to pay *just* her school expenses. [She would use the account only for her school expenses.]

Misplaced phrases

Prepositional phrases and **verbal phrases,** especially those attached at the end of sentences, might seem to modify the wrong words.

FAULTY: I learned to saddle horses, to pack mules, and to guide nervous riders *on Big Lake last summer*. [*On Big Lake* and *last summer* mistakenly modify *riders*.]

REVISED: *On Big Lake last summer*, I learned to saddle horses, to pack mules, and to guide nervous riders.

FAULTY: Make reservations early to have a luxury horseback ride through rugged mountain country *at the Big Lake resort corral*. [*At the Big Lake resort corral* appears to modify *country*.]

REVISED: *To have a luxury horseback ride through rugged mountain country*, make reservations early at the Big Lake resort corral.

Misplaced clauses

Relative clauses may appear to modify the wrong **noun** or **pronoun** when they are not placed next to the word they modify.

FAULTY: A three-day ride could take you past trout brooks and lakes above the timberline *that takes off from a base camp each morning*. [The italicized clause appears to modify *timberline* instead of *ride*.]

REVISED: A three-day ride *that takes off from a base camp each morning* could take you past trout brooks and lakes above the timberline.

See also **dangling modifiers.**

 misspelled words, common   Of all the words in the English language, only a small number are commonly misspelled by many writers. If you want to improve your **spelling,** find out which words you misspell. Have someone read the words on the following list while you spell them. Mark the words you miss and make up your own cue cards for those words. To familiarize yourself with words, look them up in your dictionary, noting syllabic divisions, pronunciation, and meaning. Then write each word on a separate card or a page of a notepad, along with a sentence that uses the word. To aid your memory, you might try mnemonic devices such as capitalizing the syllables you misspell (for example, "calenDAR") or writing a statement that calls attention to the problem (for example, *"manageable* has *age* before *able"*). Sometimes it helps to visualize the parts of the word, separating *tomorrow*, for example, into *to* and *morrow* or *Wednesday* into *Wed nes day*. Make cards also for other words that are your individual spelling demons. Then once a week review your cue cards and occasionally have someone test you by reading the words to you. See also **spelling** and **homonyms.**

COMMONLY MISSPELLED WORDS

absence	amount	biggest	competent
acceptable	analysis	boundary	competition
accessible	angel/angle	breath/breathe	complement
accidentally	announcement	bulletin	conceited
accommodate	apparent	bureaucracy	conceive
accompanied	appearance	business	concentrate
accomplish	approach		condemn
accuracy	appropriate	cafeteria	confident
achievement	approximate	calculator	conscience
acknowledge	argument	calendar	conscientious
acquaintance	article	careless	consensus
acquire	aspirin	carrying	consistent
across	associate	category	continuous
actually	athlete	cemetery	controlled
address	attach/attack	census	controversy
admission	attendance	certain	convenience
advice/advise	authentic	changeable	coolly
affect/effect	average	changing	course/coarse
against		channel	courteous
aggression	bargain	chief	criticism
aisles	basically	choose/chose	criticize
alcohol	beautiful	coming	curiosity
all right	beginner	commercial	
a lot	believe	commitment	dealt
amateur	beneficial	committee	deceive
among	benefited	comparative	decide

definitely	financially	jealousy	ninety
dependent	forty	judgment	ninth
descend	friend		noticeable
describe	fulfill	knowledge	
desirable			obstacle
desperate	gauge	laboratory	occasionally
develop	government	laid	occurred
different	grammar	led	occurrence
dining	guarantee	leisure	official
disagree	guard	lenient	omitted
disappear	guidance	liable	operate
disappoint		library	opinion
disastrous	harass	license	opportunity
disease	height	lightning	opposite
discipline	here/hear	likelihood	ordinarily
discussion	heroes	loneliness	originally
divide	hindrance	lose/loose/losing	
divine	hoping	luxury	paid
	huge	lying	pamphlet
efficient	humorous		parallel
eighth	hurrying	magazine	particular
elaborate	hypocrite	magnificent	past/passed
embarrass		maintenance	peculiar
environment	ideally	manageable	perceive
equipped	ignorant	management	performance
especially	imaginary	marriage	permanent
every	immediately	material	personnel
exaggerate	immensely	mathematics	persuade
excellent	incidentally	meant	physical
except	incredible	medicine	piece/peace
exercise	independent	mere	planned
exhaust	indispensable	miniature	pleasant
existence	individually	minutes	politician
expense	initiative	mischievous	pollute
experience	innocuous	missile	possess
experiment	inoculate	mortgage	possibly
explanation	intelligent	muscle	practically
extremely	interest	mysterious	precede
	interference		preferred
familiar	interrupt	naturally	prejudice
family	irrelevant	necessary	preparation
fascinate	irresistible	neither	principle/principal
favorite	irritated	nickel	privilege
February	it's/its	niece	probably

procedure	restaurant	succeed	unconscious
proceed	rhythm	success	until
professor	ridiculous	sufficient	usage
prominent	roommate	summary	usually
pronunciation		surely	
psychology	sacrifice	surprise	vacuum
pursue	safety	suspicious	valuable
	sandwich		various
quantity	satellite	teammate	vegetable
questionnaire	scarcity	technical	view
quiet/quite/quit	schedule	technique	villain
quizzes	secretary	temperature	visible
	seize	temporary	
realize	sense	tendency	warrant
really	separate	than/then	weather/whether
receive	sergeant	their/there/	Wednesday
receipt	several	they're	weird
receive	sheriff	thorough	where/were
recipe	shining	though	woman/women
recognize	significant	thought	writing
recommend	similar	tomorrow	written
referring	sincerely	to/too/two	
rehearsal	sophomore	tragedy	yield
relief	speak/speech	transferred	
relieve	statistics	tremendous	
religious	stopping	tries	
remembrance	strategy	truly	
reminisce	strength	twelfth	
repetition	studying	typical	

⚠ mixed constructions   A mixed construction contains two or more grammatical structures that do not logically fit together. The error may occur when a writer pauses after starting a sentence and then loses track of how the sentence began.

FAULTY: By passing the new law extends employability to many disabled Americans. [The sentence begins with a **prepositional phrase** and does not have a **subject** of the **verb** *extends*.]

REVISED: By passing the new law, the U.S. government extends employability to many disabled Americans. [The subject is *the U.S. government*.]

FAULTY: Because the new law forbids discrimination against disabled Americans means that many qualified Americans are more likely to be hired. [The sentence begins with a subordinate **clause** and does not have a subject of the verb *means*.]

REVISED: Because the new law forbids discrimination against disabled Americans, many qualified disabled Americans are more likely to be hired.

FAULTY: By not requiring preferential treatment of people with disabilities results in equal opportunity for job candidates who are not disabled. [The sentence begins with a prepositional phrase and does not have a subject for the verb *results*.]

REVISED: Not requiring preferential treatment of people with disabilities results in equal opportunity for job candidates who are not disabled. [The preposition *by* is omitted, making *treatment* the subject of *results*.]

Mixing subordinating and coordinating conjunctions

Mixing subordinating **conjunctions** and coordinating conjunctions in a sentence may result in a mixed construction. The faulty construction can be revised with either the subordinating or the coordinating conjunction.

FAULTY: *Though* speculation on the existence of worlds similar to ours dates back to ancient civilizations, *but* there is still no compelling evidence for extraterrestrial life.

REVISED: *Though* speculation on the existence of worlds similar to ours dates back to ancient civilizations, there is still no compelling evidence for extraterrestrial life.

REVISED: Speculation on the existence of worlds similar to ours dates back to ancient civilizations, *but* there is still no compelling evidence for extraterrestrial life.

Watch particularly for sentences that begin with *although, even though, though, if,* and *even if.* See also **conjunctions.**

Faulty predication

Faulty predication is a mixed construction in which the subject and verb (**predicate**) do not make sense together.

FAULTY: The reason for the Americans with Disabilities Act of 1990 *was because* many Americans had been denied access to the workplace. [Avoid the construction *reason . . . is (was) because.*]

REVISED: The reason for the Americans with Disabilities Act of 1990 was *that* many Americans had been denied access to the workplace. [*That* replaces *because.*]

REVISED: The Americans with Disabilities Act of 1990 was enacted because many Americans had been denied access to the workplace. [*Reason* is omitted.]

FAULTY: A violation of the act *is when* employers do not make reasonable accommodations for people with disabilities. [The **linking verb** *is* cannot logically link the adverbial *when* clause with the subject *violation.*]

REVISED: A violation of the act occurs when employers do not make reasonable accommodations for people with disabilities. [*Occurs* replaces *is.*]

FAULTY: The *use of* the law will protect people with disabilities. [It is *the law* that *will protect people with disabilities*; *The use of* is redundant.]

REVISED: The law will protect people with disabilities.

See also **shifts.**

mixed metaphors   (See **metaphors**)

▼ **modals**   Modals are **helping verbs** that alter the meaning of verbs, indicating possibility, necessity, capability, willingness, and the like.

Columbus *can* be seen as a flawed hero.

Columbus *might* be seen as a flawed hero.

Columbus *must* be seen as a flawed hero.

The verbs most commonly thought of as modals are *can, could, may, might, must, ought, shall, should, will,* and *would.* Unlike other verbs, they do not change form to indicate **number** and **person:** I *can* see, she *can* see, we *can* see.

modifiers   Modifiers are words, **phrases,** and **clauses** that limit, broaden, describe, define, identify, or explain other parts of a sentence. Modifiers function as **adjectives** (modifying nouns and pronouns) or **adverbs** (modifying verbs, adjectives, or other adverbs).

Adjectives

WORD: Exposure to the sun's *ultraviolet* rays can cause *health* problems. [*Ultraviolet* and *health* are adjectives modifying *rays* and *problems.*]

PHRASE: Habitual tanning leads to early aging *of the skin.* [The **prepositional phrase** *of the skin* modifies *aging.*]

PHRASE: Many skin changes *previously linked to normal aging* are now known to be caused by exposure to ultraviolet light. [The **participial phrase** *previously linked to normal aging* modifies *changes.*]

CLAUSE: Some people *who worry about sun tanning* go to tanning parlors. [The **relative clause** *who worry about sun tanning* modifies *people.*]

Adverbs

WORD: Tanning under tanning lamps is *no less* risky than tanning under the sun. [*Less* modifies *risky*, and *no* modifies *less.*]

PHRASE: Ultraviolet light is invisible *to the human eye.* [The prepositional phrase *to the human eye* modifies *invisible.*]

CLAUSE: Tanning lamps may be more dangerous than the sun *because their rays penetrate the skin more deeply than sunlight does.* [The **subordinate clause** beginning *because* modifies the independent clause.]

See also **dangling modifiers** and **misplaced modifiers.**

money   (See **numbers**)

months of the year   (See **capitalization**)

mood of verbs   Mood enables verbs to express attitudes and intentions. The most common mood, the **indicative,** states a fact or asks a question.

The Greek philosopher Socrates *left* no writings.

How *do* we *know* what he *thought* and *taught?*

The **imperative** mood makes a request or a command.

Read the works of Plato to learn about Socrates.

An imperative sentence typically begins with the verb (in its base form) and addresses the audience. The **subjunctive mood** is usually the most troublesome. It indicates conditions contrary to fact: wishes, recommendations, and possibilities.

If she *were* to read Plato's *Phaedrus*, she would learn what Socrates thought about rhetoric.

moral, morale   *Moral* as a noun means "lesson" or "general truth."

He couldn't see the *moral* of the story.

Morale means "state of mind or spirit."

The team's *morale* was at a low point.

Ms.   A blend of *Miss* and *Mrs., Ms.* is a title that can be used before a woman's name when marital status is not relevant. *Ms.* is widely used in business and professional life, though academic and professional titles such as *Dr.* and *Professor* take precedence. When a woman prefers *Mrs.* or *Miss* to other titles, that preference should be honored. Some women use *Ms.* in social situations, in which case *Ms. Smith* is correct for the wife of John Smith, but *Ms. John Smith* is not. If the wife of John Smith retains her family name, she could use the title *Ms. Ford* but not *Mrs. Ford.*

musical works   (See **titles**)

myself   (See **reflexive pronouns**)

N

names   (See **capitalization** and **proper nouns**)

negative constructions   Negation is usually indicated by the **adverbs** *not* and *never* and the **adjective** *no*.

We can*not* honor your request. [*Not* modifies the verb *can honor*.]

We will *never* honor your request. [*Never* modifies the verb *will honor*.]

We will honor *no* request from you. [*No* modifies the noun *request*.]

▼ As adverbs, *not* and *never* modify **verbs**, adjectives, and adverbs.

I *do not understand* your meaning. [*Not* modifies the verb *do understand*.]

We closed the show because there was *not nearly enough* interest. [*Not* modifies the adverb *nearly*.]

There was *not* enough interest to justify the costs. [*Not* modifies the adjective *enough*.]

As an adjective, *no* modifies **nouns.**

> We had *no desire* to continue the show. [*No* modifies the noun *desire.*]

> We had *no immediate desire* to continue the show. [*No* precedes the adjective *immediate* and modifies the noun *desire.*]

The **double negative** is a sentence fault in which two negatives perform the same function.

> FAULTY: We will *never* honor *no* request from you.

> REVISED: We will *never* honor a request from you.

> REVISED: We will honor *no* request from you.

nominalizations   A nominalization is a **noun** derived from a **verb.**

> We will make an *evaluation* of your report. [The noun *evaluation* is derived from the verb *evaluate.*]

Nominalizations usually contribute to **wordiness:** they are usually longer than the verbs from which they are derived, and they usually require additional words.

> WORDY: Our *intention* is to make a full *evaluation* of your report.

> REVISED: We *intend* to fully *evaluate* your report.

Nominalizations sometimes reduce wordiness.

> WORDY: The fact that we intend to evaluate your report is no reason for you to be worried.

> REVISED: Our *intention* to evaluate your report is no reason for you to worry. [The nominalization *intention* eliminates the wordier phrase *the fact that we intend.*]

By summarizing previously stated ideas, nominalizations can facilitate coherence, allowing writers to connect ideas.

> These *interpretations* will change the way we think about inventories.

nominative absolutes   (See **absolute**s)

nominative case   (See **case**)

noncount nouns   (See **mass nouns**)

▲ **nonrestrictive elements**   A nonrestrictive element is a **modifier** that does not identify, limit, or define the word it modifies. Although it probably offers important information, the nonrestrictive element could be removed from the sentence without altering the identity of the modified word.

> Sri Lanka, *formerly called Ceylon,* achieved independence from Great Britain in 1948. [The phrase *formerly called Ceylon* is not necessary for identifying the country being discussed here; Sri Lanka is already identified by name.]

In contrast to a **restrictive element**, a nonrestrictive element is set off from the sentence with **commas** or occasionally with **dashes** or a **colon.** Words, **phrases,** and **clauses** may be nonrestrictive.

Words

The ancient Greeks had another name for Sri Lanka: *Taprobane.*

The Arabs had still another name, *Serendip.*

The two names—*Taprobane and Serendip*—are no longer used.

Phrases

"Serendipity," *the English word for an unexpected gift,* is derived from the Arab name for Sri Lanka. [**appositive** phrase]

Declaring itself a republic in 1972, the nation changed its name from Ceylon to Sri Lanka. [**participial phrase**]

In the mid-1600s, the Dutch took possession of the island. [**prepositional phrase**]

Clauses

The Dutch ceded the island to the British, *who developed coffee, coconut, rubber, and tea plantations.* [**relative clause**]

The country's economy still depends mainly on these crops, *though graphite is another important product.* [**adverb clause**]

Modifiers of **proper nouns** are almost always nonrestrictive, because the name identifies the person or thing.

CAUTION: The distinction between restrictive and nonrestrictive is important to writers because meaning is often affected by whether or not the element is set off from the sentence. Avoid setting off restrictive elements as if they were nonrestrictive. The following sentences, for example, have different meanings.

FAULTY: People, *who live in Sri Lanka,* speak Sinhala, Tamil, or English. [By treating the relative clause as nonrestrictive the sentence implies that all people live in Sri Lanka and speak Sinhala, Tamil, or English.]

REVISED: People *who live in Sri Lanka* speak Sinhala, Tamil, or English. [By treating the relative clause as restrictive the sentence describes only the people living in Sri Lanka.]

non sequiturs   (See **fallacies in logic**)

nonsexist language   Because there are increasing numbers of women in the workplace, terms such as *fireman* and *chairman* are no longer acceptable to many readers. To be sensitive to your audience, avoid such terms, replacing them with expressions such as *firefighter* and *chair* or *chairperson.*

Masculine nouns

Do not use *man* and its compounds generically. Instead, use a term that encompasses both genders, which in many cases is a more descriptive term.

businessman	businessperson, executive, manager, or some other specific term
congressman	member of Congress, representative
mail man	mail carrier
man hours	work hours
mankind	humanity, people
manmade	manufactured, synthetic
policeman	police officer
salesman	salesperson, sales representative, sales clerk, or some other specific term

Masculine pronouns

The pronouns *he, him*, and *his* can no longer be assumed to refer to both male and female. But avoiding them is difficult because English has no singular generic pronoun that is acceptable in all situations. In **colloquial** usage, *they, them*, and *their* are often used in a singular sense.

COLLOQUIAL: Every smoker has to make *their* own decision about smoking. [*Their* refers to the singular subject, *smoker.*]

But such usage is not widely accepted. Writers must therefore select the most suitable of several options.

PLURAL: *Smokers* have to make *their* own decisions about smoking.

ELIMINATED PRONOUN: Every smoker has to make *a* decision about smoking.

RECIPROCAL PRONOUNS: Every smoker has to make *his or her* own decision about smoking. [To avoid wordiness, use this option sparingly and only when you want to emphasize the individuals.]

SECOND PERSON, *YOU*:   As a smoker, *you* have to make *your* own decision about smoking. [Use this option only when you want to directly address your audience.]

Stereotyping and patronizing terms

Avoid words that cast men or women in particular roles or that imply that women are subordinate to men. Here are some acceptable substitutes:

career girl	professional woman, attorney, manager, or other specific term
coed	student
fisherman	angler
gal Friday	assistant, secretary, or other specific term
housewife	homemaker, consumer, parent, or other specific term
Keats and Miss Dickinson	Keats and Dickinson
lady lawyer	lawyer
laundress	launderer
maiden name	family name, surname, birth name
male nurse	nurse
poetess	poet
Workmen's Compensation	Worker's Compensation

nonstandard usage   Nonstandard usage (such as *themself, we knowed,* and *ain't got no*) is a variety of English that is not acceptable for educated speakers and writers. Although some nonstandard words and phrases are common in casual speech, they are never acceptable in formal speaking and writing. To identify nonstandard forms, consult your dictionary and your handbook.

nor, or   *Nor* and *or* are coordinating **conjunctions** used to indicate alternatives. As correlative conjunctions, *or* is paired with *either* and *nor* is paired with *neither.*

> I could have *either* enrolled in technical college *or* continued at my summer job.

> I liked *neither* the work *nor* the pay.

See also **agreement of subjects and verbs** and **parallelism**.

noun clauses   **Subordinate clauses** functioning as **nouns.**

noun phrases   A noun phrase is a **noun** plus its **modifiers:** *the work environment, a stress-related headache, an ergonomically sound work-station.* **Gerund phrases, infinitive phrases,** and occasionally **prepositional phrases** can function as nouns.

> *Sitting for many hours at a computer* puts strain on the neck and back. [gerund phrase as **subject**]

> The purpose of ergonomics is *to relieve that strain.* [infinitive phrase as **subject complement**]

> *After work* is the time for less stressful activities. [prepositional phrase as subject]

Gerund and infinitive phrases as subjects take singular verbs.

> *Adapting to changes in the work environment* has taken its toll in the form of stress. [The gerund phrase is the subject and takes the singular verb, *has taken.*]

> *To understand how today's work environment differs from earlier environments* requires a study of the history of humanity. [The infinitive phrase is the subject and takes the singular verb *requires.*]

nouns   A noun is the name of anything that may be a **subject** or an **object** in a sentence. Nouns name persons, places, or things (including concepts, actions, and qualities). Nouns may serve the following functions.

> **Subject:** *Turtles* have outlasted the dinosaurs.
> **Appositive:** An ancient *species*, turtles survive without adaptation.
> **Direct** object: Whatever killed the *dinosaurs* did not kill the *turtles.*
> **Indirect** object: Let's give *turtles* their due.
> **Object complement:** We might name them the ultimate *survivors.*
> **Subject complement:** Turtles are *residents* of all land masses.

Object of preposition: With their protective *shells*, they don't worry about ultraviolet *rays*.

Absolute: Their *shells* lending protection from the sun's rays, turtles have little problem with skin cancer.

Noun number

A noun naming one person or thing is **singular;** a noun naming more than one thing is **plural.** Most plural nouns are formed by adding -*s* to the singular form.

SINGULAR	PLURAL
book	books
magazine	magazines
desk	desks

Nouns ending in *s, sh, ch, x,* or *z* are made plural by adding -*es.*

SINGULAR	PLURAL
fax	faxes
pass	passes
watch	watches

Common nouns and proper nouns

Nouns may be classified as *common* or *proper.* A common noun is the name for a general type of person, place, or thing: *girl, engineer, turtle, dinosaur, shell, protection, problem, cancer, species.* A proper noun is the name for a particular person, place, or thing; it is capitalized: *Emydidae, Tyrannosaurus, Michelangelo, London, Republican.* Nouns naming relatives are capitalized only when they are used as names:

My *father* was not able to attend my graduation, but *Mom* was there.

See also **capitalization.**

Possessive case of nouns

Possessive nouns show ownership or connection.

This is my *brother's* computer. [ownership]
I have been reading *Gus Lee's China Boy.* [authorship]
Today's newspaper hasn't arrived yet. [connection]

For more on forming possessive nouns, see **apostrophes.**

See also **abstract words/concrete words** and **collective nouns.**

number   (See *amount*)

▼ **number**   Number is a property of **nouns, pronouns,** and **verbs** that indicates whether they are referring to one person, place, or thing (**singular**) or more than one (**plural**).

> The *report is* nearly finished, and you will have *it* tomorrow. [singular]
>
> The *reports are* nearly finished, and you will have *them* tomorrow. [plural]

numbers   Rules for using numbers vary. When you are using a great many numbers, write as words all whole numbers from zero to ten, and write as figures all numbers above ten. But never begin a sentence with a figure.

> The meeting was attended by *80* people.
>
> *Eighty* [not *80*] people attended the meeting.
>
> I am a *48*-year-old student.

When you are using only an occasional number, spell out all numbers that can be written in two words or less.

> The meeting was attended by *fifteen hundred* people.

In a sentence that contains several related numbers, normally all the numbers are written as figures.

> In this month alone, *256* jobs were lost in Baraboo, *24* in Kenosha, and *6* in Fond du Lac.

Use figures for decimals (*4.5*), percents (*6 percent*), and units of measurement (*8 miles*). Fractions attached to whole numbers are expressed as figures, but fractions not accompanied by a whole number are written out *(4 1/4, one-fourth)*. Use figures for chapter and page references.

> I found the quotation in *Chapter 4* on *page 38.*

Use figures for exact amounts of money: *$16.95, $12.5 million, 65 cents*. Round amounts may be expressed in words: *sixty cents, forty dollars, six million cats.*

> The plurals of figures are usually formed by the addition of *s* (*6s,*
13s), though some usage calls for an apostrophe before the *s* (*6's, 13's*). In referring to decades, do not add the apostrophe before the *s* (*1990s,*

1860s). When omitting the first two digits of a decade, follow **apostrophe** rules for omissions: *'90s, '60s.*

Numbers in addresses and dates

Use figures in addresses (*15 Ninth Avenue*) and street numbers over ten (*2359 14th Street*). Also, use figures in dates.

> The events of *February 6, 1969,* are long forgotten. [A comma follows both the day and the year.]

> The newspapers dated *6 February 1969* are long buried. [No commas are required when the day precedes the month.]

> The events of *February 1969* are long forgotten. [A comma does not separate the month and the year.]

Do not use ordinal numbers following dates, as in *February 6th;* however, *the sixth of February* is appropriate within sentences.

Numbers for time

Hours and minutes are written as figures when followed by *a.m.* or *p.m.* but hours are written as words when followed by *o'clock* (*12:35 a.m., twelve o'clock*).

O

---

object complements   An object complement is a **noun**, a **pronoun**, or an **adjective** in the **predicate** that completes the meaning of the direct **object**. A noun or pronoun complement renames the direct object, and an adjective complement **modifies** or describes the direct object.

> The refrigerator company named Shirley Fitzsimmons *section manager of the year.* [The noun object complement *manager* renames the direct object *Shirley Fitzsimmons.*]

> The company called her work *admirable and outstanding.* [The two adjectives in the object complement *admirable* and *outstanding* describe the direct object *work.*]

Object complements follow words such as *call, choose, elect, make,* and *name.* See also **complements.**

objective case   (See **case**)

objects

SECTION OVERVIEW
Direct objects
Indirect objects
Objects of prepositions

An object is a **noun** or **pronoun** influenced by a transitive **verb, a verbal,** or a **preposition. Phrases** and **clauses** that function as nouns may also be objects. Pronoun objects are in objective **case** *(me, us; you; her, him, it, them; whom).* There are three types of objects: direct objects, indirect objects, and objects of prepositions. See also **object complements.**

Direct objects

A direct object receives the action of a verb or verbal and usually follows the verb or verbal in a sentence.

subject	verb	direct object

The Netherlands   shares   a *border*   with Belgium.

subject	infinitive	direct object

People of the Netherlands want you   to call   them Netherlanders. [The infinitive phrase, *you to call them Netherlanders,* is the direct object of *want,* and *them* is the direct object of *to call* in the infinitive phrase; *you* is the subject of *to call.*]

subject	verb	direct object

You   can also call   them   the Dutch.

Direct objects may be modified by **adjectives.**

The seaport city of Rotterdam ships *essential cargo* all over the world. [The direct object *cargo* is modified by *essential.*]

A direct object can usually answer the question *what?* or *whom?* after the verb. In each of the example sentences, the direct object answers a question:

The Netherlands shares what?
You can call whom?
The seaport city of Rotterdam ships what?

Indirect objects

An indirect object answers the questions *to or for whom?* or *to or for what?* Usually an indirect object appears after the verb and before the direct object.

The Red Cross sends *refugees* the relief they need. [*Refugees* answers the question *sends relief to whom?*]

You can give the *Red Cross* gifts of money and food. [*Red Cross* answers the question *give money and food to what?*]

Indirect objects commonly follow verbs such as *allow, assign, ask, give, grant, pay, send, show, tell,* and *write.*

Objects of prepositions

In a **prepositional phrase,** an object, either a noun or a pronoun, follows the **preposition.**

A militia is an organization of *citizens* trained for military *service* in *times* of national *emergency.* [*Citizens* is the object of *of, service* the object of *for,* times the object of *in,* and *emergency* the object of *of.*]

Objects of prepositions may be modified by **adjectives** and by other prepositional phrases.

A militia is an organization of citizens trained for military service *in times of national emergency.* [*In times* modifies *service,* and *of national emergency* modifies *times.*]

Pronouns as objects of prepositions are in the **objective case.**

When the emergency is over, militia members have civilian status returned to *them.*

Objects of prepositions answer the questions *what?* or *whom?* after the preposition: *in what? of what? to whom?*

objects of prepositions (See **objects**)

of, have   Use *have,* not *of,* after verbs such as *could, should, would,* and *might.*

We *should have* (not *should of*) known what to expect.

off of, off from   Avoid using *of* or *from* with *off,* because they add no further meaning.

He fell *off* (not *off of* or *off from*) the porch.

OK, O.K., okay   All three spellings are acceptable, but reserve this term for informal usage.

We received the final *OK* (or *O.K.* or *okay*) from the project manager.

on, upon   Both *on* and *upon* are acceptable **prepositions** for indicating spatial relations. However, many writers consider *upon* too formal for most occasions.

PREFERRED: The waves rippled *on* the surface of the water.

ALSO ACCEPTABLE: The waves rippled *upon* the surface of the water.

on account of   The less wordy *because of* is preferred.

Importing mongooses into the United States is illegal *because of* (not *on account of*) their destructive behavior.

or   A coordinating **conjunction** used to connect an alternative word, phrase, or clause. *Or* is also paired with *either* as a correlative conjunction: *either . . . or*. See **nor.**

oversimplification   (See **fallacies in logic**)

owing to the fact that   The less wordy *because* is preferred.

Importing mongooses into the United States is illegal *because* (not *owing to the fact that*) these Old World mammals are fiercely destructive hunters.

P

---

parallelism   Parallelism results when two or more grammatically equivalent sentence elements are joined.

Not only had the big bankers of 1929 failed to stop the Panic, but as time went on the inability of financiers generally to cope with the down trend, their loss of confidence in their own economic convictions, and the downfall of the banking system itself all advertised their helplessness.

—FREDERICK LEWIS ALLEN

This sentence has two parallel **independent clauses** (introduced by *not only* and *but*) and three parallel **objects** of the preposition *with*. Here is the sentence with the parallel elements arranged more visibly:

> *Not only* had the big bankers of 1929 failed to stop the Panic,
> *but* as time went on the inability of financiers generally to cope *with*
> the down trend,
> their loss of confidence in their own economic convictions, and
> the downfall of the banking system itself
> all advertised their helplessness.

Parallelism is a useful stylistic device providing **emphasis** and conciseness. Any sentence element can be written parallel to equivalent elements: **nouns** with nouns, **verbs** with verbs, **prepositional phrases** with prepositional phrases, adverb **clauses** with adverb clauses, and so forth. As the example sentence illustrates, however, the principle of parallelism does not require that elements be alike in every way. The three objects of *with* have different modifiers.

⚠   CAUTION: Faulty parallelism results when dissimilar elements are joined.

FAULTY: The Great Depression affected people in all walks of life: farmers, industrial workers, formerly respected bankers, and the attitudes of college students. [*Farmers, workers,* and *bankers* are specific instances of the noun *people*; *attitudes* are not.]

REVISED: The Great Depression affected people in all walks of life: farmers, industrial workers, formerly respected bankers, and college students.

FAULTY: Overproduction of goods and having easy money policies both contributed to the Depression. [The **verbal phrase** *having easy money policies* is not parallel to the **noun phrase** *overproduction of goods.*]

REVISED: Overproduction of goods and easy money policies both contributed to the Depression.

FAULTY: Two colossal effects of the Depression were the rise to power of both Adolf Hitler in Germany and the election of Franklin Delano Roosevelt in the United States. [The sentence elements following the correlative **conjunctions** *both (Adolf Hitler)* and *and (the election of . . .)* are not equivalent.]

REVISED: Two colossal effects of the Depression were both the rise to power of Adolf Hitler in Germany and the election of Franklin Delano Roosevelt in the United States.

As these sentences illustrate, faulty parallelism can usually be corrected by *deleting words* (the first and second example sentences) and *moving words* (the third example sentence). To avoid faulty parallelism, make sure that any correlative or coordinating **conjunctions** connect equivalent grammatical elements. See also **coordination.**

paraphrases   A paraphrase is a restatement that conveys the meaning of the original in the paraphraser's words. In contrast to a summary, a paraphrase is usually not a condensed version of the original. Here is a statement and a paraphrase of it:

> ORIGINAL: The word *poverty* is too general, too vague. Let me try to make it more concrete by suggesting that it has three parts: employment, income, and material standard of life.   —JOHN HOLT

> PARAPHRASE: John Holt concretizes the word *poverty* by breaking it into three parts: "employment, income, and material standard of life."

To be accurate and true to the original, the three parts of poverty are quoted.

> CAUTION: When you paraphrase, be careful to use your own words and phrases; do not just rearrange the original words.

> ORIGINAL: That is the miracle of Greek mythology—a humanized world, men freed from the paralyzing fear of an omnipotent Unknown. The terrifying incomprehensibilities which were worshiped elsewhere, and the fearsome spirits with which earth, air and sea swarmed, were banned from Greece.   —EDITH HAMILTON

> FAULTY PARAPHRASE: The miracle of Greek mythology is that men were freed from the paralyzing fear of an Unknown who was omnipotent. Banned from Greece were the terrifying incomprehensibilities worshiped elsewhere and the frightening spirits in earth, air, and sea.

> BETTER PARAPHRASE: Greek mythology, says classical scholar Edith Hamilton, shows how the Greeks took charge of their world, refusing to be bound by unknown forces and natural occurrences that they did not understand. Instead of worshiping things they didn't know, they explained them in myths.

The faulty paraphrase, by using much the same words as the original, gives no evidence that the writer has understood the passage. See also **indirect quotation** and pages 125–126.

parentheses   Parentheses enclose interrupting elements, setting them off from the rest of the sentence with a greater separation than other paired marks such as **commas** and **dashes.** They usually add explanatory information that might otherwise disrupt a sentence.

Horace Mann *(1796–1859)* was a leader in U.S. education.

To improve the quality of teaching, he established the first state normal schools *(teacher-training institutions).*

Other punctuation with parentheses

When **commas** are required with parentheses, they almost always follow the parentheses.

By establishing the first state normal schools (teacher-training institutions), Horace Mann sought to improve the quality of teaching.

A **period** goes outside the parentheses when the enclosed element is part of a sentence, as illustrated above. When the enclosed element is a complete sentence, the preceding sentence ends with a period and the text within parentheses ends with a period.

We can also thank Mann for our coeducational institutions of higher learning. (As President of Antioch College, he showed that women and men can both attend the same school.)

Use **brackets** to enclose brief interruptions within parentheses.

We can also thank Mann for our coeducational institutions of higher learning. (As President of Antioch College *[1853–1859]*, he showed that women and men can both attend the same school.)

parenthetical elements   Parenthetical elements are words, **phrases,** and **clauses** that interrupt the flow of a sentence. They may be enclosed by **commas, dashes,** or **parentheses.**

Victoria, *queen of Great Britain and Ireland and empress of India,* had the longest reign in English history. [The parenthetical **appositive** consists of the **noun** *queen* with its modifiers.]

She acquired the title "empress of India" late in her reign *(but only through the efforts of Benjamin Disraeli).* [Parenthetical **prepositional phrase**; note that final period is outside close parenthesis.]

Queen Victoria was known worldwide for her high moral character—*though not for her intelligence.* [parenthetical negative phrase]

See also **nonrestrictive elements.**

participial phrases   A participial phrase is a **verbal phrase** that functions as an **adjective,** modifying **nouns** or **pronouns.** It consists of a **participle** and its **modifiers, objects,** or **complements.**

> *Aiming to reduce the budget deficit in installments,* the Gramm-Rudman Act was passed by Congress in 1985. [The present participle *aiming* modifies *Gramm-Rudman Act* and is modified itself by an **infinitive phrase.**]

> *Passed by Congress in 1985,* the Gramm-Rudman Act aims to reduce the budget deficit. [The past participle, *passed,* modifies *Gramm-Rudman Act* and is modified itself by two **prepositional phrases.**]

⚠   CAUTION: *Dangling participles.* A participial phrase is said to dangle when its connection with the word it modifies is ambiguous. Put another way, dangling participles occur when the implied **subject** of the participle does not coincide with the subject of the sentence. To avoid this sentence fault, revise either the phrase or the rest of the sentence so that the doer of the action of your participle is the same as the subject of the sentence.

> FAULTY: *Intended to reduce the deficit to near zero by 1991,* success was obviously not achieved by the Act. [The participial phrase appears to modify *success,* not *Act.*]

> REVISED: Success was obviously not achieved by the Act, which was intended to reduce the deficit to near zero by 1991. [The phrase has been moved and expanded to a clause, now clearly modifying *Act.*]

> REVISED: Intended to reduce the deficit to near zero by 1991, the Act obviously did not achieve success. [The main part of the sentence is revised from passive **voice** to active voice with *Act* as subject, making the participial phrase clearly modify *Act.*]

See also **dangling modifiers.**

> FRAGMENTS.   Participial phrases written as **sentences,** beginning with a capital letter and ending with a period, are sentence **fragments.**

> FAULTY: The budget cuts divided evenly between defense and domestic programs. [The past participle *divided* cannot function as a verb.]

> REVISED: The budget cuts were divided evenly between defense and domestic programs. [A verb, *were,* has been added.]

participles Participles are **verbals** that function as **adjectives.**

> *Uncontrolled* anger can lead to violence. [*Uncontrolled* modifies *anger.*]

> *Smoldering* anger can lead to conflagration. [*Smoldering* modifies *anger.*]

Participles have present and past forms: *mixing, mixed; washing, washed; seeing, seen; making, made.* For regular **verbs,** add *-ing* to form the present participle; form the past participle the same way you form the past tense: add *-d* or *-ed.* But with **irregular verbs** the past tense and past participle are often formed differently.

VERB TENSE AND PARTICIPLE FORMS, REGULAR AND IRREGULAR VERBS

	PRESENT	*PRESENT PARTICIPLE*	*PAST*	*PAST PARTICIPLE*
REGULAR	want	wanting	wanted	wanted
	promote	promoting	promoted	promoted
	direct	directing	directed	directed
IRREGULAR	come	coming	came	come
	do	doing	did	done
	write	writing	wrote	written

Participles as verbs

Unlike the present tense and past tense verb forms, the present and past participles cannot function as verbs in sentences. Using participles in place of verbs makes sentence **fragments** or **nonstandard** verb usage:

FAULTY: Anger *reflecting* deep and sincere feelings. [sentence fragment]

REVISED: Anger *reflects* deep and sincere feelings. [The present tense verb *reflects* replaces the present participle *reflecting.*]

FAULTY: Because we were angry, we *done* things we regretted later. [nonstandard verb usage]

REVISED: Because we were angry, we *did* things we regretted later. [The past tense verb *did* replaces the past participle *done.*]

But a participle can function as a verb when accompanied by a **helping verb.**

Our anger *was reflecting* deep and sincere feelings. [past progressive form]

Because of anger, we *have done* things we regretted later. [present perfect tense]

Many wrongs *have been committed* out of anger. [present perfect tense]

But many positive social actions *have been motivated* by anger. [present perfect tense]

PROGRESSIVE FORMS OF VERBS. To express an action in progress in either the present, the past, or the future use a form of *be* (*am, is, are, was, were, be, being, been*) with the present participle:

I *was writing* my paper when the fire alarm sounded. [past progressive]

I *am waiting* anxiously to return to my room. [present progressive]

The helping verb *be* must be preceded by a **modal** (*can, could, may, might, must, shall, should, will, would*):

FAULTY: I *be finishing* my paper later.

REVISED: I *will be finishing* my paper later. [future progressive]

PASSIVE VOICE. To form the **passive voice,** use the past participle of a **transitive verb** with a form of *be* (*am, is, are, was, were, be, being, been*).

My paper *will be finished* by noon. [passive voice; future tense]

I hope that late papers *are accepted*. [passive voice; present tense]

Participles in absolutes

A participle may function as the verbal in an **absolute.**

Anger being a volatile emotion, people are wise to control it. [The **participial phrase** *being a volatile emotion* modifies *anger;* together they make the absolute.]

Because absolutes modify the entire sentence, not a particular word, using them is sometimes a useful strategy for revising **dangling modifiers.**

FAULTY: Being a volatile emotion, people are wise to control their anger. [The participle *being* appears to modify *people*; the example sentence above is a possible revision.]

▼ CAUTION: With verbs describing emotional qualities, such as *amuse, bore, disappoint, interest,* and *surprise,* use the present participle when the word it modifies causes the action.

> It was a *boring* book. [*Boring* modifies *book*; the book bored me.]
>
> The movie was even less *interesting*. [*Interesting* modifies *movie*; the movie did not interest me.]

Use the past participle when the word it modifies is the receiver of the action.

> *Bored* by the book, I went for a walk. [*Bored* modifies *I*; I was bored.]
>
> *Interested* in the people I met, I enjoyed my walk. [*Interested* modifies *I*; I was interested in the people.]

parts of sentences Sentences are composed primarily of **subjects, predicates,** and **modifiers** in various **sentence patterns.** Basic to every sentence is a subject and a predicate, or **verb.**

Subject

A subject tells what a sentence is about. The simple subject may be a single **noun** or **pronoun,** a **phrase,** or a **clause.**

> The *Sahara* is the world's largest desert. **[noun]**
>
> *Visiting a desert* might be an interesting experience. [**gerund** phrase]
>
> *What I could learn* might surprise me. [Noun **clause**; in the noun clause the **pronoun** *I* is the subject of *could learn.*]

The simple subject may have **modifiers.**

> This *vast* desert extends across northern Africa. [The **adjective** *vast* modifies *desert.*]
>
> *Extending east to west and north to south,* the Sahara makes up over 3 million square miles. [The **participial phrase** modifies *Sahara.*]

Predicate

A predicate is a verb and any **modifiers, objects,** and **complements** necessary for completing the sentence. A verb makes a declaration about a subject.

> Rainfall in the Sahara *ranges* from five to ten inches a year.
>
> Dry periods with no rain *are* common.

Verbs may be modified by **adverbs** and adverbial phrases and clauses.

> These dry periods *occasionally* last for years. [*Occasionally* modifies the verb *last.*]

> But vast aquifers lie *beneath the surface.* [The **prepositional phrase** modifies *lie.*]

> These aquifers were formed *when the Sahara was wetter.* [The adverbial **clause** modifies *were formed.*]

Predicates can have complements (subject complements, object complements) and objects (direct objects, indirect objects, objects of prepositions) depending on the nature of the verb.

> The aquifers are an abundant *source* of water. [*Source* is a subject complement following the **linking verb** *are.*]

> Deposits of iron ore, oil, and natural gas make the *Sahara* an important *territory.* [*Sahara* is the direct object of the **transitive verb** *make,* and *territory* is the object complement renaming *Sahara.*]

> These natural resources give the *desert* worldwide *importance.* [*Desert* is the indirect object and *importance* is the direct object following the transitive verb *give.*]

See also **sentence patterns.**

Modifiers

Modifiers may appear in both subject and predicate; they may be in the form of words, phrases, or clauses.

> *Nighttime* temperatures *in the Sahara* may drop *below freezing.* [The adjective *Nighttime* and the prepositional phrase *in the Sahara* modify the subject *temperatures;* the prepositional phrase *below freezing* modifies the verb *may drop.*]

> *Daytime* temperatures, *which have been recorded at more than 135 degrees Fahrenheit*, are the *opposite* extreme. [The adjective *Daytime* and the **relative clause,** *which have been recorded at more than 135 degrees Fahrenheit*, modify the subject *temperatures*; the adjective *opposite* modifies the subject complement *extreme.*]

parts of speech   Words are classed as parts of speech according to their function in a sentence.

PARTS OF SPEECH

Nouns	name a person, place, or thing (*letter, computer, Johnson, Mitchell Hall*).
Pronouns	substitute for nouns (*we, she, they, someone, which, that*).
Verbs	express action or state of being (*do, see, become, try, wish*).
Adjectives	modify (describe, limit, explain, or alter) nouns and pronouns (*blue, long, ready, quick, English*).
Adverbs	modify verbs, telling manner (*well*), time (*now*), frequency (*often*), place (*there*), direction (*forward*), or degree (*hardly*); adjectives and adverbs, usually as intensifers (*very, too, quite*); and whole sentences, as with transitional adverbs (*however, therefore*).
Prepositions	relate their objects to other parts of sentences (*of* the page, *in* a minute, *for* the last time).
Conjunctions	join one element of a sentence to another. There are three kinds: coordinating (bacon *and* eggs, high *but* dry), correlative (*either . . . or*), and subordinating (*if* you knew, *when* he comes).
Interjections	express strong emotion, have little or no grammatical connection to other parts of a sentence, and often are punctuated as a sentence (*Oh! Wow! Ouch!*).

Because a word's part of speech is determined by its function in a particular sentence, words frequently shift from one part of speech to another.

All I want is a cold drink of *water.* [noun]

I *water* my plants once a week. [verb]

I recently purchased a small *water* hose. [adjective]

Water! [interjection]

passive voice   A **verb** form consisting of a form of **be** and a past **participle** to indicate that the subject of a sentence is being acted upon rather than performing the action. See **voice**.

past participles   (See **participles**)

past perfect tense   (See **tenses of verbs**)

percent, percentage   In sentences, use the word *percent* (instead of the symbol %) with **numbers.**

So far we've met *40 percent* of our goals.

Use *percentage* to indicate a proportion or share.

The *percentage* of completion is not surprising.

▼ *Percentage* introduced by *the* takes a **singular** verb (as in the preceding example); when the word is introduced by *a,* the verb is singular or **plural** depending on meaning.

A large percentage of the trees *have died.* [The meaning is plural.]

A moderate percentage of the new crop *is doing* well. [The meaning is singular.]

perfect tenses   (See **tenses of verbs**)

periods   The period is the primary mark of **punctuation** to end **sentences.** It ends statements and mild commands.

Omar Khayyam was an eleventh-century Persian poet and mathematician.

Read his *Rubaiyat* to discover his hedonistic philosophy.

The period also ends **indirect questions.**

After reading the *Rubaiyat,* you may question what kind of a mathematician he was. [The direct question would be *What kind of a mathematician was he?*]

Other uses of periods

ABBREVIATIONS.   Periods are sometimes used with **abbreviations.**

a.m. (ante meridiem)	Mr. (mister)
B.C. (before Christ)	Ph.D. (Doctor of Philosophy)
etc. (et cetera)	St. Paul (Saint Paul)

Use only one period at the end of a sentence that ends in an abbreviation.

I usually get home from work at 7:30 *a.m.* [not *7:30 a.m.*]

INITIALS IN NAMES. Use a period, followed by a space, for abbreviating names.

H. L. Mencken   Samuel F. B. Morse   I. M. Pei

WITH NUMBERS. Use periods as decimal points in **numbers.**

$341.68   5.2 percent   12.6 miles

With other punctuation

QUOTATION MARKS. With **quotations,** periods go inside the end **quotation marks,** even when only a single word is quoted.

> Omar's hedonism is illustrated in the lines, "Come, fill the Cup, and in the fire of Spring / Your Winter garment of Repentance fling."
> —Tr. EDWARD FITZGERALD

> The poetry was written in Persian quatrains called *"ruba i."*

When you parenthetically cite a source, the period follows the end parenthesis.

> Omar declares his urgency to enjoy life when he writes, "The Bird of Time has but a little way / To flutter—and the Bird is on the Wing" (V–7). [See also "Documenting Your Sources," page 280.]

PARENTHESES. A period goes inside **parentheses** when the enclosed remark is a complete sentence, outside the end parenthesis when the parenthetical remark is part of a sentence.

> Besides his *Rubaiyat,* Omar wrote some less popularized but noteworthy mathematical studies. (He also participated in a calendar reform.)

> Omar the Tentmaker is another name for Omar Khayyam of Naishapur (died 1123).

ELLIPSES. Periods are used with **ellipsis dots** (three spaced periods to indicate omissions in quoted material) when the ellipsis occurs after the end of a sentence. The ellipses follow the sentence period.

> Omar, troubled by the end of life, urged enjoyment of the present: "The Leaves of Life keep falling one by one. . . . Ah, make the most of what we yet may spend, / Before we too into the Dust descend."

CAUTION: Inserting a period before the end of a sentence results in a sentence **fragment.**

> **FAULTY:** Omar Khayyam was a member of a Persian astronomical commission. Whose goal was to adjust the calendar.

REVISED: Omar Khayyam was a member of a Persian astronomical commission whose goal was to adjust the calendar.

Do not insert a period simply because a sentence is long. It is stylistically appropriate to have occasional long sentences, and breaking them willy-nilly often leads to fragments.

person Person is a term used with **verbs** and **pronouns** to represent whether the **subject** names the person(s) speaking (first person), spoken to (second person), or spoken about (third person). **Personal pronouns** have **singular** and **plural** forms for each person. All **nouns** are third person and have singular and plural forms. Most verbs change form to indicate person only in third person singular (with an -s ending), but *be* has its own form for the first person singular *(am)*.

	SINGULAR	PLURAL
FIRST PERSON	I *walk*, I *am*	we *walk*, we *are*
SECOND PERSON	you *walk*, you *are*	you *walk*, you *are*
THIRD PERSON	he, she, it, Harry *walks*	they, Harry and Ann *walk*
	he, she, it, Harry *is*	they, Harry and Ann *are*

CAUTION: Avoid unintended and illogical **shifts** from one person to another.

FAULTY: *I* found a perfect book on *my* topic, but *you* can't check it out of the library. [shift from first person *I* to second person *you*]

REVISED: *I* found a perfect book on *my* topic, but *I* can't check it out of the library.

FAULTY: *Students* can use the book only in the library, and *you* can take it for only two hours. [shift from third person *students* to second person *you*]

REVISED: Students can use the book only in the library, and *they* can take it for only two hours.

personal pronouns Personal **pronouns** refer to the person(s) speaking (*I, me, mine; we, us, ours*), the person(s) spoken to (*you, yours*), or the person(s) or thing(s) spoken about (*he, him, his; she, her, hers; it, its; they, them, theirs*).

I, we

Use *I* when referring to your own actions.

I surveyed 25 people concerning their voting experiences.

In report writing, however, the use of *I* should be limited, because it may displace emphasis on the topic. Do not use *we* when you mean *I*.

-self pronouns

Do not use the **reflexive pronouns**—*herself, himself, myself, yourself*—when personal pronouns are appropriate.

FAULTY: Felicia and *myself* collaborated on the research.

REVISED: Felicia and *I* collaborated on the research.

phenomenon, phenomena   *Phenomena* is the plural of *phenomenon,* an occurrence or fact that can be perceived by the senses.

It was the strangest *phenomenon* I had ever experienced.

phrases

> SECTION OVERVIEW
> Prepositional phrases
> Gerund phrases
> Participial phrases
> Infinitive phrases
> Absolute phrases

A phrase is a group of related words that does not have a **subject** and a **verb.** The principal kinds of phrases are **prepositional, verbal** (**gerund, infinitive,** and **participial**), and **absolute.** However, other groups of words can be termed phrases: a **verb phrase** (a verb plus helping verbs, such as *have been seeing*), a **noun phrase** (a noun plus its modifiers, such as *twenty antique cars*), and phrasal **prepositions** (such as *instead of* and *such as*). Because phrases do not have subjects and verbs, they cannot be written as sentences. The result would be a sentence **fragment.**

FAULTY: Nearly 142 million acres of prairie in the central United States.

REVISED: There were once nearly 142 million acres of prairie in the central United States.

Prepositional phrases

A **prepositional phrase** consists of a **preposition,** its **object,** and any related **modifiers.**

Most *of the prairies* have been plowed under.

In the entire region, barely 1 percent *of the original prairies* remain.

Prepositional phrases usually function as **adjectives** or **adverbs.**

Many people are preserving some prairieland *for future generations.*
[adverb phrase modifying the verb *are preserving*]

They restore patches *of native prairie* as they find them. [adjective
phrase modifying the noun *patches*]

Occasionally, prepositional phrases function as nouns.

From early spring to late summer is the best time to find prairie
flowers. [Phrases as the subject of the sentence.]

Gerund phrases

Gerund phrases are verbal phrases that function as nouns. They
consist of a **gerund** (the -*ing* form of a verb) and its **objects, complements,** and **modifiers.**

Finding and saving prairie flowers is an unexpected pleasure. [The
gerund phrase is the subject of the sentence; *flowers* is the direct
object of the two gerunds *Finding* and *saving.*]

Though *containing an abundance of flowers*, prairies are mainly
grasslands. [The gerund phrase is the object of the preposition
though; abundance is the direct object of *containing*, and the
prepositional phrase *of flowers* modifies *abundance.*]

Participial phrases

Participial phrases are verbal phrases that function as adjectives.
They consist of a present or past **participle** and its objects, complements, and modifiers.

Wind *unhindered by barriers of any kind* sweeps across the
grasslands. [The phrase containing the past participle *unhindered*
modifies *wind.*]

Groves of trees *sometimes reaching far into the grasslands* are
another part of the prairie. [The participial phrase modifies *trees;
sometimes* modifies the present participle *reaching.*]

Infinitive phrases

Infinitive phrases are verbal phrases that function as adjectives,
adverbs, or nouns. The **infinitive** is the base form of the verb, the one
listed in the dictionary; it is often preceded by *to*. An infinitive phrase
consists of an infinitive and its objects, complements, and modifiers.

To appreciate prairies, visit one of the public preserves. [The
infinitive phrase modifies the verb *visit; prairies* is the direct object
of *to appreciate.*]

Late May through July is a good time *to see prairie flowers*. [The infinitive phrase modifies the noun *time*; *flowers* is the direct object of *to see*.]

All verbals have subjects, or doers of the action they express, but usually those subjects are implied. With infinitives, the subjects are sometimes expressed.

Late May through July is a good time for *prairie enthusiasts to see native flowers*. [*Enthusiasts* is the expressed subject of *to see*.]

Absolute phrases

An **absolute phrase** is a group of words consisting of a participle plus the noun or pronoun it modifies and any objects, modifiers, or complements of the phrase. The absolute phrase itself modifies an entire sentence or clause.

A few preserves have prairie marshes—*habitats attracting a variety of wildfowl*. [The participle, *attracting*, modifies *habitats*, and the absolute phrase modifies the entire **independent clause.**]

plagiarism   Plagiarism is the use of someone else's words or ideas as if they were one's own. It constitutes academic dishonesty, and schools usually have severe penalties for it. One form of plagiarism is the presentation of someone else's work under one's own name. Another is faulty or incomplete documentation in reporting research. To avoid plagiarism, make sure you understand how to cite your sources. Each discipline has its own method of citation. See "Documenting Your Sources" on page 280.

plays, titles of   (See **titles** and **italics**)

▼ **plurals**

> SECTION OVERVIEW
> Nouns
> Pronouns
> Verbs

Nouns, pronouns, and **verbs** may be **singular** or **plural.**

Nouns

To make a noun plural, normally add -*s* to its singular form (the one listed in the dictionary). To singular nouns ending in *s, z, x, ch,* and *sh*, add -*es.*

SINGULAR	PLURAL
machine	machines
needle	needles
car	cars
mass	masses
march	marches
tax	taxes

Nouns ending in *y* take an -*ies* ending when the *y* follows a consonant.

army	armies
fly	flies

When the *y* follows a vowel, the plural is formed with an -*s.*

attorney	attorneys
key	keys

Some nouns ending in *o* form their plurals with -*s* and some with -*es.* For words not listed here, check your dictionary.

piano	pianos
folio	folios
potato	potatoes
hero	heroes

A few words have more than one plural form, but usually one of the forms is more commonly used.

MORE COMMON	LESS COMMON
banjos	banjoes
buffaloes	buffalos (*or* buffalo)
cargoes	cargos
frescoes	frescos
grottoes	grottos
halos	haloes
lassos	lassoes
mottoes	mottos
tornadoes	tornados
volcanoes	volcanos
zeros	zeroes

Some nouns ending in *f* or *fe* change to *ves* in the plural, and a few use either *fs* or *ves*. Check your dictionary for words not listed here.

SINGULAR	PLURAL
leaf	leaves
life	lives
half	halves
wolf	wolves
roof	roofs
safe	safes
gulf	gulfs
scarf	scarfs *or* scarves
hoof	hoofs *or* hooves
wharf	wharves *or* wharfs

A few nouns form plurals without the addition of -*s*.

deer	deer
sheep	sheep
foot	feet
mouse	mice
child	children
man	men
woman	women
goose	geese

For the plural forms of words of foreign origin, check your dictionary. Some have variant plurals that represent different meanings. *Antennae*, for example, means the sensory appendages of certain living creatures, and *antennas* means metallic aerials for sending and receiving electromagnetic waves. Here are a few words of foreign origin, followed by the most common plural and, with some, an alternative plural.

SINGULAR	PLURAL
analysis	analyses
appendix	appendixes, appendices
basis	bases
crisis	crises
criterion	criteria
curriculum	curriculums, curricula
datum	data
focus	focuses, foci
fungus	funguses, fungi
index	indexes, indices
memorandum	memorandums, memoranda
syllabus	syllabuses, syllabi
thesis	theses

Use -'s to form the plural of letters referred to as letters and words referred to as words (see **apostrophes**).

> There are two *s*'s in the word *misspelling.*
>
> I have too many *and*'s in my sentence.

In general, to make **numbers** plural, add -*s,* not -'s.

> Let's see what happens to employment in the *1990s.*
>
> All the *fours* can move to the front of the room.
>
> The clothing rack did not have any 14s.

 CAUTION: Do not use **apostrophes** to make either common or proper nouns plural.

FAULTY PLURAL	CORRECT PLURAL
neighbor's	neighbors
parent's	parents
calendar's	calendars
Jackson's	Jacksons
Smith's	Smiths
Cass's	Casses
Barry's	Barrys

Pronouns

Personal **pronouns** have plural forms *(I, we; he, they; she, they; it, they). You* has the same form for both singular and plural. Informally, *they* is used as a generic singular for *he, she,* and *it.*

> Nearly every person waiting in line got the ticket *they* wanted.
> [*They* refers to the singular noun *person.*]

Such usage is not acceptable in most formal writing situations, including those at school and at work. See also **nonsexist language.**

Verbs

Verbs take singular or plural forms to agree with their **subjects** (see **agreement of subjects and verbs**).

> SINGULAR: The bidder *agrees* to be bound by union contracts.
>
> PLURAL: The bidders *agree* to be bound by union contracts.

Unlike nouns, which normally form their plural with an -*s* ending, an -*s* ending added to the base form of a verb means present tense singular third person.

BASE FORM	THIRD-PERSON SINGULAR	THIRD-PERSON PLURAL
see	She *sees*.	They *see*.
bark	It *barks*.	They *bark*.
run	A car *runs*.	Cars *run*.
burn	The light *burns*.	Lights *burn*.

A verb's plural form is normally the base form of the verb, which is the form listed in the dictionary. An exception is the verb *be*, which has *are* as its present tense plural form *(The papers are here)*. See also **number.**

plus *Plus* is a **preposition** referring to an addition. As a preposition, it is followed by an **object,** not by a **clause,** so it should not be used in place of *and.*

> FAULTY: In the old days, top management made the rules and decisions, *plus* it didn't ask for employee input.

> REVISED: In the old days, top management made the rules and decisions, *and* it didn't ask for employee input.

poem titles (See **titles**)

possessive adjectives (See **possessive case**)

possessive case The possessive **case** is a way of showing possession or connection in **nouns** or **pronouns.**

> *Africa's* wildlife is sometimes relocated to better food sources.

> A *night's* food for a hippopotamus might be as much as 150 pounds of green grass.

> Often there is not enough grass to sustain *their* appetites.

The possessive case of nouns and most **indefinite pronouns** is formed with *-'s* (see **apostrophes**). Personal and relative pronouns and adjectives have special possessive case forms.

POSSESSIVE PRONOUNS AND ADJECTIVES

PRONOUNS	ADJECTIVES
mine	my
yours	your
his	his
hers	her

its	its
ours	our
theirs	their
whose	whose
whosever	whosever

Possessive pronouns refer to a noun or another pronoun; possessive adjectives modify a noun.

> Drought has forced some African nations to reduce the size of *their* wildlife populations through managed kills. [possessive adjective modifying *populations*]
>
> This decision, difficult though it was, was *theirs* to make. [possessive pronoun referring to *nations* in the previous sentence]
>
> By such "culling," many animals are saved from starvation and *their* meat is given to local people *whose* crops have failed. [possessive adjectives *their* and *whose*]

The possessive pronouns *its* and *whose* can refer to nonhuman antecedents.

> Hippopotamuses *whose* food sources have dried up are dying of starvation.

The use of possessive nouns to refer to inanimate objects is less common.

FAULTY	REVISED
the book's cover	the cover of the book
the building's front door	the front door of the building
the computer's monitor	the monitor of the computer

Use possessive adjectives with **gerunds.**

> *Their culling* of wildlife thus saves both animals and people. [possessive adjective modifying the gerund *culling*]

 CAUTION: Do not use an apostrophe with possessive pronouns.

FAULTY PLURAL	CORRECT PLURAL
it's	its
our's	ours
your's	yours
their's	theirs
who's	whose

Only contracted personal and relative pronouns take apostrophes: *it's* means "it is" or "it has"; *who's* means "who is" or "who has."

post hoc fallacy   (See **fallacies in logic**)

precede, proceed   *Precede* means "to come before"; *proceed* means "to go forward."

> Does the preface *precede* the table of contents or follow it?
>
> You can *proceed* with Part II of the test after you have completed Part I.

predicate adjectives   (See **subject complements**)

predicate nouns   (See **subject complements**)

predicates   The predicate is the part of a **sentence** that makes a declaration about the **subject**. It consists of a **verb** and any **complements, objects,** and **modifiers.**

> Almost 16 million Americans *live in mobile homes.* [The predicate consists of the verb, *live,* and a **prepositional phrase** that modifies the verb.]
>
> Half the people living in mobile homes *have incomes of less than $20,000 a year.* [The predicate consists of the verb *have,* followed by the direct **object** *incomes* and a prepositional phrase that modifies *incomes.*]
>
> *Do* you *know the average age of mobile home residents?* [Predicate of a **question;** the verb *do know* is followed by the direct object *age,* which is modified by a prepositional phrase.]

Compound predicates have more than one verb.

> Mobile home residents *worry about severe thunderstorms* and *greatly fear tornadoes.* [two verbs: *worry* and *fear*]

CAUTION: Don't separate the two parts of a compound predicate with a comma or other punctuation.

> FAULTY: Mobile home residents *worry about severe thunderstorms, and greatly fear tornadoes.*

See also **parts of sentences.**

prefixes   Prefixes are groups of letters added to the beginning of a word to change its meaning: *co + operate = cooperate; ex + president =*

ex-president; inter + national = international. Most prefixes are added with no connecting **hyphen:** *anti + knock = antiknock; extra + ordinary = extraordinary; hyper + active = hyperactive; poly + ethylene = polyethylene; super + conductivity = superconductivity.* A few prefixes are connected with hyphens: *all-, ex-, quasi-,* and *self-: all-inclusive, ex-wife, quasi-scientific, self-help.* Use hyphens also to attach prefixes to **proper nouns** and adjectives as well as **numbers:** *pro-American, pre-1960.* Use hyphens also when the prefix might create a confusing word: *re-create* (meaning "to create again"). See also **suffixes.**

prepositional phrases   A **preposition** and its **object** plus any **modifiers** make up a prepositional **phrase.** These phrases usually function as **adjectives** or **adverbs.**

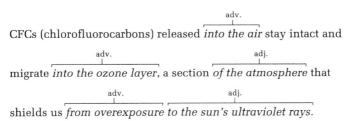

In the example, the prepositional phrases modify **verbs** (*released, migrate, shields*) and **nouns** (*section, overexposure*). Sometimes prepositional phrases themselves have modifiers.

> *At least by the year 2030,* the Clean Air Act requires phasing out all refrigerants that contain chlorine. [*At least* modifies the prepositional phrase.]

⚠ CAUTION: Be careful that your prepositional phrase modifies the intended word.

> **FAULTY:**   A valve reverses the flow of refrigerant to give off heat inside the house instead of exhausting it outdoors *in a heat pump.* [The phrase *in a heat pump* appears to modify *exhausting* instead of *reverses.*]
>
> **REVISED:**   *In a heat pump,* a valve reverses the flow of refrigerant to give off heat inside the house instead of exhausting it outdoors.

⚠ Do not write a prepositional phrase as a sentence; the result would be a sentence **fragment.**

FAULTY: A common problem with aging air-conditioning equipment is leakage. *Usually from a tiny pinhole at a pipe joint.*

REVISED: A common problem with aging air-conditioning equipment is leakage, *usually from a tiny pinhole at a pipe joint.*

⟁ prepositions   A preposition relates its **object** to other parts of a sentence. The nature of the relationship (time, space, condition, cause) is determined by the preposition and the context.

The statements *by* women in the military are disturbing.

The statements *about* women in the military are disturbing.

The statements *to* women in the military are disturbing.

The statements *among* women in the military are disturbing.

The statements *against* women in the military are disturbing.

The statements *of* women in the military are disturbing.

A preposition, its object, and any modifiers together make up a **prepositional phrase.**

▼ Choosing the right preposition is complicated enough for native speakers of a language. For ESL speakers it is particularly difficult, since preposition use is determined mainly by **idiom.** Both native and ESL speakers can sharpen their preposition sense by paying close attention when reading and listening. Notice how other writers use their prepositions, and make your own cue cards, with a separate card for each preposition. Write the preposition and the sentence in which it occurs; then write another sentence of your own using the preposition. Review your cue cards periodically.

COMMON PREPOSITIONS

about	at	by means of	in addition to
above	because of	concerning	in back of
according to	before	despite	in place of
across	behind	down	inside
after	below	during	in spite of
against	beneath	except	instead of
along	beside	except for	into
along with	between	excepting	like
among	beyond	for	near
around	but	from	next
as	by	in	of

off	over	to	up
on	past	toward	upon
onto	regarding	under	up to
out	since	underneath	with
out of	through	unlike	within
outside	throughout	until	without

present participles   (See **participles**)

present perfect tense   (See **tenses of verbs**)

present tense   (See **tenses of verbs**)

pretty   Avoid using *pretty* to mean "somewhat" or "considerable."

> **INFORMAL:**   You did a *pretty* good job of stating your opinion.
>
> **REVISED:**   You did a good job of stating your opinion.
>
> **REVISED:**   You stated your opinion well.

principal, principle   *Principal* is both a **noun** and an **adjective.** As a noun, it means "chief person" or a sum of money owed, on which interest is calculated; as an adjective it also can mean "chief."

> All the *principals* were present for the rehearsal. [noun]
>
> The *principal* actors were present. [adjective]

Principle is a noun and has several meanings, all of them abstract: "a basic truth," "a moral standard," "a natural law."

> She acted on *principles,* not on common sense.

proceed   (See ***precede***)

 pronoun reference

> SECTION OVERVIEW
> More than one possible antecedent
> Intended antecedent is an adjective
> Antecedent is implied
> Separation between pronoun and antecedent is too great

Personal and **relative pronouns** refer to nouns, called **antecedents.**

> Adolescents do not always think of *their* heroes as fallible human beings. [*Adolescents* is the antecedent of *their*.]

Pronouns get meaning from their antecedents. Ambiguous pronoun reference may occur in various ways: there is more than one possible antecedent, the intended antecedent is an **adjective,** the antecedent is only implied but not present, and the separation between the pronoun and the antecedent is too great.

More than one possible antecedent

FAULTY: Whether their heroes are someone they know or celebrities admired from afar, adolescents are vulnerable when *they* fall. [Does *they* modify adolescents or *heroes?*]

REVISED: Whether their heroes are someone they know or celebrities admired from afar, adolescents are vulnerable when *their idols* fall.

Intended antecedent is an adjective

FAULTY: In adolescents' view, *they* see their heroes as flawless. [As a noun in possessive case, *adolescents'* functions as an adjective.]

REVISED: Adolescents view their heroes as flawless.

Antecedent is implied

FAULTY: *They* say that kids are extremely judgmental about their heroes. [There is no antecedent for *they.*]

REVISED: *Some people* say (or *It is said*) that kids are extremely judgmental about their heroes.

Separation between pronoun and antecedent is too great

FAULTY: All too often, heroes fall from the pedestals their young fans put them on, *who* may be athletes, politicians, and other luminaries.

REVISED: All too often, heroes, who may be athletes, politicians, and other luminaries, fall from the pedestals their young fans put them on.

You can correct faulty pronoun reference by clarifying the relationship between the pronoun and its intended antecedent. In some cases, you can substitute a **noun** for the unclear pronoun. Sometimes you can accomplish the revision by moving parts of the sentence.

CAUTION: *Possessive nouns.* Be careful to avoid sentences with phrases such as *In Leslie Marmon Silko's book Ceremony,* and then following the phrase with a pronoun: *In Leslie Marmon Silko's book Ceremony, she describes. . . .* The problem is that the possessive noun *Leslie Marmon Silko's* functions as an adjective and cannot serve as the antecedent of *she*. Instead, begin *In her book <u>Ceremony</u>, Leslie Marmon Silko describes. . . .*

This, which, and it in broad reference. Avoid using *this, which,* and *it* to refer to a whole idea or sentence. These pronouns should refer to specific nouns.

> FAULTY: Leslie Marmon Silko describes how Native Americans have been treated as second-class citizens. *This* shows how they have been misunderstood as a displaced people.

> REVISED: Leslie Marmon Silko describes how Native Americans have been treated as second-class citizens. *This treatment* shows how they have been misunderstood as a displaced people.

Nonsexist language. Avoid using masculine pronouns (*he, him, his*) to refer to antecedents of unspecified gender.

> FAULTY: The American Indian has long been paying for *his* prior inhabitation of the continent.

> REVISED: American Indians have long been paying for *their* prior inhabitation of the continent.

See also **nonsexist language.**

pronouns

> SECTION OVERVIEW
> Personal pronouns
> Relative pronouns
> Interrogative pronouns
> Demonstrative pronouns
> Indefinite pronouns

Pronouns substitute for **nouns,** performing all the same sentence functions as nouns: *she* might be a subject referring to *Michele; them* might be an object referring to *horses.* But only nouns name things. When you read the noun *horses,* you visualize a certain kind of animal; but the pronoun *them* gives you no such image. Pronouns can only stand for nouns—their **antecedents. Pronoun reference** therefore must always be evident. There are several kinds of pronouns: **personal** (including **reflexive** and intensive), **relative, interrogative, demonstrative,** and **indefinite.**

Personal pronouns

Personal pronouns refer to the person speaking or writing (first person), the person(s) spoken or written to (second person), or to the person(s) spoken or written about (third person). Personal pronouns can be **singular** or **plural**. (See also **cases** and **possessive case**.)

PERSONAL PRONOUNS		
	SINGULAR	*PLURAL*
FIRST PERSON	I, me, my, mine	we, us, our, ours
SECOND PERSON	you, your, yours	you, your, yours
THIRD PERSON	he, him, his	they, them, their, theirs
	she, her, hers	they, them, their, theirs
	it, its	they, them, their, theirs

CAUTION: Reflexive and intensive pronouns (*myself, ourselves, yourself, yourselves, himself, herself, itself, themselves*) should be used only with antecedent nouns and other pronouns. Do not use them in place of personal pronouns.

FAULTY: Write the letter to the program assistant or *myself.*

REVISED: Write the letter to the program assistant or *me.*

Avoid faulty spellings for these words: *himself* (not *hisself*), *ourselves* (not *ourself*), *themselves* (not *themself* or *theirselves*). *Yourself* refers to one person, *yourselves* to more than one.

Relative pronouns

The **relative pronouns** (*who, whom, whose, which, that*) and their compounds (*whoever, whomever, whosever, whichever*) do more than stand in the place of nouns. They also introduce **relative clauses** and connect relative clauses to the nouns they **modify.**

On your way up the California coast toward Oregon, stop at Eureka, *which* has some fabulous refurbished Victorian homes. [In the relative clause, *which* is the subject of the verb *has*; its antecedent is *Eureka,* and the relative clause modifies *Eureka.*]

The town of Eureka has some 25,000 residents, *who* collectively make it the largest population center on the North Coast of California. [In the relative clause, *who* is the subject of *make,* its antecedent is *residents,* and the relative clause modifies *residents.*]

Who and its related forms refers to people, *which* to nonhuman antecedents. *That* refers mainly to things and is sometimes omitted when it introduces a noun **clause:**

We know [*that*] *you will enjoy the trip.*

CAUTION: Often the omission of *that* causes misreading. Especially in writing, it is good practice to include *that.*

> FAULTY: Historians will recall California's Fort Ross was a Russian fur-trading port.
>
> REVISED: Historians will recall *that* California's Fort Ross was a Russian fur-trading port.

⚠ A clause introduced by a relative pronoun cannot function independently as a sentence. The result would be a sentence **fragment.**

> FAULTY: *Which* is what I meant to say in the first place.
>
> REVISED: The sentence as I restated it is what I meant to say in the first place.

Interrogative pronouns

Interrogative pronouns (*who, whom, whose, which, what*) introduce **questions** and **indirect questions.**

> *Who* wants to make a trip to the North Coast of California? [direct question]
>
> I asked *who* wanted to make a trip to the North Coast of California. [indirect question]

Unlike relative pronouns, interrogative pronouns can introduce **independent clauses,** as the first example sentence illustrates.

Demonstrative pronouns

Demonstrative pronouns (*this, these, that, those*) point out persons, places, and things.

> *This* is the trip I've been waiting for.

The demonstratives are often used as **adjectives,** especially when the thing they refer to would not otherwise be named in the sentence.

> For all *these reasons,* I want to make this trip. [The phrase *these reasons* summarizes a previous statement.]

This use of demonstrative adjectives is effective for relating a sentence to the previous one. See **pronoun reference.**

Indefinite pronouns

Indefinite pronouns do not refer to specific persons or things and do not require antecedents.

I hope I can convince *someone* to make the trip with me. [The indefinite pronoun *someone* refers to no one in particular and has no antecedent.]

These are some of the common indefinite pronouns:

any, another, anyone, anybody, anything
some, someone, somebody, something
one, none, no one, nobody, nothing, many, few, much
each, each one, several, all, both, either, neither
everyone, everybody, everything

Some of the indefinites (*any, some, each, every*) can function also as adjectives.

Some people like to make reservations in advance.

Most of the indefinites are grammatically **singular** and therefore take singular verbs and pronouns.

Everyone who *visits* Bodega Bay *thinks* about the movie *The Birds* and *keeps* looking over *his or her* shoulder.

Each town and port along the North Coast *has its* own attraction.

▼ *One* and *other* have plural forms (*ones, others*) and possessive forms (*one's, other's*).

The jeweler told her, "The bracelet you want to see is not for sale, but we have wider *ones* that you might like."

One also has a reflexive form (*oneself* or *one's self*). Compounds of *one, other,* and *body* also have possessive forms (*another's, anybody's, someone's, each one's, one another's*). When an indefinite pronoun or adjective is used with *else, else* takes the possessive form (*somebody else's*). See also **agreement of pronouns and antecedents.**

proper adjectives   A modifier derived from a **proper noun;** it is capitalized: *English, Californian.* (See **adjectives.**)

proper nouns   A name for a particular person, place, or thing; it is capitalized: *John Smith, Cincinnati, Tuesday.* (See **nouns.**)

punctuation   Punctuation is a system of signals telling readers how the parts of written discourse relate to one another. For example, a **period** signals the end of a sentence, a **colon** that an explanation will follow, and a **comma** that sentence parts are parallel, in a series, or being set off as a unit. Punctuation corresponds roughly to intonations and other physical signals in speech. When speaking, you probably pause and let your voice drop at the end of a **sentence,** and you often have smaller pauses between **clauses** and longer **phrases.** If you want to gain **emphasis** or drama, you can increase the length of your pauses. To express strong feelings, you can shout. At the end of some of your questions, you make your voice rise. Punctuation replaces these and other vocal signals.

Ends of sentences are punctuated with **periods, question marks,** or **exclamation points. Semicolons** function as "soft" periods, usually marking the end of independent **clauses** but not of complete thoughts. **Commas** show relationships within sentences, as do **colons, dashes, quotation marks, parentheses, brackets,** and **ellipsis dots.** Other marks are used within words: **apostrophes, hyphens, italics (underlining),** and **slashes.** Each of these punctuation marks is explained in a separate entry.

Q

question marks   A question mark ends a **sentence** that asks a direct **question.**

Do you know anything about fuels for the future?

Question marks do not end **indirect questions.**

Margaret asked if I knew anything about fuels for the future.

When quoting a question, place the question mark inside the final quotation mark.

Margaret asked, "Do you know anything about fuels for the future?"

When you ask a question that includes a quotation, the question mark goes outside the final quotation mark.

Did Margaret say, "I need to know something about fuels for the future"?

When both the sentence and the quotation are questions (a rare occurrence), use one question mark and place it inside the end quotation mark.

Did Margaret ask, "Do you know anything about fuels for the future?"

questions   Sentences that ask questions begin with an **interrogative word** (such as *who, what, why, where*) or with a **verb** preceding the **subject,** and they end with a **question mark.**

> *Who* are the rural homeless? [interrogative **pronoun**]
>
> *Can* we *do* something to aid the rural homeless? [inverted order]
>
> *Are* the rural homeless a social concern? [inverted order]

▼ As these sentences illustrate, some questions begin with a form of *be* or one part of a verb phrase. Other questions begin with a form of *do.*

> *Do* you *know* the scope of rural homelessness?

Questions signaled by inverted order are sometimes called *yes/no* questions, because they can be answered with yes or no.

▼   Statements that end in a "tag" that asks a question are called **tag questions.**

> Some areas are providing shelter for the rural homeless, *aren't they?*
>
> Other areas are not yet aware of the problem, *are they?*

An affirmative statement with a negative tag, like the first tag question example, assumes a yes answer: *Yes, some areas are providing shelter for the rural homeless.* A negative statement with an affirmative tag, such as the second example, anticipates a no answer: *No, other areas are not yet aware of the problem.* See also **indirect questions** and **question marks.**

quotation, quote   *Quotation* is a noun, *quote* a verb.

> After I had *quoted* extensively from the article, I decided not to use the *quotations* (not *quotes*) after all.

quotation marks   The primary use of quotation marks is to enclose the words of another person.

> The report stated, "More and more couples want flexible work schedules."

Material enclosed in quotation marks should be an exact repetition of the original. **Indirect quotations** are written in the words of the person repeating them and are not enclosed in quotation marks.

> The report stated that a greater percentage of couples would like to have flexible work schedules.

Other uses of quotation marks

TITLES. Titles of works published as part of larger works are enclosed in quotation marks. These titles include short stories, poems, essays, reports, articles in magazines and journals, chapters in books, episodes of radio and television programs, and short musical works.

> "The New Scoop on Vitamins" [article in a magazine]
>
> "To a Locomotive in Winter" [poem]
>
> "Everything That Rises Must Converge" [short story]
>
> "Dancing Particles" [short musical work]

See **italics (underlining)** for treatment of titles of works published independently.

WORDS. Use quotation marks sparingly to enclose words you use in a special sense.

> The term "flextime" is generally used to refer to flexible work schedules.

Quotation marks with other punctuation

INTRODUCING THE QUOTATION. Ordinarily, a comma precedes the first quotation mark, but omit the comma when you introduce a direct quotation with *that* or when your sentence does more than introduce the quotation.

> According to some employers, "Allowing employees to set their own hours improves productivity."
>
> Employers say that "flexible work time is favored particularly by women."
>
> Companies that allow flexible work schedules have been referred to as "the most family-friendly companies in America."

Long or formal quotations are often introduced with **colons.**

> Douglas Fraser, former president of the United Auto Workers, comments: "The younger generations are more interested in time off their jobs than were their fathers and grandfathers. They have other values—living a fuller life with their family and having more time for recreation and social activities."

Quotations longer than four typed lines are usually marked by indentation rather than quotation marks. Indent the quotation ten spaces from the left margin and omit the quotation marks.

ENDING THE QUOTATION.   Whether you quote sentences or single words, place **periods** and **commas** inside the end quotation mark, **colons** and **semicolons** outside the end quotation mark. **Dashes, question marks,** and **exclamation points** go inside or outside depending on meaning—inside if the mark applies to the quotation and outside if it applies to the surrounding sentence.

> Flextime can involve "job-sharing, unconventional hours, leaves of absence, part-time employment, and permission to work at home"— all of which are currently in use.

> "The most common use of flextime, according to this definition, is part-time work"; shortened work weeks are a close second.

When you parenthetically cite the source of the quotation, place the period after the close parenthesis.

> Companies that allow flexible work schedules have been referred to as "the most family-friendly companies in America" (Johnson 68). [See page 280 on citing sources.]

When interrupting a quotation, use whatever punctuation is appropriate for the sentence:

> "Companies with unbending schedule policies," the report said, "will no longer be the norm." [Commas are appropriate because the quoted sentence continues.]

> "Rigid managers believe that people aren't performing unless they're at their desk," according to the report. "Other managers have found that people with alternative work schedules are more productive." [The period after *report* is appropriate because both quotations are complete sentences.]

See also **quotations.**

quotations   Quotations are the exact words of another person, enclosed in **quotation marks** and usually separated from the rest of the sentence by a **comma** or a **colon.**

> The facts are clear: "One out of five children in America live in poverty." [formally introduced quotation]

> These are children who live in a family whose "annual income is less than $13,359 for a family of four." [quotation as an integral part of the sentence]

> "These children," says the report, "lack adequate nutrition, health care, education, and safety." [interrupted quotation]

Quotations must be word-for-word copies of the original. If you need to alter them to suit your sentence, use **ellipsis dots** to show omissions and **brackets** to insert your own comments or clarifications. **Indirect quotations,** or **paraphrases,** are often advantageous to a writer because the ideas of another person can be stated in one's own words and style, thus fitting more smoothly into the piece of writing; they are not set off with quotation marks. Long quotations, those over four typed lines, should be set off with indentation, not quotation marks. See also pages 272–274 on research writing.

R

---

raise, rise   *Raise* is a transitive **verb** that takes an **object;** *rise* is an intransitive verb that does not take an object.

The derrick *raises* the huge unit to the top of the building.

The huge unit *rises* to the top of the building.

Raise is formed regularly; *rise* is an **irregular verb.**

BASE FORM	PAST TENSE	PAST PARTICIPLE
raise	raised	raised
rise	rose	risen

The huge unit *rose* to the top of the building. [past tense of *rise*]

The huge unit *has risen* to the top of the building. [present perfect tense of *rise*]

real, really   Avoid using *real* as an **adverb,** and use *really* sparingly.

Unfortunately, the rumor was *really* [not *real*] accurate.

reason is because   Use *reason . . . is that* or *because,* not *reason . . . is because.*

The *reason* he left the firm *is that* [not *because*] he wanted to continue his education.

He left the firm *because* he wanted to continue his education.

redundancies   Redundant phrases say the same thing twice and consequently are a cause of **wordiness.** In the examples listed below, the words in italics could be omitted without altering meaning:

consensus *of opinion*	red *in color*
cooperate *together*	tall *in height*
quite complete	oblong *in shape*
basic fundamentals	*true* fact
repeat *again*	*really* true
return *again*	modern world *of today*

reference   (See **pronoun reference**)

reflexive pronouns   The *-self* **pronouns** (*herself, himself, itself, myself, yourself, yourselves, ourselves, themselves*) are reflexive (serving as **objects** as well as **subjects**) or intensive (emphasizing their **antecedents**).

> Throughout the book, Martha has written notes to *herself*. [*Herself* is reflective of its antecedent, *Martha*.]
>
> She *herself* has written the notes. [*Herself* intensifies its antecedent, *She*.]

Reflexive pronouns should be used only with antecedent nouns or pronouns.

> **FAULTY:**   You can return the books later to Kathryn or *myself*. [There is no antecedent for *myself*.]
>
> **REVISED:**   You can return the books later to Kathryn or *me*.

Do not use the forms *hisself* (for *himself*), *themself* or *theirselves* (for *themselves*), and *ourself* (for *ourselves*).

regular verbs   Regular **verbs** show **person, tense,** and **number** in the following ways: an *-s* ending for the present-tense first-person singular (*wants*), no ending for other present-tense forms (*want*), and a *-d* or *-ed* ending for the past tense and the past **participle** (*wanted, have wanted*). See **verbs.**

relative adjectives and adverbs   Relative adjectives and adverbs, like **relative pronouns,** connect **relative clauses** to the words they **modify.** A relative adjective (*whose, whosever, which, that*) modifies a word in its own **clause,** refers to an **antecedent** in another clause, and connects its own clause to the other clause.

> Left-handed people are a minority group *whose* problems are little understood. [*Whose* means *group's* and modifies *problems;* it connects its clause, *whose problems are little understood,* to the independent clause.]

Introducing relative clauses

A relative adverb (*when, why, how,* or *where*) functions as an adverb within its own clause and introduces a relative clause that modifies nouns denoting time or place.

> There was a time *when* left-handedness was thought to be evil. [The *when* clause describes the noun *time.*]

> CAUTION: Avoid using *that* in place of *when* or *where.*

> FAULTY: There was a time *that* left-handedness was thought to be evil. [See revision above.]

Avoid using *when* or *where* to modify words that do not indicate time or place.

> FAULTY: It was a situation *where* the word *sinister* came to be used synonymously for left-handedness and trouble. [*Situation* does not refer to place.]

> REVISED: It was a situation *in which* the word *sinister* came to be used synonymously for "left-handedness" and "trouble."

See also **nonrestrictive and restrictive modifiers.**

Introducing noun clauses

Relative adjectives and adverbs also introduce noun **clauses.**

> You may wonder *what* problems left-handed people have. [*What* modifies *problems*, and the entire noun clause is the direct **object** of *may wonder.*]

> *How* handedness is determined is still not clearly understood. [*How* is an adverb in the noun clause *How handedness is determined;* the noun clause functions as the **subject** of *is understood.*]

relative adverbs   (See **relative adjectives and adverbs** and **relative clauses**)

relative clauses   Relative clauses, sometimes called *adjective clauses*, are subordinate **clauses** that modify **nouns** or **pronouns** and usually immediately follow the words they modify.

> New Zealand is an island nation *that has two main ethnic groups, European and Maori.* [The relative clause, introduced by the **relative pronoun** *that*, modifies *nation.*]

The Maori, *whose ancestry is Polynesian*, probably migrated to the islands by 1400. [The relative clause, introduced by the **relative adjective** *whose*, modifies *Maori*.]

Relative clauses are connected to other clauses by means of relative pronouns, relative adjectives, or relative adverbs.

RELATIVE PRONOUNS, ADJECTIVES, AND ADVERBS		
which	what	who (whose, whom)
whichever	whatever	whoever (whosever, whomever)
that	where	why
what	when	

When a relative pronoun functions as an **object** in a relative clause, do not put a second object in the clause.

FAULTY: New Zealand, *which* James Cook described *it* after his journeys, became interesting to the English for settlement. [*Which* functions as the direct object of *described*; *it* is redundant.]

REVISED: New Zealand, *which* James Cook described after his journeys, became interesting to the English for settlement.

See also **restrictive and nonrestrictive elements.**

▼ **relative pronouns**   A relative pronoun connects a **relative clause** to another **clause**. In addition, it represents a **noun** or **pronoun** (its **antecedent**) in another clause, and functions as a **subject** or an **object** within its own clause.

Tropical rain forests, *which* cover about 7 percent of the earth's surface, are important to modern medicine. [The relative pronoun *which* connects the relative clause to the main clause; *which* refers to *rain forests* and functions as the **subject** of its own clause.]

Rain forests yield medicines *that* 75 percent of the world's population relies on for health care. [The relative pronoun *that* connects the relative clause to the main clause; *that* refers to *medicines* and functions as the object of the preposition *on* in the relative clause.]

People *who* suffer from Hodgkin's disease may take medicine derived from the periwinkle of Madagascar. [The relative pronoun *who* connects the relative clause to the main clause; *who* refers to *people* and functions as the subject of the relative clause.]

People for *whom* the rain forests are important medicinally would suffer if the forests continue to be destroyed. [The relative pronoun *whom* connects the relative clause to the main clause; *whom* refers to *people* and functions as the object of the preposition *for* in the relative clause.]

Relative pronouns come in three cases: the nominative, the objective, and the possessive. Most relative pronouns don't change form to indicate their case, but a few do.

CASES OF RELATIVE PRONOUNS

NOMINATIVE	OBJECTIVE	POSSESSIVE
who	whom	whose
which	which	
that	that	
whoever	whomever	whosever
whichever	whichever	

The pronoun *who* (*whom, whose*) normally refers to a person, *which* normally to a thing, and *that* to a thing or to a group of people (such as *team* and *committee*). *That* is used with **restrictive** clauses; *which* is usually reserved for **nonrestrictive** clauses; and *who* is used in both.

Quinine, *which* is used to treat malaria, comes from trees in Africa, Asia, and South America. [*Which* refers to a thing, *Quinine;* it introduces a nonrestrictive clause and is the subject of that clause.]

The green canopies *that* stretch across continents are quickly disappearing. [*That* refers to a thing, *canopies;* it introduces a restrictive clause and is the subject of that clause.]

People *who* destroy the rain forests disregard their medicinal value. [*Who* refers to *People;* it introduces a restrictive clause and is the subject of that clause.]

Relative pronouns are often omitted, especially in speech. In writing, including them may be necessary for clarity.

Seventy percent of known anticancer agents are part of the bounty [*that*] *rain forests supply.*

repetition   Repetition of words, phrases, or sentence patterns can be used intentionally to achieve **emphasis** and coherence. Each time a key word or phrase occurs or a structural pattern is repeated, it draws the reader's attention.

> EMPHASIS: But, in a larger sense, *we cannot dedicate—we cannot consecrate—we cannot hallow*—this ground.   —ABRAHAM LINCOLN,
> "Address at the Dedication of the
> Gettysburg National Cemetery"

> COHERENCE: After the *nuclear* disaster at Chernobyl, Italian voters halted their *nuclear* construction, Austrian voters decided never to operate their single *nuclear* plant, and Swedish voters decided to shut down all their *nuclear* plants by the year 2010. [In addition to repetition of the key word *nuclear*, clauses beginning *X voters* are similarly constructed and contain related ideas. See also **parallelism.**]

CAUTION: The fact that repetition attracts attention is also a reason for avoiding its unintentional use.

> CLUMSY REPETITION: People must learn ways *which* will improve the environment *which* they share with other creatures *which* inhabit this globe.

> REVISED: People must learn ways *to improve* the environment *they share* with all other creatures *that* inhabit this globe.

Sometimes synonyms are more effective than repetition.

> In Europe, efforts have been made to *stop overcrowding the planet.* East Germany *brought births and deaths into balance* in 1969. West Germany's *population stopped growing* in 1972. And by 1986 eleven other European nations reported *zero population growth.* [four ways of stating the same idea]

restrictive and nonrestrictive elements   Some **modifiers** are essential to a sentence because they *restrict*, or limit, the meaning of the words they modify; other modifiers, although they add important information, are not essential to the meaning of the sentence. The first type of modifier is called *restrictive* and the second *nonrestrictive.* Restrictive and nonrestrictive elements are usually subordinate **clauses** or **phrases.**

> Everything *you do* exists first as electricity and chemistry in your brain. [Restrictive subordinate clause; it cannot be removed from the sentence without altering the meaning.]

> The idea *of the brain as a computer* is inadequate. [The restrictive **prepositional phrase** is essential to the meaning of the sentence.]

The brain is simply a brain, *which is unlike anything else.* [Non-restrictive subordinate clause; although the clause contributes useful information, the essential meaning of the sentence would not change if you removed it.]

Can the brain, *with all its sophisticated synapses and neurons,* understand everything? [Nonrestrictive prepositional phrase; the essential meaning of the sentence would not change if you removed it.]

CAUTION: Nonrestrictive elements, because they don't limit the meaning of the words they modify, are set off from the sentence with **commas** (sometimes with **dashes**). Restrictive elements are not set off with punctuation. Because the distinction is one of meaning, it is an important one for writers to make.

FAULTY: Even people, who can't remember their mothers' birthdays, have brains far superior to the most powerful computer. [Set off with commas, the relative clause does not limit the meaning of *people;* the sentence implies that all people cannot remember their mothers' birthdays.]

REVISED: Even people *who can't remember their mothers' birthdays* have brains far superior to the most powerful computer. [Restrictive clause limits the meaning of *people;* the sentence is not referring to all the people in the world, only those *who can't remember their mother's birthdays.*]

Use these guidelines in making the distinction between restrictive and nonrestrictive elements:

1. A modifier that modifies a proper **noun** (one that names a specific person, place, or thing) is usually nonrestrictive, because the name is sufficient identification. (*Aleksandr Luria, noted Soviet psychologist*)

2. A *that* clause is almost always restrictive (*a fact that we all know well*).

3. A nonrestrictive modifier at the beginning of a sentence is followed by a comma, one at the end of the sentence is preceded by a comma, and one in the middle is enclosed with two commas.

See also **commas.**

run-on sentences   A sentence fault in which a writer has omitted punctuation between two **independent clauses.** See **fused sentences.**

S

salutation   (See "Business Letters" under Part Four, "Specialized Writing.")

scarcely   Because of its negative meanings, *scarcely* should not be used with *not* and other negatives.

> We *could scarcely* (not *couldn't scarcely*) see the other side of the road because of blowing snow.

See *can't hardly* and **double negatives.**

seasons   (See **capitalization**)

secondly   (See *firstly*)

semicolons   The main use for a semicolon is to separate two independent **clauses** not joined with a coordinating **conjunction.**

> Teamwork in business has been shown to be efficient and productive; individual competition is not necessarily the best way to get things done.

Even when the second clause is related to the first with a **transitional adverb** (such as *however, then, moreover, thus, therefore*), a semicolon separates the two clauses.

> Teamwork pools the knowledge of specialists in various fields; however, this collaboration requires clear task definition and support from management.

> Each specialist contributes his or her own expertise; the effect, therefore, is power planning.

Sometimes semicolons separate items in sentences that are complicated with modifiers set off with commas.

> A power team might include designers and engineers, who could draft the plans; manufacturing specialists, who could consider the dynamics of production; and marketing managers, who could work out how to advertise and sell the product.

⚠   CAUTION: Do not use a **comma** when a semicolon is required between independent clauses; the result would be a **comma splice.**

FAULTY: The sum of the team is more than what individual members could contribute alone, scientists call this effect *synergy.*

REVISED: The sum of the team is more than what individual members could contribute alone; scientists call this effect *synergy.*

⚠ Do not use a semicolon in place of a comma; the result would be a type of **fragment.**

FAULTY: People working alone draw only on their own expertise; a system that is much less efficient than combining the expertise of several people. [The force of the semicolon makes a fragment of the second part of the sentence.]

REVISED: People working alone draw only on their own expertise, a system that is much less efficient than combining the expertise of several people. [A comma is appropriate punctuation.]

⚠ Another type of fragment occurs when writers use a semicolon where a **colon** is required.

FAULTY: Ineffective teams result from three main factors; lack of leadership, lack of incentive, and lack of direction.

REVISED: Ineffective teams result from three main factors: lack of leadership, lack of incentive, and lack of direction.

Think of semicolons as soft **periods.** Semicolons are often interchangeable with periods, especially when they come between closely related ideas. They are not interchangeable with commas and colons.

sentence faults   (See specific fault: **comma splices, fragments, fused sentences, shifts**)

sentence fragments   (See **fragments**)

sentence patterns   English **sentences** fall into five basic sentence patterns, each determined by the type of **verb**—transitive or intransitive—and the **objects** or **complements** it takes. All sentence patterns can include **modifiers.**

BASIC SENTENCE PATTERNS
(Verbs are italicized.)

PATTERN 1: SUBJECT, INTRANSITIVE VERB

People *vote*.

People *vote* in elections. [**prepositional phrase** modifying *vote*]

People aged 18 to 25 *vote* in elections in limited numbers. [**participial phrase** *aged 18 to 25* modifying *People* and prepositional phrase modifying *vote*]

There *are* more registered voters in the 58 to 65 age group. [**inverted order** with the subject *voters* following the verb *are;* prepositional phrase modifying *voters*]

Where *are* the younger voters? [**question** with the subject *voters* following the verb *are*]

Pattern 1 sentences can have modifiers, but they do not have subject or object complements and direct or indirect objects.

PATTERN 2: SUBJECT, LINKING VERB, AND SUBJECT COMPLEMENT

Some spiders *are* endangered. [*Endangered* is an **adjective** subject complement describing the subject, *spiders.*]

Three kinds of arachnids *are* endangered species. [*Species* is a **noun** subject complement renaming the subject, *kinds.*]

Be (plus its forms *am, is, are, was, were, being, been*) is the most common linking verb. Others are *seem, become, appear, turn, grow, look, remain, smell, taste, feel,* and *sound.*

A few insects *are becoming* endangered species too. [The subject complement, *species,* renames the subject, *insects.*]

The number of endangered butterflies *is growing* larger each year. [The subject complement, *larger,* describes the subject, *number.*]

A subject complement renames or describes the subject.

PATTERN 3: SUBJECT, TRANSITIVE VERB, DIRECT OBJECT

The child *bit* a snake. [*Snake* is the direct object.]

The mother *rushed* the child to a hospital. [*Child* is the direct object.]

A doctor *examined* the child and *sent* him and the relieved mother home. [*Child* is the direct object of the first verb *examined; him* and *mother* are direct objects of the second verb *sent.*]

A direct object names the receiver of the action of the verb.

PATTERN 4: SUBJECT, TRANSITIVE VERB, INDIRECT OBJECT, DIRECT OBJECT

> Advertisers *send* people junk mail. [*People* is the indirect object; *mail* is the direct object.]
>
> Advertisers wanting to persuade people to buy their products *send* Americans an average of 216 pieces of junk mail yearly. [*Americans* is the indirect object; *average* is the direct object. The phrases are modifiers.]

An indirect object names the person or thing to whom or for whom the action of the verb is performed. Verbs that commonly take indirect objects are *ask, tell, write, give, send, pay, assign,* and similar ones.

PATTERN 5: SUBJECT, TRANSITIVE VERB, DIRECT OBJECT, OBJECT COMPLEMENT

> The judge *declared* the man guilty. [*Man* is the direct object; *guilty* is an adjective object complement modifying *man.*]
>
> Accused of defecting to the Soviet Union, the man *pronounced* himself an unwitting counterspy. [*Himself* is the direct object; *counterspy* is a noun object complement renaming *himself.*]

Object complements describe or rename the direct object; they usually follow the direct object.

Sentence patterns are one of the means you have for achieving **sentence variety**. See also **sentence types**.

sentences   A sentence is a group of related words that makes a statement or asks a question. It contains a **subject** (a **noun** or **pronoun** and **modifiers**) and a **predicate** (a **verb** and its **objects, complements,** and modifiers) in at least one **independent clause**.

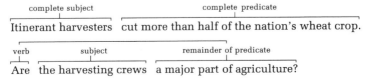

complete subject   complete predicate

Itinerant harvesters cut more than half of the nation's wheat crop.

verb   subject   remainder of predicate

Are the harvesting crews a major part of agriculture?

Sentences may have **objects, complements,** and **modifiers.**

<pre>
              subject   verb   direct object
          ┌──────┴──────┐   ┌────┴───┐   ┌──────┴──────┐
</pre>
The high cost of combines   prevents   grain farmers

<pre>
           prepositional phrase
      ┌──────────────┴──────────────┐
</pre>
from doing their own harvesting. [The **prepositional phrase** *from doing their own harvesting* modifies the verb.]

<pre>
             subject   verb   subject complement
       ┌───────┴────────┐ ┌─────┴─────┐   ┌───────┴───────┐
</pre>
The custom harvesters   might be called   the cowboys

<pre>
     prepositional phrase
   ┌──────────┴──────────┐
</pre>
of the wheat fields. [The prepositional phrase *of the wheat fields* modifies *cowboys.*]

Sentences may have more than one **clause.**

<pre>
                         independent clause
   ┌─────────────────────────────┴─────────────────────────────┐
</pre>
The reapers first cut the winter wheat of the southern plains;

<pre>
                     independent clause
   ┌──────────────────────────┴──────────────────────────┐
</pre>
from there they move north to the ripening crops. [**compound sentence**]

<pre>
            subordinate clause   independent clause
   ┌───────────────┴───────────────┐   ┌───────────────┴───────────────┐
</pre>
As the grain ripens in the wheat belt,   farmers call their custom

harvesters. [**complex sentence**]

<pre>
        indepen-   subordinate clause
   ┌───────┴────────┐   ┌──────────────────┴──────────────────┐
</pre>
The itinerant cutters, who live a nomadic life from May into

<pre>
                 dent clause
   ┌───────────────┴───────────────┐
</pre>
autumn, travel in trailer-home caravans. [complex sentence; independent clause interrupted by a subordinate clause]

Parts of sentences may be modified by **phrases.**

<pre>
              independent clause   participial phrase
   ┌──────────────────┴──────────────────┐   ┌────────┴────────┐
</pre>
Families travel together and work together,   meeting old friends

along the way. [The phrase modifies *families.*]

two prepositional phrases	independent clause

Despite dependence on the weather, the harvesters find the

seasons quite regular. [*On the weather* modifies *dependence,* and *despite dependence* (plus *on the weather*) modifies the main verb, *find.*]

For further discussions, see **sentence patterns, sentence types,** and **sentence variety.** For sentence faults, see **comma splices, fragments, fused sentences,** and **shifts.**

sentence types   Sentences are classified in various ways. Two classification schemes are discussed here: grammatical types (**simple, compound, complex,** and **compound-complex**) and rhetorical types (**declarative, interrogative, imperative,** and **exclamatory**).

Grammatical types of sentences

SIMPLE SENTENCES.   A simple sentence consists of one **independent clause** with as many **modifiers** as necessary.

Design is critical.

The design of a product can enhance its function and make it more attractive to buyers. [The sentence has a **compound predicate**—two verbs *can enhance* and *make,* with one subject, *design.*]

COMPOUND SENTENCES.   Compound sentences contain two or more independent clauses and no **subordinate clauses.**

The field of industrial design is growing, and graphic designers are becoming increasingly influential in the world market. [two independent statements joined by the coordinating **conjunction** *and*]

Nearly everything you use or see has been designed by someone; however, you probably give very little thought to the designer. [two independent clauses separated by a **semicolon**]

COMPLEX SENTENCES.   Complex sentences contain one independent clause and at least one subordinate clause.

Although you may not have thought about it before, consider the design of your reading lamp, of the light bulb *you screw into it,* and of the cord *with which you attach it to an electrical current.* [The subordinate clauses are italicized.]

Then think about *why your desk was designed the way <u>it was</u>* and
how the drawer pulls evolved into their present shape. [The two
subordinate clauses are italicized and a third is underlined.]

COMPOUND-COMPLEX SENTENCES.   Compound-complex sentences have
at least two independent clauses and at least one subordinate clause.

Industrial designers are coming to be recognized as essential
members of the production team *who can help American business
compete with foreign competitors;* as a result, they now work with
people in marketing, sales, engineering, manufacturing, and
purchasing. [The subordinate clause is italicized.]

Rhetorical types of sentences

DECLARATIVE SENTENCE.   A **declarative sentence** makes an assertion. It ends with a **period.**

Responding to a demand for wilderness areas, Congress passed the
National Wild and Scenic Rivers Act in 1968.

So far, over 150 rivers have been designated as wild or scenic.

Normal sentence order of a declarative sentence is **subject** first, then
verb. In the first sentence above, *Congress* is the subject and *passed* is
the verb. In the second sentence, *rivers* is the subject and *have been
designated* is the verb.

INTERROGATIVE SENTENCE.   An **interrogative sentence** asks a question. It ends with a **question mark.**

Do you know how many miles are represented in those 150 rivers?

Where can I find a wild and scenic river?

The normal interrogative sentence begins with an **interrogative word**
(such as *where, who,* and *how*) or with a verb. See also **questions.**

IMPERATIVE SENTENCE.   An **imperative sentence** is a type of declarative sentence that expresses a mild command. It ends in a period.

To see a landscape that has not been dammed, drained, channeled,
overdeveloped, or choked with pollution, travel a wild and scenic
river.

Contact the National Park Service or the U.S. Forest Service to get
information about a wild and scenic river near you.

With imperative sentences the subject is an unstated *you,* and the verb
is the base form of the verb (with no added ending): *do, go, be, forget,
ask.*

EXCLAMATORY SENTENCE.   An **exclamatory sentence** is an emphatic expression. It is often an incomplete sentence. It is followed by an **exclamation point.**

Splendid!
Go now! This minute!
We won!

Exclamations are rare in academic and professional writing.
See also **sentences** and **sentence patterns.**

sentence variety   **Sentence** variety is one of the means you have for creating lively and interesting writing. You can vary your **sentence types, sentence patterns,** word order and choice, and sentence length. Sentence variety is best examined as part of revision. Read your work aloud. If you find that you have begun a number of sentences with subordinate **clauses** (beginning with *After* or *Because,* for example), revise them: put some of the subordinate clauses at the end of their sentences, convert them to **phrases** or sentences, or perhaps even omit them entirely. If you find yourself stopping frequently for periods, try combining some sentences by making some independent clauses into subordinate clauses or phrases. Or if you find yourself panting for a period as you read aloud, your sentences are probably too long; break some of them up. Don't begin many sentences with *and* or *but.* You may have been taught never to do it, but judicious use of the conjunction makes a smooth connection between sentences.

Here is a paragraph that lacks sentence variety. Compare it with the revision that follows it.

LACK OF VARIETY: The Siberian railroad covers more than 5,000 miles. It is a trip that under good conditions takes seven days. My shorter trip from Omsk to Moscow lasted nearly 44 hours. The trip past endless birch forests and tiny villages soon became monotonous. The food on the train was unappetizing in appearance and taste. The railroad food could be supplemented by entrepreneurial vendors who would readily sell food and drink at every stop. Examples of the food they offer are ice cream, beer, boiled potatoes, and sliced bread. Train travel is inexpensive in Russia. The Siberian trip cost me $4.00.

REVISION: The Siberian railroad covers more than 5,000 miles, a trip that under good conditions takes seven days. When I traveled the shorter distance from Omsk to Moscow, the monotonous ride past endless birch forests and tiny villages lasted nearly 44 hours. To make the trip even more tedious, the food on the train was unappetizing in both appearance and taste, though it could be supplemented by entrepreneurial vendors who would readily sell food and drink—such as ice cream, beer, boiled potatoes, and sliced bread—at every stop. To counterbalance the drabness of the trip, train travel in Russia is inexpensive. The entire Siberian trip cost me only $4.00.

In the revision, the paragraph achieves variety through varied sentence patterns, synonyms, and word order and with combined phrases and subordinate clauses. The revised paragraph also gains meaning with connecting phrases (*to make the trip even more tedious, to counterbalance the drabness of the trip*) and **emphasis** with the single short sentence at the end. See also **subordination.**

sequence of tense (See **tenses of verbs**)

series punctuation (See **commas**)

set, sit *Set* is a **transitive** verb meaning "to put" or "to place" and takes a direct **object.**

> You can *set* your papers on the desk. [*Papers* is the direct object of *set*.]

Except for the third-person singular present tense form *sets* and the present participle and progressive form *setting, set* has only one form: *set* (present), *set* (past), and *set* (past participle).

> She *set* her papers on the desk yesterday. [past tense]

Sit means "to rest" as in a chair or on a perch. As an **intransitive verb,** it does not take a direct object. Its forms are *sit* (present), *sat* (past), *sitting* (present participle and progressive form), and *sat* (past participle).

> Does it make any difference where we *sit*?
>
> We *have sat* in the same seats every day.
>
> Our papers are *sitting* on the desk. [Inanimate objects and nonhuman beings can *sit*.]

sexist language (See **nonsexist language**)

shall, will At one time, *shall* was used with *I* and *we* to indicate some future action, *will* for all other uses. In current American usage, however, *will* is used almost exclusively.

I *will* let you know what we decide.

You *will* hear from me soon.

Shall is sometimes still used to ask **questions** or to emphasize a point.

Shall I call you when we have made our decision?

All members of the committee *shall* remain until a decision is reached.

See also **modals.**

 shifts

> SECTION OVERVIEW
> Shifts in person
> Shifts in number
> Shifts in tense
> Shifts in mood
> Shifts in voice and subject

Keep your sentences consistent and clear by avoiding shifts in **person, number, tense, mood, voice,** and **subject.**

Shifts in person

Do not make illogical shifts between first **person** (*I, we*), second person (*you*), and third person (*he, she, it, they,* and all nouns):

FAULTY: If a person dresses well for a job interview, *you* stand a better chance of making a good impression. [Shift from third person, *a person,* to second, *you.*]

REVISED: If a person dresses well for a job interview, *he or she* stands a better chance of making a good impression.

REVISED: If you dress well for a job interview, *you* stand a better chance of making a good impression.

REVISED: People who dress well for a job interview stand a better chance of making a good impression.

Shifts in number

PRONOUNS.   Make sure your **pronouns** are the same **number** as their **antecedents.**

FAULTY: A person applying for a job can increase *their* chances of getting an interview if *they* have an impressive resumé. [shift from singular (*person*) to plural (*their, they*)]

REVISED TO SINGULAR: A person applying for a job can increase *his or her* chances of getting an interview if *he or she* has an impressive resumé.

REVISED TO PLURAL: People applying for a job can increase *their* chances of getting an interview if *they* have an impressive resumé.

MORE CONCISE REVISION: Job applicants can increase *their* chances of getting an interview if *they* have an impressive resumé.

See also **agreement of pronouns and antecedents.**

NOUNS. Nouns related contextually should be consistent in number.

FAULTY: With attention to details, college students can create a good *resumé.* [shift from plural (*students*) to singular (*resumé*)]

REVISED TO CONSISTENT PLURAL: With attention to details, college students can create good *resumés.*

Shifts in tense

Shifts in **tense** are often necessary for representing time accurately.

Students who *prepare* their resumés early in their college careers *will be able* to update them easily. [The italicized verbs accurately represent present and future time.]

But verbs that do not accurately represent time or that shift without reason may be confusing.

FAULTY: Your resumé *is* your promotional brochure, a digest of your job qualifications. It *will increase* your chances of getting a job and *tells* a potential employer who you are. [The use of the future and present tenses is inconsistent.]

REVISED: Your resumé *is* your promotional brochure, a digest of your job qualifications. It *increases* your chances of getting a job and *tells* a potential employer who you are. [All verbs are present tense.]

REVISED: Your resumé *is* your promotional brochure, a digest of your job qualifications. It *will increase* your chances of getting a job and *tell* a potential employer who you are. [Both verbs in the second sentence are future tense.]

WOULD. The **modal** *would* is commonly used to indicate willingness or customary action.

Potential employers *would* frequently meet with placement personnel about job opportunities.

Avoid shifting to *would* when past tense is more accurate.

FAULTY: The first time the personnel manager from Unitech Corporation *met* with the placement personnel, he *would* announce that he needed five engineers.

REVISED: The first time the personnel manager from Unitech Corporation *met* with the placement personnel, he *announced* that he needed five engineers.

Writing about another piece of writing. Be especially careful of shifts in tense when you are writing about other pieces of writing (such as stories, novels, essays, poetry) or films. Conventionally, use present tense verbs to describe what others have written, whether you are writing about what the author does in a work or about what characters within the story do. Verbs not describing the other piece of writing take whatever tense is appropriate.

The informational brochure from our college placement service *advises* students to carefully inventory their skills, responsibilities, and successes. Your placement service *may have prepared* a similar brochure.

Shifts in mood

Shifts in **mood** sometimes occur between **imperative** and **indicative** verbs.

FAULTY: When writing your resumé, *eliminate* extraneous information, and you *should have* only one page. [Sentence shifts from the imperative verb *eliminate* to the indicative *should have.*]

REVISED: When writing your resumé, *eliminate* extraneous information and *have* only one page. [Both verbs are in the imperative mood.]

Shifts in voice and subject

The **voice** used most commonly in English sentences is the *active* voice, in which the subject is the doer of the action of the verb.

On your resumé you *should* ordinarily *omit* references to your religion, political persuasion, and national origin. [The subject, *you*, does the omitting.]

In the *passive* voice, the doer of the action is expressed in a prepositional phrase or not at all.

References to your religion, political persuasion, and national origin *should* ordinarily *be omitted* on your resumé [by you]. [The subject, *references*, is not the doer of the action.]

Shifts between active and passive voice are sometimes useful for keeping **subjects** consistent. However, shifts to passive voice that also involve shifts in subjects may make reading difficult. In this sample passage and its revisions, the subjects are underlined and the verbs are italicized.

FAULTY: On your resumé, you *should* ordinarily *avoid* naming your religion, political persuasion, and national origin. Photographs also *should be omitted*, because you never *know* how employers *will react* to them. You *can* even *omit* references, although they *can be listed* on a separate sheet that you *take* with you to an interview. [The underlined subjects shift from you to photographs, you, employers, you, they, and you. The italicized verbs shift from active (*should avoid*) to passive (*should be omitted*), active (*know, will react, can omit*), passive (*can be listed*), and active (*take*).

REVISED: On your resumé, you *should* ordinarily *avoid* naming your religion, political persuasion, and national origin. You *should* also *omit* photographs, because you never *know* how employers *will react* to them. You *can* even *omit* references, although you *can list* them on a separate sheet that you *take* with you to an interview. [In this revision, the subjects are consistently *you*, and the verbs are consistently active voice.]

REVISED: On your resumé, naming your religion, political persuasion, and national origin *should* ordinarily *be avoided*. Photographs also *should be omitted*, because it *is* never *known* how employers *will react* to them. Even references *can be omitted*, although they *can be listed* on a separate sheet *to be taken* along to an interview. [In this revision, the sentence subjects are consistently items on the resumé, and the verbs (except *will react*) are consistently passive voice.]

As these two revisions illustrate, you can vary the focus and emphasis of your writing by your choice of subject.

INFINITIVES.   The subjects of **infinitives** are sometimes unclear because of shifts in voice.

FAULTY: References *can be listed* on a separate sheet *to take* with you to an interview. [After the passive verb *can be listed*, the implied subject of the active infinitive, *to take*, is not clear.]

REVISED: References *can be listed* on a separate sheet *to be taken* with you to an interview. [The passive infinitive is consistent with the passive verb.]

See also **mixed constructions.**

short story titles   (See **titles** and **quotation marks**)

should of Do not use *of* in place of *have* (as in *I should of called you*). See ***of, have.***

simile A simile is a figure of speech that compares two unlike things, usually with the stated *like* or *as:*

> For some children, *homework is like a snarling beast* that demands their quality time in the evening.

Like other figures of speech (**metaphor** and personification), similes are useful for describing things that are difficult to represent directly.

simple, simplistic *Simple* means "uncomplicated"; *simplistic* means "oversimplified" and "ignoring the complexities." *Simplistic* is a negative term, whereas *simple* is either positive or negative depending on the circumstances.

> The *simple* truth was that he had taken a *simplistic* view of the entire problem.

simple sentences A simple sentence consists of one **independent clause** that expresses a complete thought.

> Acetylsalicylic acid is just aspirin.
>
> Acetylsalicylic acid, known for a century to relieve aches and pains and now supposed to ward off heart attacks, is just everyday, over-the-counter, penny-a-pill aspirin. [one **subject,** *acid,* and one **verb,** *is,* with **modifiers**]
>
> Buy aspirin. [the **imperative** verb *buy* with the subject *you* understood]

See also **sentence types.**

since The most common use for *since* is to indicate time relationships.

> We've completely repainted the house *since* you left for school.

It also sometimes has the meaning "because," although the meaning may be ambiguous.

> *Since* you left for school, we've rented out your room. [This sentence could mean "because you left school" or "after you left school."]

As a result of the ambiguity, many writers avoid using *since* when they mean "because."

singular   **Nouns, pronouns,** and **verbs** may be singular or **plural.**

Nouns

A singular noun represents one person, place, or thing. The singular form of a noun is the one listed in the dictionary, for example, *book, article, text, disk, candy, motorcycle.* For singular possessive forms, see **apostrophes.**

Pronouns

The singular personal pronouns are *I, me, my, mine; you, your, yours; he, him, his; she, her, hers; it, its.* The singular forms of the compound personal pronouns are *myself, yourself, himself, herself,* and *itself.* Singular pronouns are used with singular **antecedents.** See **agreement of pronouns and antecedents.**

Verbs

A verb is singular whenever its **subject** is singular. First **person** and second person singular verbs do not have endings; third person singular verbs in present **tense** normally end in *-s.* Here are some examples of singular regular and irregular verbs:

SINGULAR PRESENT TENSE REGULAR VERBS		
FIRST PERSON	*SECOND PERSON*	*THIRD PERSON*
I wait	you wait	she waits
I answer	you answer	Charles answers
I wash	you wash	Brian washes
SINGULAR PRESENT TENSE IRREGULAR VERBS		
FIRST PERSON	*SECOND PERSON*	*THIRD PERSON*
I am	you are	he, she, it is
I have	you have	Roosevelt has
I do	you do	Felicia does

See **agreement of subjects and verbs.**

sit, set   (See *set, sit*)

slang   Slang is a style of language that is usually characteristic of given localities, age groups, and social or cultural groups. It is usually short-lived (do you know anyone who uses *flummox* anymore, or *hubba-hubba* or *snuffy?*), though some words pass into general usage (such as *jazz, jaywalk, Uncle Tom,* and *cram*). Slang is the spice of everyday language, but it is usually avoided in formal writing. What is a "real cool" term one day may be "old hat" the next. See also **colloquial, diction, jargon, nonstandard usage,** and **standard English.**

slash   To separate lines of poetry run in with your text, use the slash with one space before and one space after.

> Did Arthur Hugh Clough foresee twentieth-century values in his satirical comment "Thou shalt not steal; an empty feat, / When 'tis so lucrative to cheat"?

Use the slash (with no space before and after) to indicate options.

> This course is graded on a *pass/fail* basis.

> CAUTION: Many people object to the *his/her, he/she, s/he,* and *and/or* options because they are often stylistically clumsy and unnecessary.

some body, somebody; some one, someone   *Somebody* and *someone* are indefinite pronouns meaning "an unspecified person." *Some body* is a noun modified by an indefinite adjective, and *some one* is a pronoun modified by an indefinite adjective.

> *Somebody* told James that his argument needed *some body.*

> *Someone* left the door unlocked, and *some one* of us is responsible.

someplace, somewhere   *Someplace* is informal usage for *somewhere*, meaning "at some unspecified place."

> I know my book is *somewhere* (not *someplace*) in this room.

some time, sometime, sometimes   *Sometime* is an adverb that means "at an indefinite future time"; *sometimes* is an adverb that means "now and then"; *some time* is a noun plus an adjective and means "a span of time."

> I'll have the report finished *sometime.*

> *Sometimes* I wonder if I will ever get it finished.

> All I need is *some time* without interruptions.

sort of   (See ***kind of***)

specially   (See ***especially***)

specific words   (See **general words**)

⚠ spelling

> SECTION OVERVIEW
> Computer spell-checkers
> Attentive reading
> Spelling rules

Words ordinarily have only one acceptable spelling—the one found in most dictionaries. Writers observe these uniform spellings so that their readers are not distracted from the ideas expressed. This section treats several ways of achieving spelling correctness: computer spell-checkers, attentive reading, and spelling rules. See also **misspelled words, common** and **homonyms.**

Computer spell-checkers

A computer spell-checker checks documents for misspelled words, comparing every word with the words in its dictionary. It flags discrepancies, suggests possible alternative spellings, and allows you to make corrections. Spell-checkers are extremely useful, especially if you compensate for their shortcomings. One shortcoming is that the checkers will flag all **proper nouns, proper adjectives,** and other specialized words not included in their dictionaries, all of which you need to check yourself. More of a problem are the words the checker does not flag: **homonyms** and other words that may be spelled correctly but are not the words you meant to write: words such as *of* for *have, well* for *will, dose* for *does,* and *denied* for *derived.* Other problematic words are those that have several forms, such as pronouns and verbs. You might, for example, have written *your* when you meant *you, ask* instead of *asks, want* instead of *wanted,* or *lead* instead of *led.* As a consequence, even with a computer spell-checker you must proofread carefully—perhaps even more carefully than without it, because the remaining misspellings are difficult to locate. Instead of looking specifically for errors, you should probably read for meaning, giving close attention to each word and mark of punctuation but also making certain that you have used the words you intended.

Attentive reading

One of the most effective ways of improving your spelling is attentively reading the words of other writers, attempting to visualize the way each word looks. This method can be helpful for learning new words or those familiar words you habitually misspell. When you see a word you want to remember, stop reading for a few seconds and look closely at the entire word, visualizing it as a whole, and then focus on trouble spots. These may be the vowels in unaccented syllables, such as the first *e* in *implement* or the second *i* in *participate.* Sometimes the final syllables of words are troublesome, such as the *-sion* of *extension* and the *-ent* of *independent.* To aid your visualization, write the word once or twice, perhaps capitalizing or underlining the trouble spot (for example, *independENT*), and later read it again.

Spelling rules

Spelling rules describe the ways that letters go together to make up words. As aids to correct spelling, rules are variously effective, and too many of them are probably a hindrance. All the rules have some exceptions. Four of the most dependable rules are explained here: doubling a final consonant, using *ie* or *ei*, keeping or dropping a final *e*, and adding an ending to a final *y*.

DOUBLING A FINAL CONSONANT.   When adding a **suffix** such as *-ing* or *-ed* to a word that ends in a consonant, double the consonant if you need to keep the internal vowel short—for example, *hop, hopping; omit, omitted.* This rule applies when all three of the following conditions are true:

1. The word ends in a consonant preceded by a single vowel (*a, e, i, o, u*),
2. The word is one syllable or the accent is on the final syllable, and
3. The suffix begins with a vowel.

The following examples illustrate the rule (*qu* is the equivalent of a consonant):

stop	stopped	occur	occurrence
begin	beginning	win	winner
commit	committed	allot	allotted
equip	equipped	prefer	preferred
sad	sadder	rid	riddance

This rule does not apply for suffixes beginning with a consonant. Affix such suffixes directly to the word: *commit, commitment; sad, sadness.* A few words that end in a hard *c* take a *k* before an *-ed, -ing*, or *-y* ending—for example, *picnicking, panicky, trafficked.*

USING *IE* OR *EI*.   The familiar rhyme about using *ie* or *ei* is true most of the time—enough times to make it worth remembering: *i* before *e* except after *c* when the sound is long *e*. The following words follow the rule:

I BEFORE *E*

belief	grieve	priest
fiend	niece	reprieve
fierce	piece	siege

EXCEPT AFTER *C*

ceiling	deceit	receipt
conceited	perceive	receive

SOUND IS NOT LONG *E*

beige	freight	sleigh
eight	height	weight

Among the exceptions to the rule are *either, leisure, neither, species,* and *weird.*

KEEPING OR DROPPING A FINAL *E*.   To add an ending to a word that ends in a silent *e*, drop the *e* when the ending begins with a vowel.

DROP THE *E* BEFORE A VOWEL

believe + able = believable	move + able = movable
hope + ing = hoping	sure + est = surest
love + able = lovable	write + ing = writing

Keep the final *e* when the suffix begins with a consonant.

KEEP THE *E* BEFORE A CONSONANT

lone + ly = lonely	move + ment = movement
love + ly = lovely	agree + ment = agreement
sure + ly = surely	hate + ful = hateful

When the letter preceding the final *e* is *c* or *g*, the *e* is dropped only when the suffix begins with *e* or *i*.

AFTER *C* OR *G*, DROP THE *E* ONLY BEFORE *E* OR *I*

change + ing = changing	change + able = changeable
notice + ing = noticing	notice + able = noticeable
manage + er = manager	manage + ment = management

CHANGING A FINAL *Y*.   To add an ending to a word with a final *y* preceded by a consonant, change the *y* to *i* except when your ending is *-ing.*

FINAL *Y* PRECEDED BY A CONSONANT

apply + ed = applied	apply + ing = applying
busy + ness = business	study + ing = studying
easy + est = easiest	try + ing = trying

When the final *y* is preceded by a vowel (*a, e, i, o, u*), keep the final *y*.

FINAL *Y* PRECEDED BY A VOWEL

buy + s = buys	play + ful = playful
employ + ment = employment	stay + ed = stayed

split infinitives   An **infinitive** is termed *split* when its **verb** form is separated from its marker *to* with a word or a phrase: *to* clearly *define; to* forcefully *disagree; to* virtually and, without a doubt inexplicably, *see*. Split infinitives are often stylistically awkward, as illustrated by the third example in the preceding sentence (which could be revised to read *to see virtually and, without a doubt, inexplicably*). Single-word interruptions are preferable when the alternative would be more awkward.

> *To* finally *understand* the need for medical research on women's ailments, funding agencies must admit to different medical histories. [*Finally* would be awkward and unclear if placed somewhere else in the sentence.]

standard English   Standard English is the variety of English used by educated writers in schools, businesses, and professions. Standard English includes all words not labeled **nonstandard, slang,** or **colloquial** by your handbook or dictionary, by accurate punctuation and spelling, and by generally accepted grammar and usage. You find Standard English described and explained in handbooks and dictionaries. Sometimes called *edited English,* because most people do not achieve the "standard" without some effort at revision, Standard English is the variety of English that usually appears in printed material.

states and countries   (See **abbreviations** and **ZIP codes**)

subject complements   A subject complement is a **noun,** a **pronoun,** or an **adjective** in the **predicate** that completes the meaning of the **subject.** A noun or pronoun functioning as a subject complement renames the **subject,** and an adjective complement **modifies** or describes the subject.

A paramecium is a microscopic one-celled *animal.* [noun subject complement; *animal* renames *paramecium*]

The paramecium is *slipper-shaped.* [adjective subject complement; *slipper-shaped* describes *paramecium*]

Subject complements follow **linking verbs** (such as *be* [*is, am, are, was, were, being, been*], *seem, become, appear, grow, remain, look, feel, sound, taste,* and *smell*). Because noun and pronoun subject complements rename subjects, they are in the same **case** as the subject: nominative.

The committee members are *Aronson, you, and I.*

subjective case (See **case**)

subject of sentence The subject of a sentence names the thing that the **predicate,** or **verb,** makes an assertion about.

Honduras has been called a "banana republic."

The *term* describes the primary crop of Honduras.

A simple subject may be a word or a group of words that functions as a **noun.** The simple subject may be modified by other words to make up the complete subject. In the sentences below, a slash separates the complete subject from the predicate (the verb plus its **modifiers** and **complements**).

Hardly a one-crop country today, *Honduras* / still depends heavily on its banana exports. [*Hardly a one-crop country today* modifies the simple subject, *Honduras.*]

It / has diversified to include coffee, corn, sugar, cocoa, and tobacco as major crops. [The **pronoun** *it,* referring to *Honduras* in the preceding example, is the subject.]

A *majority* of banana plantations / are Honduran-owned today.

Being a banana republic / has many economic disadvantages. [The **gerund phrase** *Being a banana republic* is the subject.]

A subject is compound when it has two or more nouns or pronouns plus their modifiers.

Northeastern Honduras and *the east coast of Nicaragua* are called the "Mosquito Coast" after the Miskito Indians. [*Honduras and Nicaragua* is a compound subject.]

Whether a subject is **singular** or **plural,** the verb must agree with it (see **agreement of subjects and verbs**).

> **SINGULAR AND PLURAL SUBJECTS**
>
> *SINGULAR*
> *Honduras* is mountainous.
> The *north* has a Caribbean coast.
> The *Pacific Ocean* borders on the southwest.
>
> *PLURAL*
> *Hondurans* speak Spanish.
> The *plains* have sparse populations.
> Most *Hondurans* are Mestizos.

subjunctive mood   The subjunctive **mood** of **verbs** indicates conditions contrary to fact: wishes, recommendations, and possibilities. Subjunctive forms show up mostly with the verb *be.*

> If you *were* to examine the causes of violence in schools, you would find that drugs and gangs account for 18 percent of the incidents. [subjunctive verb *were*]
>
> The school board recommended that guns *be checked* at the school doors. [subjunctive verb *be checked*]
>
> God *be* with you.
>
> I move that the meeting *be adjourned.*

Compare the meanings of the *if* clauses in the following sentences, one in **indicative mood,** the other in subjunctive:

> INDICATIVE: If Sharon *was* in class, I didn't see her.
>
> SUBJUNCTIVE: If Sharon *were* in class, she could solve this problem.

See also **mood, indicative mood,** and **imperative mood.**

subordinate (dependent) clauses

> SECTION OVERVIEW
> Adverb clauses
> Adjective clauses
> Noun clauses

A subordinate **clause** is a subject-verb combination that cannot stand alone as a sentence but functions within a sentence as an **adverb,** an **adjective,** or a **noun.** Subordinate clauses are connected to **independent** (or main) **clauses** by subordinating **conjunctions** (such as *because, after, when, though, before*), **relative pronouns** (*who, which, that, whoever, whichever*), **relative adjectives** (*whose, whosever, which, that*), or **relative adverbs** (*where, why, when, how*). A sentence with an independent clause and a subordinate clause is a **complex sentence.**

Adverb clauses

Adverb clauses ordinarily **modify** verbs but sometimes modify adjectives or other adverbs. Adverb clauses begin with subordinating conjunctions and, like adverbs, indicate time, place, cause, manner, result, condition, concession, and comparison.

> **TIME:** *Before you have your next cup of coffee,* ask yourself if coffee is bad for you.
>
> **CAUSE:** *Because conditions differ so greatly from person to person,* the best answer is "It depends."
>
> **CONDITION:** *If you're wondering about the effects of caffeine on your health,* try going without it for a few weeks.
>
> **CONCESSION:** Caffeine in moderation may have no ill effects on you, *though overdosing may cause insomnia or nervousness.*
>
> **RESULT:** Caffeine withdrawal is so difficult *that few try it.* [The adverb clause modifies the adverb *so.*]

Adverb clauses are sometimes elliptical; that is, only part of the clause is expressed.

> **COMPARISON:** Tea ordinarily has less caffeine *than* coffee [*does*].
>
> **TIME:** Withdrawal from caffeine is difficult *when* [*it is*] *necessary.*

Adjective clauses

An adjective clause modifies a noun or pronoun and usually immediately follows the word it modifies. It is introduced by a relative pronoun, relative adjective, or relative adverb that stands for the word the clause modifies.

> People *who have ulcers* should avoid coffee. [The clause modifies *People,* and *who* stands for *People*: *people have ulcers.*]
>
> There are no conclusive studies *that recommend caffeine avoidance for everyone.* [The clause modifies *studies,* and *that* stands for *studies*: *studies recommend caffeine avoidance for everyone.*]
>
> Many people experience no harmful effects from ingesting caffeine, *which for them is only a mild stimulant.* [The clause modifies *caffeine,* and *which* stands for *caffeine*: *caffeine for them is only a mild stimulant.*]

See also **restrictive and nonrestrictive elements.**

Noun clauses

Whereas adverb and adjective clauses *modify* other sentence elements, a noun clause functions as a **subject, direct object, subject**

complement, as an **object** of **preposition,** or an **appositive** within another clause. It is therefore an integral part of the sentence.

> *Whoever has high serum cholesterol* should consider reducing caffeine intake. [The noun clause is the subject of *should consider.*]
>
> Studies have not concluded *that caffeine is harmful for everyone.* [The noun clause is the direct object of *have concluded.*]
>
> The benefits or harm of caffeine depends on *your overall health.* [The noun clause is the object of the preposition *on.*]

Noun clauses are introduced by conjunctions (such as *that, if,* and *whether*), relative pronouns (*who, whom, what, which, whoever, whatever, whichever*), relative adjectives (*whose, which, what*), and relative adverbs (*when, where, why, how*). When the conjunction *that* introduces the clause, it may be unexpressed.

> Some people actually think [*that*] *caffeine makes them sleep better.*

CAUTION: Do not omit *that* in noun clauses when doing so would cause misreading.

> FAULTY: These people feel *the benefits outweigh the disadvantages.* [Someone might read *benefits* as a direct object of *feel,* whereas the entire noun clause is the direct object.]
>
> REVISED: These people feel *that the benefits outweigh the disadvantages.*

subordinating conjunctions   (See **conjunctions**)

subordination   Subordination makes one grammatical element of a **sentence** dependent on another element. Single words, **phrases,** and **clauses** may be subordinated.

> The first communications satellite was NASA's Echo 1, *an inflatable sphere without instruments.* [**appositive** phrase]
>
> Later satellites, *starting with the Telstar satellites,* carried electronic equipment. [**participial phrase**]
>
> *Because they avoid the limitations from the curvature of the earth,* space satellites can amplify and rebroadcast signals back to earth. [**subordinate** (adverbial) **clause**]

Subordination is an effective stylistic device because it allows you to de-emphasize less important ideas. Observe how each sentence below is altered when part of it is subordinated:

UNEMPHATIC: The first synchronous-orbit satellite was launched in 1963, and it helped to bring about lower-cost transoceanic communications.

REVISED: The first synchronous-orbit satellite, *launched in 1963,* helped to bring about lower-cost transoceanic communications. [A less important element is subordinated.]

UNEMPHATIC: NASA led the way with its early satellite launchings; then several other countries developed their own satellite systems.

REVISED: *After NASA led the way with its early satellite launchings,* several other countries developed their own satellite systems. [One clause is subordinated, showing a sequential relationship.]

CAUTION: Be careful not to load your sentences with too much subordination.

OVERSUBORDINATED: Artificial satellites are launched into orbit around the earth by rockets, which take them to about 22,300 miles from the earth, where the satellites circle the earth once every 24 hours—the same time it takes the earth to rotate once on its axis—in a synchronous orbit.

REVISED: Artificial satellites are launched into orbit around the earth by rockets, which take them to about 22,300 miles from the earth. There the satellites circle the earth once every 24 hours—the same time it takes the earth to rotate once on its axis—in a synchronous orbit.

See also **sentence variety.**

subsequently   (See *consequently*)

such as   (See *as*)

suffixes   Suffixes are syllables added at the end of words to change the meaning and often the part of speech of the words: *magic + ian = magician*; *brother + hood = brotherhood*; *friend + ly = friendly.* See **spelling** on rules for adding suffixes.

superlative forms   (See **adjectives** and **adverbs**)

supposed to, used to   *Supposed* and *used* are past **participle** forms of **verbs** and therefore must end in -*d.*

Applicants for the position are *supposed to* participate in a group interview.

The company is *used to* having only the most qualified people apply for work.

sure, surely   *Sure*, an **adjective**, is sometimes used **colloquially** in place of the **adverbs** *surely* or *certainly*. In all but the most informal writing situations, use *surely* or *certainly* when an adverb is required.

INFORMAL: That is *sure* the best book I've read this year.

REVISED: That is *surely* the best book I've read this year.

REVISED: That is *certainly* the best book I've read this year.

syllables   (See **hyphenation**)

T

▼ **tag questions**   A tag **question** is a question added to the end of a sentence.

Spring came a little early this year, *didn't it?*

Kalvin doesn't want to attend the meeting, *does he?*

Tag questions are asked to verify information or simply to invite conversational response. They are seldom needed in formal writing. An affirmative sentence (such as the first example) takes a negative tag and assumes an affirmative answer: "Yes, spring did come early." A negative sentence (such as the second example) takes an affirmative tag and assumes a negative answer: "No, he doesn't seem to want to attend the meeting." Notice how **expletives** and **demonstrative pronouns** are used in the following questions:

That will be your decision, *won't it?* [*It* is used with *that*.]

Those aren't the only choices, *are they?* [*They* is used with *those*.]

There is a chance you could be wrong, *isn't there?* [*There* is used with *there*.]

take   (See **bring**)

▲ tenses of verbs

SECTION OVERVIEW
Summary of tenses
Uses of the present tense
Uses of the past perfect tense
Use of progressive forms
Sequence of tenses

Summary of tenses

Tense in **verbs** (from the Latin *tempus,* "time") refers to the ability of verbs to indicate the time of an action in relation to the time when the action is being described in speaking or writing. By changes in their forms, verbs can show *present, past,* and *future* time, as well as more complex time relations in the *perfect* tenses and the *progressive* forms. Observe how meaning changes as the verb tense *continue* changes in the following sentences:

PRESENT: Car theft *continues* to be a major problem.

PAST: Car theft *continued* to be a major problem.

FUTURE: Car theft *will continue* to be a major problem.

PRESENT PERFECT: Car theft *has continued* to be a major problem.

PAST PERFECT: Car theft *had continued* to be a major problem [before we increased our security measures].

FUTURE PERFECT: Car theft *will have continued* to be a major problem [before new legislation is enacted in the next century].

PRESENT PROGRESSIVE: Car theft *is continuing* to be a major problem.

To the base form of the regular verb *continue,* adding an *-s* shows present tense for third-person **singular;** adding *-ed* shows past tense and creates the past **participle,** a form combined with **helping verbs** to create the perfect tenses; and adding *-ing* makes the present participle, a form combined with helping verbs to create progressive forms. **Irregular verbs** are formed differently, as illustrated in the following chart (showing how verbs change form to show tense).

SUMMARY OF TENSES

	REGULAR VERBS	IRREGULAR VERBS
PRESENT	I (you, we, they) talk, she (he, it) talks	I (you, we, they) write, she (he, it) writes
PAST	I (you, we, they, she, he, it) talked	I (you, we, they, she, he, it) wrote
FUTURE	I (you, we, they, she, he, it) will talk	I (you, we, they, she, he, it) will write
PRESENT PERFECT	I (you, we, they) have talked she (he, it) has talked	I (you, we, they) have written she (he, it) has written
PAST PERFECT	I (you, we, they) had talked she (he, it) had talked	I (you, we, they) had written she (he, it) had written
FUTURE PERFECT	I (you, we, they, he, she, it) will have talked	I (you, we, they, she, he, it) will have written

PROGRESSIVE

PRESENT	I am talking, you (we, they) are talking she (he, it) is talking	I am writing, you (we, they) are writing she (he, it) is writing
PAST	I (she, he, it) was talking you (we, they) were talking	I (she, he, it) was writing you (we, they) were writing
FUTURE	I (you, we, they, she, he, it) will be talking	I (you, we, they, she, he, it) will be writing
PRESENT PERFECT	I (you, we, they) have been talking she (he, it) has been talking	I (you, we, they) have been writing she (he, it) has been writing
PAST PERFECT	I (you, we, they, she, he, it) had been talking	I (you, we, they, she, he, it) had been writing
FUTURE PERFECT	I (you, we, they, he, she, it) will have been talking	I (you, we, they, she, he, it) will have been writing

Uses of the present tense

The present tense has several uses in addition to representing current action.

Action occurring now: If your car is unlocked, it *is* at risk of being stolen.

Habitual or recurring action: Most car thefts *occur* with unlocked cars.

General truth: A vehicle theft *happens* in the United States every nineteen seconds.

Reference to published ideas or words, such as reports, works of literature, movies, poems: An FBI report *cites* special risk to late-model cars.

Fixed future time: The informational meeting *begins* at 7:30 this evening.

Uses of the past perfect tense

The past perfect tense indicates action completed before another past action.

The car was stolen because we *had forgotten* to lock it. [The action of forgetting occurred before the action of stealing.]

CAUTION: Avoid using the past perfect tense when simple past tense is appropriate.

FAULTY: The car *had disappeared* yesterday.

REVISED: The car *disappeared* yesterday.

Use of progressive forms

The progressive forms show continuing action. They consist of the *-ing* form of the verb plus a form of **be.**

Car thefts *are increasing* at an alarming rate.

CAUTION: Avoid overusing the progressive forms when the simple tense forms are appropriate.

WORDY: From 1985 to 1989, car thefts in the United States *were increasing* by 42 percent.

REVISED: From 1985 to 1989, car thefts in the United States *increased* by 42 percent.

Sequence of tenses

You can represent true time relationships by using the correct sequence of tenses. In sentences with more than one verb, the verbs do not always refer to the same time of action. The following chart summarizes some of the possible relationships.

SEQUENCE OF TENSES

INDEPENDENT CLAUSE	*SUBORDINATE CLAUSE*	*EXAMPLE*
Present tense	Present tense (same time action)	The report *says* that 80 percent of auto thefts *are* automobiles.
Present tense	Past tense (earlier action)	The report *says* that 1.63 million vehicles *were stolen* in 1990.
Present tense	Present perfect (action extending from past to present)	The FBI *reports* that most thefts *have occurred* in major cities.
Present tense	Future tense (action to come)	If you *have* a luxury car, you *will* more likely *experience* auto theft.
Past tense	Past tense (earlier action)	Automobile alarms *became* popular when New York *passed* a law requiring insurance discounts on cars with antitheft devices.
Past tense	Past perfect (earlier action)	The victim *knew* he *had left* his car unlocked.
Past tense	Present tense (general truth)	The victim *knew* also that locked cars *are* less likely to be stolen.
Present perfect or Past perfect tense	Past tense	Car alarm sales *have increased* since New York and other states *enacted* laws requiring insurance discounts on cars with such devices.
Future tense	Present tense (same time action)	Even if you *have* a car alarm, a new luxury car *will risk* being stolen.

Future tense	Past tense (earlier action)	Your car will be safer if you bought an alarm system disabling the starter.
Future tense	Present perfect tense (earlier future action)	If you *have locked* your car and *parked* it in a locked garage, it *will* most likely not *be stolen.*
Future perfect tense	Present	You *will have thwarted* a few car thieves if you *take* a few safety measures.
Future perfect tense	Present perfect tense	You *will have gained* a little peace of mind after you *have done* everything you can to prevent car theft.

Sentences using the **modal** *would* express wishes and other conditions contrary to fact.

> I *would like* to know what the assignment is.

> It *would be* better to know the worst.

When a condition contrary to fact is expressed in a **subordinate clause,** use past perfect tense in the subordinate clause and *would* in the **independent** (main) **clause.**

> If he *had known* then what he knows now about car theft, he *wouldn't have left* his car unlocked.

See also **verbs, shifts.**

than, then   *Than* is a subordinating **conjunction** used in comparisons; *then* is an **adverb** that indicates time or sequence.

> I would rather write an essay on political speeches *than* give one.

> First you decide how you will use a computer; only *then* do you begin shopping for one.

that, which   *That* introduces **restrictive** clauses; *which* most commonly introduces **nonrestrictive** clauses but sometimes also introduces restrictive clauses.

> Overeaters Anonymous is one of the many weight-loss groups *that* lend support to overeaters. [restrictive]

> Another respected support group is TOPS, *which* stresses positive reinforcement while its members "Take Off Pounds Sensibly." [nonrestrictive]

the   The indefinite **article,** used to precede a noun when the thing the noun represents is known to the reader.

their, there, they're   *Their* is a possessive **pronoun** signifying ownership or relationship, and *they're* is a **contraction** of *they are.*

> My groupmates decided that *they're* going to allow me to be *their* recorder.

There is an **adverb** signifying place or an **expletive** standing in place of a delayed subject.

> You can stack the extra chairs over *there.*

> *There* were no questions following the address. [The subject *questions* comes after the verb *were.*]

theirselves, themselves   *Theirselves* is **nonstandard** for *themselves.*

> The committee members congratulated *themselves* [not *theirselves*] on completing their work so early.

Themself is another nonstandard form that should not replace *themselves.* See also **reflexive pronouns.**

then   (See ***than***)

there   (See **expletives** and **their, there, they're**)

thirdly   (See ***firstly***)

till, until   *Till* and *until* can be used interchangeably to mean "before" or "up to the time of."

> We wouldn't leave *until* (or *till*) we knew she was all right.

time   (See **colons** and **numbers**)

titles   The title of a work is its name and as such has its first, last, and all main words capitalized.

> "The Trouble with Spot"
> Once upon a Rooftop

The titles of works should be set in **italics** (underlined) or **quotation marks.** Italics mark titles of published books, plays, magazines, newspapers, journals, long poems, films, television and radio programs, and musical works.

A Small Place (novel)

A Doll's House (play)

Newsweek (magazine)

Fresh Aire IV (album of music)

Quotation marks set off titles of shorter works, those published within larger, complete works, and unpublished pieces; examples are essays, short stories, articles in magazines and journals, chapters in books, episodes of radio and television programs, most poems, and short musical works.

"Barn Burning" (short story)

"Cultural Shock in Reverse" (essay)

"Nice Day for a Lynching" (poem)

"Sun Singer" (song)

CAUTION: The titles of your essays and other written works are marked by their placement in title position. Do not italicize (underline) them or enclose them in quotation marks.

to, too, two   *Two* is the word for the numeral 2; *too* means "also" or "more than enough."

Two people on this job are one *too* many.

To is a preposition having many meanings, among them "toward" and "as far as."

Leif Ericsson sailed *to* America five centuries ahead of Columbus.

To is also the marker for an **infinitive.**

Ericsson probably intended *to land* in Greenland.

toward, towards   Interchangeable words meaning "in the direction of."

We watched as the hot-air balloon glided *toward* (or *towards*) us.

transitional adverbs (conjunctive adverbs)   Transitional adverbs (sometimes called *conjunctive adverbs*) relate **clauses** or **phrases** to one another. Because they are **modifiers,** they cannot be used as

conjunctions to join **words, phrases,** or **subordinate clauses.** Common transitional adverbs serve a number of functions: they show addition, comparison, contrast, result; they introduce examples; and they indicate time sequence.

TRANSITIONAL ADVERBS

ADDITION	*CONTRAST*	*EXAMPLES*
in addition	however	for example
also	nevertheless	for instance
moreover	on the contrary	in fact
next	on the other hand	specifically
then	otherwise	*TIME*
finally	*RESULT*	meanwhile
COMPARISON	therefore	subsequently
likewise	consequently	finally
similarly	then	then
in comparison	as a result	next

Transitional adverbs are used most commonly to connect the ideas expressed in **independent clauses.**

> The ancient Greeks pretended to retreat from Troy; *however,* they left a gift of a wooden horse.

> The Trojans ignored warnings and took the horse into their city; *then* Greek warriors emerged and opened the city gates for the Greek army.

When a transitional adverb begins a second independent clause, it is preceded by a **semicolon.** Failure to practice this rule of punctuation results in a **comma splice** or a **fused sentence.** The transitional adverb is usually followed by a **comma,** although sometimes the comma is omitted.

 CAUTION: To avoid comma splices, distinguish between transitional adverbs and coordinating conjunctions *(and, but, or, nor, for, so, yet).* None of the coordinating conjunctions is longer than three letters, and all of the transitional adverbs are at least four letters long. Notice also that transitional adverbs, unlike conjunctions, can often function in several locations in their clauses. The transitional adverbs in the preceding examples could have appeared elsewhere in their clauses.

The ancient Greeks pretended to retreat from Troy; they left a gift of a wooden horse, however.

The Trojans ignored warnings and took the horse into their city; Greek warriors *then* emerged and opened the city gates for the Greek army.

transitive verbs   Verbs that take **objects**. (See **verbs**.)

try and, try to   *Try and* is a **colloquial** substitute for *try to.*

Try to (not *try and*) finish the work before Thursday.

two   (See ***to, too, two***)

type   (See ***kind***)

U

▼ **uncountable nouns**   **Nouns** representing things that normally cannot be counted, such as *information, literature,* and *sugar*. See **mass nouns (noncount nouns).**

underlining   (See **italics**)

uninterested   (See ***disinterested***)

unique   Because it is an absolute adjective, *unique* cannot logically be modified by **intensifiers** such as *very* and *quite.*

Corinne had a *unique* (not *very unique*) way of writing her C's.

until   (See ***till***)

upon   (See ***on***)

used to   (See ***supposed to***)

V

variety in sentences   (See **sentence variety**)

verbal phrases   A verbal **phrase** is a word group made up of a **verbal (infinitives, participles, gerunds)** and related **modifiers** and other words. It may be an **infinitive phrase,** a **gerund phrase,** or a **participial phrase.** As opposed to **verb phrases,** which are made up of main verbs and helping verbs and serve as predicates, a verbal phrase does not function as a verb. Instead, it functions as a **noun,** an **adjective,** or an **adverb.**

> *Founded in 1754 by grant of King George II,* Columbia University was first called King's College. [participial phrase as adjective modifying *Columbia University*]

> After *being closed during the American Revolution,* it was reopened as Columbia College in 1784. [gerund as noun, object of the **preposition** *after*]

> *To reflect the addition of graduate and professional schools,* the name Columbia University was adopted in 1896. [infinitive as adverb modifying the verb *was adopted*]

⚠ CAUTION: Do not write a verbal phrase as a **sentence;** the result would be a sentence **fragment:**

> **FAULTY:**   Columbia College and Barnard College remaining as undergraduate schools.

> **REVISED:**   Columbia College and Barnard College remained as undergraduate schools.

verbals   A verbal is a word formed from a verb but not functioning as a verb. It can be an **infinitive,** a **gerund,** or a **participle:**

VERB	INFINITIVE	VERBALS PRESENT PARTICIPLE AND GERUND	PAST PARTICIPLE
need	to need	needing	needed
go	to go	going	gone
get	to get	getting	got, gotten
be	to be	being	been

V–Z

Verbals function as **adjectives, nouns,** and **adverbs.**

> The *bargaining* unit would not agree to the compromise. [adjective]
>
> The *bargaining* continued long into the night. [noun as **subject**]
>
> It seemed that the executive board didn't want *to bargain.* [noun as direct **object**]
>
> Under those circumstances, it was hard *to bargain.* [adverb modifying *hard*]

▼   *Verbals as direct objects*

For the most part, use an infinitive for the hypothetical, unexperienced, or hoped for object.

> I hope *to graduate* in two more years.

In general, use a gerund for actual experiences.

> I enjoy *taking* courses in my major.

See **verbs** ("Verbs followed by infinitives and gerunds").

verb phrases   A verb phrase is a **verb** consisting of a main verb and **helping verbs:** *has been seen, should be going, does need, can have, was leading.* Unlike **verbal phrases,** verb phrases serve as **predicates.**

> About one million insect species *have been identified.*
>
> On a square yard of moist soil, you *could find* at least 500 types.

⚠ verbs

> SECTION OVERVIEW
> Form and meaning
> Unintentional shifts in verb forms
> Regular and irregular verbs
> Transitive, intransitive, and linking verbs
> Helping verbs
> Verbs followed by infinitives and gerunds

A verb is the part of a **sentence** that expresses action, occurrence, or state of being. With its **objects, modifiers,** and **complements,** it forms the **predicate. Subjects** and predicates together make sentences.

> The metric system *measures* meters and kilograms.
>
> A meter *is* a unit of length and a kilogram a unit of mass.

Form and meaning

By changes in form, verbs can express various meanings.

TIME OF THE ACTION

Present: Business *realizes* the need for metric.

Past: Business *realized* the need for metric.

Future: Business *will realize* the need for metric.

Present Perfect: Business *has realized* the need for metric.

Past Perfect: Business *had realized* the need for metric.

Future Perfect: Business *will have realized* the need for metric.

(See **tenses of verbs.**)

CONTINUING ACTION

Present Progressive: Business *is realizing* the need for metric.

Past Progressive: Business *was realizing* the need for metric.

Future Progressive: Business *will be realizing* the need for metric.

Present Perfect Progressive: Business *has been realizing* the need for metric.

Past Perfect Progressive: Business *had been realizing* the need for metric.

Future Perfect Progressive: Business *will have been realizing* the need for metric.

(See **tenses of verbs,** "Use of progressive forms.")

ATTITUDES AND INTENTIONS

Indicative: Change *is* inevitable.

Imperative: Make the change soon.

Subjunctive: If the change *were made* now, we could communicate better with other nations.

(See **mood, indicative mood, imperative mood, subjunctive mood.**)

RELATIONSHIP BETWEEN SUBJECT AND VERB

Active: The British Commonwealth *has set* a deadline for conversion.

Passive: A deadline for conversion *has been set* by the British Commonwealth.

(See **voice.**)

THE NUMBER OF THE SUBJECT

Singular: The labor union *thinks* the cost of conversion *is* too high.

Plural: Labor unions *think* the costs of conversion *are* too high.

(See **singular, plural,** and **agreement of subjects and verbs.**)

PERSON OF THE SUBJECT

First: I *worry* about the change. We *worry* about it too.

Second: You *worry* about the change.

Third: She *worries* about the change, and he *worries* about it too. They all *worry* about the change.

(See **person.**)

In the third-person singular, verbs in the present tense take an *-s* ending.

The new automobile *reports* kilometers per hour.

Nearly everyone *hates* to think of the inconvenience of change.

CAUTION: Do not omit needed endings.

Faulty: If she *ask* for an extension, the officer might grant it.

Revised: If she *asks* for an extension, the officer might grant it.

Faulty: If she *need* to miss the deadline, she should have made arrangements.

Revised: If she *needed* to miss the deadline, she should have made arrangements.

Unintentional shifts in verb forms

Avoid unintentional **shifts** in verb forms.

SHIFT IN TENSE

Faulty: Stephen Crane's *Maggie: A Girl of the Streets is* a remarkable novel that *gave* a realistic view of nineteenth-century life. [shift from present to past]

Revised: Stephen Crane's *Maggie: A Girl of the Streets is* a remarkable novel that *gives* a realistic view of nineteenth-century life.

SHIFT IN PROGRESSIVE FORM

Faulty: Houseplants *remove* toxic chemicals from the air. The plants *are managing* this cleanup with microbes in their soil. [Shift from present to present progressive]

Revised: Houseplants *remove* toxic chemicals from the air. The plants *manage* this cleanup with microbes in their soil.

SHIFT IN MOOD

Faulty: Buy houseplants like dracaena and bamboo palm, and you *should place* them in rooms where you have toxic substances. [shift from imperative to indicative]

Revised: Buy houseplants like dracaena and bamboo palm, and *place* them in rooms where you have toxic substances.

SHIFT IN VOICE

Faulty: As soon as you *finish* revising your paper, it *should be turned* in for a grade. [shift from active to passive]

Revised: As soon as you *finish* revising your paper, *turn* it in for a grade.

SHIFT IN NUMBER

Faulty: When a writer *needs* more information, they *go* to a source of that information. [shift from singular to plural]

Revised: When writers *need* more information, they *go* to a source of that information.

SHIFT IN PERSON

Faulty: I *was canoeing* down the Sauk River when, all of a sudden, you *were* able to see a doe and two half-grown fawns. [Shift from first person to second person.]

Revised: I *was canoeing* down the Sauk River when, all of a sudden, I *was* able to see a doe and two half-grown fawns.

(See also **shifts.**)

 CAUTION: Do not omit needed verbs. The result would be a type of sentence **fragment.**

Faulty: Sulfuric acid an extremely corrosive liquid.

Revised: Sulfuric acid *is* an extremely corrosive liquid.

Regular and irregular verbs

Verbs may be regular or **irregular.** Regular verbs form the past **tense** and the past **participle** with -*ed* added to the base word *(want, wanted);* irregular verbs change in different ways. The present participle of both regular and irregular verbs has -*ing* added to the base form *(want, wanting).*

		PRESENT	
BASE FORM	*PAST TENSE*	*PARTICIPLE*	*PAST PARTICIPLE*
amend	amended	amending	have amended
measure	measured	measuring	have measured
define	defined	defining	have defined
report	reported	reporting	have reported
relate	related	relating	have related
include	included	including	have included

EXAMPLES OF REGULAR VERBS

EXAMPLES OF IRREGULAR VERBS

		PRESENT	
BASE FORM	*PAST TENSE*	*PARTICIPLE*	*PAST PARTICIPLE*
be (is, am, are)	was, were	being	have been
come	came	coming	have come
do (does)	did	doing	have done
give	gave	giving	given
go	went	going	gone
lie	lay	lying	lain

See a more complete list of irregular verbs under the **irregular verbs** entry. Verbs may take **helping,** or auxiliary, verbs (such as *do, have, can,* and *will*) to indicate time, voice, and other meanings. As such, they may be called **verb phrases.**

Transitive, intransitive, and linking verbs

Some verbs take **objects,** and some do not. Those that take objects are called **transitive,** meaning that the action is carried from the subject to the object.

Automakers *have included* kilometers per hour on cars. [The object *kilometers* receives the action of the verb *have included.*]

Soft-drink makers *sell* their products in liters. [The object *products* receives the action of the verb *sell.*]

Verbs that do not take objects are intransitive.

Some changes *are creeping* in.

Very few government agencies *have converted* to metric.

Some intransitive verbs have a special, linking function, in which the nouns or adjectives that follow them rename or describe the subject. These are **linking verbs.**

The Department of Education *is* perhaps the greatest laggard. [The linking verb *is* connects the **subjective complement** noun *laggard* to the subject of the sentence *Department of Education.*]

Massive conversion *appears* not imminent. [The linking verb *appears* connects the subjective complement adjective *imminent* to the subject of the sentence *conversion.*]

To find out whether a verb is transitive or intransitive, consult a dictionary.

▼   *Helping verbs*

Use **helping verbs** with care. **Modals** have only one form: *can, could, may, might, must, shall, should, will, would.* The other helping verbs are forms of **be**, *do*, and *have* (which can also function as main verbs). *Be* and its forms *am, is, are, was, were, being,* and *been* have two uses as helping verbs:

WITH PRESENT PARTICIPLES TO FORM PROGRESSIVE TENSES
We *are wondering* when this paper is due.
We *were thinking* it was not due until Thursday.

WITH PAST PARTICIPLES TO FORM PASSIVE VOICE
The paper *was assigned* only yesterday.
The assignment *has been given* already.

Do and its forms *does, did, doing,* and *done* have three uses as helping verbs:

TO ASK QUESTIONS
Did you *attend* the meeting last night?

TO EXPRESS NEGATION
I *did* not *attend* the meeting.

TO EMPHASIZE THE VERB
But I *did attend* the meeting last week.

Have and its forms *has, had,* and *having* are used with past **participles** to form the perfect **tenses:**

I *have known* Liu for two years. [present perfect]
I *would have recognized* her anywhere. [present perfect with modal *would*]

▼   *Verbs followed by infinitives and gerunds*

A number of English verbs are likely to take **infinitives** as **objects;** others are often followed by **gerunds.**

INFINITIVE: Promise *to call* when you get home.
GERUND: Practice *writing* on the word processor.

VERBS LIKELY TO BE FOLLOWED BY INFINITIVES

agree	choose	get	mean	say
aim	consent	happen	neglect	start
appear	continue	have	offer	stop
arrange	dare	hesitate	ought	swear
ask	decide	hope	plan	threaten
attempt	deserve	hurry	prefer	try
be able	dislike	intend	prepare	use
beg	expect	leave	promise	wait
begin	fail	like	refuse	want
care	forget	love	remember	wish

VERBS LIKELY TO BE FOLLOWED BY GERUNDS

admit	consider	finish	practice	resist
advise	delay	imagine	quit	resume
appreciate	deny	mind	recall	risk
avoid	dislike	miss	report	suggest
can't help	enjoy	postpone	resent	tolerate

Use these lists as general guidelines, and be sensitive to exceptions. For example, you might say "I *stopped to see* her," meaning that you saw her; but you might also say "I *stopped seeing* her," meaning that you are no longer seeing her.

After verbs such as *do, help, feel, let, see, hear,* and *make,* the *to* of a following infinitive is often omitted.

Will you help us *write* our reports tomorrow?
Our instructor might let us *work* together.

verb tenses   (See **tenses of verbs**)

very   As an intensifier **adverb,** *very* is often unnecessary and may actually weaken the effect of the word it modifies.

WEAK: Candido was *very* excited about receiving the award.

REVISED: Candido was excited about receiving the award.

⚠ **voice (active or passive)**   The voice of a transitive **verb** indicates whether the subject is acting or being acted upon. In **active voice,** the subject does the acting; in **passive voice** the subject is acted upon.

ACTIVE: Earthquakes *have shaken* parts of California.

PASSIVE: Parts of California *have been shaken* by some of the quakes.

Because the grammatical subject of a passive sentence does not correspond to the the subject being acted upon by the verb, writers usually prefer active voice. Passive verbs are longer too, consisting of a form of *be* and the past **participle** of the verb: *is examined, was examined, has been examined, will have been examined.* One of the major objections to sentences with passive voice is that they do not state who performed the action of the verb.

Data concerning the earthquakes *have been examined.*

Reports *will be filed.*

Converting passive voice to active and active voice to passive

To convert passive voice to active, change the verb and make the subject the doer of the action. To convert active voice to passive, change the verb and make the direct object the subject; the active subject may go in a *by* phrase following the verb.

CONVERTING PASSIVE TO ACTIVE AND ACTIVE TO PASSIVE

RECEIVER OF ACTION	*PASSIVE VERB*	*DOER OF ACTION*
The city	was shaken	by the earthquake.

DOER OF ACTION	*ACTIVE VERB*	*DIRECT OBJECT*
The earthquake	shook	the city.

▼   **CAUTION:**   Avoid mixing active and passive constructions.

FAULTY: Scientists have been studied earthquakes. [The subject, *scientists,* is the doer of the action; the verb, *have been studied,* is passive.]

REVISED: Scientists *have studied* earthquakes. [active verb]

REVISED: *Earthquakes* have been studied by scientists. [subject as receiver of the action; passive voice]

Appropriate use of passive voice

Passive voice is useful especially when a writer does not want to name the person doing the action or does not know who that person is.

Hundreds of people *were injured.*

Some of the old theories about earthquakes *have been challenged.*

▼ CAUTION: Do not use intransitive **verbs** in passive constructions.

FAULTY: Hundreds of people *were died* in the earthquake.

REVISED: Hundreds of people *died* in the earthquake.

Intransitive verbs, such as *die, fall, happen,* and *occur,* can be used only in active voice.

W

---

way, ways   *Ways* is **colloquial** for *way.*

Yes, women have come a long *way* [not *ways*].

well   (See *good*)

when, where   (See **mixed constructions**)

which, who, that   *Which, who,* and *that* are relative pronouns. *Which* refers to things, not to people. *Who* refers to people. *That* refers to things or groups of people. In strictest usage, *which* is used only in **nonrestrictive** clauses, though many writers use it interchangeably with *that* in **restrictive** clauses. *Who* can be used in restrictive and nonrestrictive clauses.

Smooth muscle, *which* lines most hollow organs, is regulated by the autonomic nervous system. [nonrestrictive clause]

The smooth muscle *that* [or *which*] lines most hollow organs is regulated by the autonomic nervous system. [restrictive clause]

Fra Filippo Lippi, *who* painted with a graceful style, was a major Florentine painter of the Renaissance. [nonrestrictive clause]

A Florentine painter *who* was an important influence on northern Italian painters of the Renaissance was Fra Filippo Lippi. [restrictive clause]

who, whom   *Whom* is the objective form of the **relative pronoun** *who* and should be used when the relative pronoun serves as a direct **object,** an indirect object, or the object of a preposition.

To *whom* are you addressing the letter?

I am addressing it to my supervisor, the person [whom] I usually report to. [*Whom* is often omitted in sentences like this.]

who's, whose   *Who's* is a contraction of *who is* or *who has*. *Whose* is the possessive form of *who*.

Who's leading the workshop today?

Whose workshop are you going to attend?

will   (See **shall**)

word choice   (See **diction** and **connotation/denotation**)

word divisions   (See **hyphens**)

wordiness

> SECTION OVERVIEW
> Unintentional repetition
> Empty words and phrases
> Inflated sentence structure

Wordiness, the opposite of conciseness, means using more words than necessary to express meaning. Unintentional **repetition,** empty words and phrases, and inflated sentence structure may obscure the idea you want to express. Wordiness often results from a mistaken effort to extend the length of a piece of writing when what is needed instead is further development of the ideas.

Unintentional repetition

Avoid saying the same thing twice.

Many job-seekers ~~out in the job market~~ overlook the importance of a well-written cover letter.

A cover letter accompanies the resumé to emphasize ~~and draw attention to~~ the applicant's special skills and experiences.

Readers may be confused when the same word is used two different ways in a sentence.

> Regarding the letter, *it* is important that *it* has a neat appearance, with no typographical errors and smudges. [*It* serves as an **expletive** and as a **pronoun** referring to *letter.*]

> **REVISED:** The letter must have a neat appearance, with no typographical errors and smudges.

Empty words and phrases

You probably know people who fill up their sentences with phrases like *due to the fact that* when they mean *because* and *in the event that* when they mean *if.* Such phrases not only take up space; they also take up readers' time. And busy readers usually resent having to waste their time. Here is a sample of those stock empty phrases that can often be revised to a single word.

EMPTY WORDS AND PHRASES	
at the present time	now *or* today
at that point in time	then
at this point in time	now
due to the fact that	because
for the purpose of	for
form a consensus of opinion	agree
in order to	to
in the event that	if
in the final analysis	finally
until such time as	until

Inflated sentence structure

Readers may be bored or turned off by wordy, pretentious sentence structures that often consist of empty verbs combined with long nouns.

> **WORDY:** Your letter should *give an honest representation of* who you are and how you qualify for the job.

> **REVISION:** Your letter should *honestly represent* who you are and how you qualify for the job.

Whenever possible, avoid using empty verbs.

VERBS THAT CONTRIBUTE TO WORDINESS			
be	conduct	give	occur
concern	do	have	perform

Passive **voice** also contributes to wordiness; use active voice whenever possible.

WORDY: The potential employer's interest in you *should be stimulated* by your introductory paragraph.

REVISED: Your introductory paragraph *should stimulate* the potential employer's interest in you.

The **expletives** *there* and *it* often lead to wordy structures, especially when they are followed by a **restrictive** clause beginning with the **relative pronouns** *that, which,* or *who.* Though expletives are useful stylistic devices, their frequent use may make your writing dull.

WORDY: *There* are some people *who* think cover letters are unnecessary.

REVISED: Some people think cover letters are unnecessary.

WORDY: *It* is the cover letter *that* presents the resumé.

REVISED: The cover letter presents the resumé.

Another source of inflated sentence structure is the use of **clauses** when **phrases** will do.

WORDY: *If you do some research about the company,* you will have an edge over applicants who do not take the trouble.

REVISED: *Doing some research about the company* will give you an edge over applicants who do not take the trouble.

WORDY: Try to match your qualifications with *what the employer needs.*

REVISED: Try to match your qualifications with *the employer's needs.*

Reducing wordiness creates a more direct style that is more likely to keep your reader interested—especially if the shorter length encourages you to add details to amplify your meaning. (See also **diction, jargon,** and **redundancies.**)

word omissions   Be careful not to omit words that are necessary to make your sentences complete, clear, or logical. Watch for faulty compound constructions, faulty comparisons, and omitted necessary **articles.**

> FAULTY: Many people cannot and have never understood nutrition labels on packaged food. [The compound verb *can understood* is not grammatical.]
>
> REVISED: Many people cannot *understand* and have never understood nutrition labels on packaged food. [The correct verb form, *understand,* is added.]
>
> FAULTY: The information on the new labels is supposedly clearer than the old labels. [*Information* and *labels* cannot logically be compared.]
>
> REVISED: The information on the new labels is supposedly clearer than *the information on the old labels.* [The information on the new labels is compared to the information on the old labels.]
>
> FAULTY: Designations of serving size are more consistent. [The comparison begun with *more consistent* is incomplete.]
>
> REVISED: Designations of serving size are more consistent in the new labels. [The comparison is completed.]
>
> FAULTY: The meat industry fought against the new labeling harder than anyone. [Because the meat industry is compared to everyone who fought against the new labeling including itself, *anyone* is illogical.]
>
> REVISED: The meat industry fought against the new labeling harder than anyone *else.* [The meat industry is compared to all others who fought against the new labeling.]
>
> FAULTY: Many Americans do not know what a gram, ounce, and calorie are. [The article *a* cannot precede *ounce.*]
>
> REVISED: Many Americans do not know what a gram, *an* ounce, and *a* calorie are. [Each noun in the series is preceded by the appropriate article.]

See also **compound predicates.**

would of   Do not use *of* in place of *have.*

> I *would have* [not *would of*] been late.

(See *of, have.*)

Y
---

yet   (See **but, yet**)

your, you're   *Your* is the possessive form of *you*. *You're* is a **contraction** of *you are.*

Tell me about *your* trip to Colorado.

If I do, *you're* going to hear a long story.

yourself   (See **reflexive pronouns**)

Z

ZIP code   In addressing mail, always abbreviate the state name according to the Postal ZIP code, which calls for two capital letters and no periods.

ZIP CODE ABBREVIATIONS FOR STATES			
AK	Alaska	MA	Massachusetts
AL	Alabama	MD	Maryland
AR	Arkansas	ME	Maine
AZ	Arizona	MI	Michigan
CA	California	MN	Minnesota
CO	Colorado	MO	Missouri
CT	Connecticut	MS	Mississippi
DE	Delaware	MT	Montana
FL	Florida	NC	North Carolina
GA	Georgia	ND	North Dakota
HI	Hawaii	NE	Nebraska
IA	Iowa	NH	New Hampshire
ID	Idaho	NJ	New Jersey
IL	Illinois	NM	New Mexico
IN	Indiana	NV	Nevada
KS	Kansas	NY	New York
KY	Kentucky	OH	Ohio
LA	Louisiana	OK	Oklahoma

OR	Oregon	UT	Utah
PA	Pennsylvania	VA	Virginia
RI	Rhode Island	VT	Vermont
SC	South Carolina	WA	Washington
SD	South Dakota	WI	Wisconsin
TN	Tennessee	WV	West Virginia
TX	Texas	WY	Wyoming

To expedite the movement of mail, the U.S. Postal Service requests that addresses on envelopes be written entirely in capital letters with no punctuation.

CARL FREDRICKSON   MANAGER
ACME PAPER CORPORATION
2368 W 181ST STREET
CHICAGO IL 60643

PART THREE

Writing a
Research Paper

Writing a Research Paper

The Community of Scholars, *251*
Types of Research, *252*
Overview of the Research Process, *254*
The Rhetoric of Research Reports, *255*
Selecting and Narrowing the Topic, *258*
Phrasing Your Research Question(s) and Tentative Thesis, *260*
Developing Your Bibliography, *262*
Searching the Library, *264*
Taking Notes on Your Reading, *270*
Organizing Your Notes: Thesis and Outline, *275*
Drafting Your Paper, *277*
Documenting Your Sources, *280*
Revising Your Paper, *286*
Format of Your Final Draft, *289*
The End, *291*
Sample Student Research Papers (MLA and APA), *292*

Many students have written a research paper of some type by the time they get to college. It may have been a short paper using three or four sources of information, a report on published critiques of a novel, poem, or short story, or even a fairly long paper that was a culmination of several weeks or months of work. Yet those of you who have never written any kind of research (or term) paper are not at a disadvantage. For all students entering college, writing a college research paper is a challenge because expectations are different from those in high school or junior high. Whatever your past experience, your instructor and this chapter will guide you through the process of research and writing so that you can produce a significant piece of writing and gain the satisfaction of knowing that from your own hard work you have acquired and reported a body of knowledge that others may find interesting and informative.

The Community of Scholars

You are about to enter a community of scholars—people who ask questions and seek answers. In a way, research is something everyone is familiar with. If you want to buy a computer, for example, you ask questions: Which type will best suit my needs? How much can I afford to pay? What do the experts say about particular brands? And so on. Then you try to answer those questions by studying computer magazines, checking your bank account, browsing at computer stores and talking with salespersons, consulting a teacher of computer courses, and so on. On the basis of your research, you come to a decision—one that can be stated somewhat like a thesis: Considering my needs, my available funds, and the best advice I could get, I will buy XXX computer.

Scholars ask questions too: What do the critics say about the published writing of Barbara Kingsolver? How do the Democratic and Republican parties compare on racism issues over the past five years? What are the psychotherapeutic benefits of meditation? Then the scholars seek answers to their questions—sometimes in the library, sometimes by surveying groups of people, sometimes with scientific experiments. They do whatever is necessary to seek answers for their questions. Sometimes their questions go unanswered, whereupon they may ask new questions or drop the subject for a time—or forever. But for the most part, research questions can be answered given the right kind and the right amount of research.

After completing their research, scholars generally report their research. In other words, they write a research paper. In their paper they describe the problem, why it was important to find an answer, how they sought their answers, and what they learned. They usually summarize the results of their research and tell their readers what they learned from their experts, statistics, or hands-on experiments. They can state an answer to their question or admit that as yet they have discovered no answer. Some research ends in a persuasive document. Researchers who want to persuade an audience to see an issue the way they do will collect evidence that supports their position and then present that evidence in a documented paper that is essentially persuasive in purpose.

For people at colleges and universities, scholarship is our job. Whether we are students or teachers, neophytes or sophisticates, we engage in scholarship. We ask questions. We study what other scholars have written. We do our own observations or experiments. And by doing these things, we seek answers to our questions. Remember that the questions scholars ask are generally of their own making. Scholars are *interested* in their questions, and, like the consumer wanting to buy a computer, they are even excited about the process of finding answers. Their questions are related to their career field or other interests, and they have some tangible knowledge when they have completed their research.

In school, often your research topic is assigned, depending upon the course of study, while at other times you have an open choice of topic. Most commonly, however, you are given a choice of topics limited to the subject under study: In a World War II history class your topic is limited to the Second World War; in an anthropology class, it is limited to some aspect of the origin, development, and behavior of humanity. By searching a particular field, you develop a familiarity with the scholarship in that field: You learn who the scholars are, how to find your way around in the journals that publish their work, what the experts have said about the topic you are researching, and so on. If this field happens to be your major, you may be laying the groundwork for further work toward your career.

Types of Research

The preceding paragraphs imply that answers to research questions can be sought in a number of ways. These ways are often classified as being of two types: primary research and secondary research.

Primary research

Primary research is hands-on work, with no go-between to interpret information. Primary researchers locate and interpret their own information. Some of their methods include interviews, surveys, controlled experiments, observations, and study of original documents. They deal with *primary evidence:* interview transcripts, survey statistics, observation records, and published documents.

Secondary research

Secondary research uses the primary research conducted by other people. All the evidence produced by secondary research is termed *secondary evidence,* which may contain interpretations and be a limited selection of the information available to the researcher. When you engage in secondary research, you read the published reports of other researchers, found generally in scholarly journals and books. For example, a review of Carolyn Chute's *The Beans of Egypt, Maine* is secondary evidence; Chute's book itself is primary evidence. A chart showing the distribution of seat-belt wearers by age and sex is secondary evidence in the health care pamphlet it appears in; the source of the statistics in the chart—the researcher's report of a survey—is primary evidence.

Sometimes secondary research takes a third step away from primary evidence in the form of published condensations or reactions to published secondary research. Encyclopedias are almost always secondary evidence, often to the extended step of being summaries of other secondary research. They are generally most useful at the beginning of research, when the researcher wants to acquire an overview of the subject.

Library research, then, is often secondary research. Unless you are using original documents or conducting your own interviews or your own experiments, you are engaging in research that depends on the credibility, accuracy, and fairness of the authors of the works you are studying. Limiting yourself to one or two sources and failing to evaluate everything you read can therefore cause a decided slant, and perhaps even unintended untruth, in your paper. But secondary research, done well, has value. To justify the need for additional information, primary researchers often begin their firsthand studies by reporting on secondary research (sometimes called, in their reports, "reviews of related literature"). Reports of this type make available the responses of experts to primary and other secondary research; it collects, summarizes, compares, and otherwise digests the reported research on a given subject; it provides information that might not otherwise be accessible to nonprofessionals.

Whether your research is primary or secondary, or both, you can report useful information.

Overview of the Research Process

At first glance, the process of writing a research paper seems quite linear: first you select a topic, then you do your research, and finally you write the paper. In practice, however, much of the activity overlaps and even falls back on itself. Some people call the process recursive, to describe the falling back, recurring action. A better term might be *concursive,* meaning that several of the research activities may occur at the same time. For example, while you're reading and taking notes, you may also be formulating and revising a tentative thesis, jotting down a working outline, and even doing some preliminary drafting. One step is not necessarily completed before you begin another. While in the process of selecting a topic, you may spend a little time at the library, take a few notes, and write a tentative thesis. In the midst of reading and note taking, you may continue to search the library, revise your tentative thesis two or three times, perform a preliminary organization of notes, and even make a stab at a portion of the first draft. However, some parts of the process obviously must follow other parts: getting the assignment comes before researching and writing, and proofreading comes after the final copy has been typed or printed.

To avoid getting deeply entrenched in research you cannot conclude, do a preliminary library search to find out whether information is available. If your topic is not working out after you are already deep into your research, alter it somewhat so that you can utilize the work you have already completed. But do avoid changing your topic midway or near the end of the process (some teachers don't allow it anyway).

The remainder of Part Three guides you through the research process, and ends with a completed sample paper. First give the entire section a quick reading to see where the research process is leading you.

The Rhetoric of Research Reports

In Part One, "Writing an Essay," you can read about the rhetorical components of writing situations: the writer, the audience, the subject, and the purpose for writing. Research writing, where the purpose is often to inform or explain, usually emphasizes the subject, though sometimes, when the purpose is to persuade, it emphasizes the interests of the audience. When you get your assignment, hold off considering your subject and the narrowed topic you will write about, and first consider the entire rhetorical situation: what your role as writer and researcher is expected to be, who your primary audience will be, how much choice you have in topic selection, on what basis you are expected to make your topic choice and, finally, the purpose for the research.

Your role as writer

In a subject matter course such as anthropology or business ethics, you are usually expected to assume the role of a student in that field—a beginning anthropologist or a future corporate employee, for example. You are expected to find books and journal articles by recognized professionals in the field and to use them with confidence and comprehension, citing their work as required by the conventions of scholarship and, where appropriate, acknowledging an author's contributions to that field. Using the vocabulary characteristic of the field further boosts your credibility. In an English class devoted to writing, you are equally expected to be a serious student of whatever subject you or your teacher selects for your research. You must search out the applicable sources of information and use them knowledgeably.

The role of researcher may be an unfamiliar one for you, but it is not an impossible one. The research process itself assists you in assuming it. By reading numerous sources of information on a given subject, you become somewhat of an expert. Plan to read more than you can possibly include in your paper, knowing that the additional reading will improve the authority of your written voice. After a while, you will also find yourself able to use the vocabulary of your subject with ease, and you will learn which names keep coming up in references and which ones are most respected. You will develop a sense of what experts in that field consider common knowledge, and you will learn to evaluate what you read. When you write your research paper, you will be able to convey this newly established credibility. You will confidently state your own research question, use the vocabulary that is appropriate, and cite only those sources you need for answering your question.

Since the emphasis of a research paper is generally on the topic, and because the genre itself is usually more formal than the short essay, most teachers advise that writers avoid the first person *I* so that the focus remains on the subject. Other forms often avoided in research papers, and again because of the level of formality, are contractions. While words such as *can't* and *won't* are acceptable in most informal writing, they lower the level of formality expected for research papers and are best spelled out in their full form.

Your audience

Your assignment will tell you something about the expectations of your audience, who in most cases of college research writing is the teacher. It is important for you to understand (and accept) that teachers differ in their expectations. Because Professor James, your history teacher, wants you to leave two-inch margins on the left and the right and to number your pages on the bottom, you are not to assume that this format is right for all situations. Some teachers may want you to lead into every piece of borrowed information by naming its source; others will not notice whether you do or do not. In some disciplines, mainly the humanities, the format of the Modern Language Association (MLA) is followed; in others, mainly the social sciences, that of the American Psychological Association (APA); and in others, still other formats. In a matter as conventional as the research paper, it is extremely important for students to learn what the expectations are and to follow them. Expectations differ according to disciplines, schools, and individuals. Outside of school, expectations differ from corporation to corporation and from institution to institution. Learning to adapt in school will lead the way for getting along as an employee.

You also need to know how much your audience knows about your subject and how detailed you should be in your writing. Sometimes teachers want you to assume a public audience, one that has no previous knowledge of the subject. In that case, you would need to be thorough in your descriptions and background information and carefully define any specialized terms you use. At other times, the teacher is a knowledgeable audience who wants you to display what you have learned about the subject. In this case also, you must be thorough, giving details, background, and defined terms to show your understanding of them. Sometimes, however, the teacher may want you to assume an audience of like-minded scholars who know the terms and background and want to know what you have discovered that is new. You may not encounter this type of assignment until later in your college career, after you have studied for a while in your major.

Your subject

A research paper is something you have to live with for a sizable chunk of your academic life. So if you have any choice at all, choose a topic that interests you, something you won't tire of next week. Don't pick a subject just because it seems easy to research or because a friend is choosing it or because someone in your family owns some books on it. Choose a topic that you want to learn about—something that interests you personally or something that will get you started toward your career interests. "Selecting and Narrowing the Topic" (p. 258) gives you some guidance in topic selection.

Your purpose

Central to the rhetoric of the research paper is the purpose for researching and writing. Sometimes people want to *report* what has been written on a given subject; their reports are often called "reviews of literature" or, as part of a larger piece of research, "reviews of related literature." They briefly summarize each work, noting contributions to the subject and often comparing and relating works. Sometimes researchers document the research done in a particular field by preparing an annotated bibliography—a list of sources briefly summarized and described. Another kind of report is an account of the writer's primary research, which describes an experimental study, an observation, a survey, an interview, and so on. Such reports often include reviews of related literature.

Many research papers are written to *inform* readers about a subject. The researcher draws together what is known and available on the subject and puts it in a readable, coherent form. Research papers written for this purpose might have titles such as "Effects of Grades on

Motivation in Tenth Graders," "Thomas Jefferson's Views on Slavery," and "The Uses of Doppler Radar for Tracking Weather Patterns." Since the primary emphasis is on the subject, these papers are written with an objective, impersonal tone.

The major purpose of still other research papers is to *persuade* the audience to a particular action or opinion. By means of the information gleaned from the research, the writer hopes to effect some change in the audience—to persuade them to stop smoking, for example, or to become vegetarian. The tone of such papers is often apparently objective because of the wealth of facts reported, but close inspection may reveal loaded words and slanted information. Whether you are a reader or a writer of persuasive research papers, look for supportive evidence based on reasoning, facts, and statements from authorities in the field.

Selecting and Narrowing the Topic

You cannot do research, of course, unless you have something to research: your topic. Two major sources of topics are yourself and your library.

Exploring your own interests

If your assignment doesn't specify a topic for your research, you need to begin exploring your own interests. To bring them to the surface, begin perhaps by brainstorming, quickly jotting down whatever thoughts enter your mind, gradually narrowing topics and making your list more specific. Or think of a topic and ask *who, what, when, where, why,* and *how.* Don't overlook the assistance you can gain from talking about research possibilities: classmates, friends, and family members are often good sounding boards.

In making your selection, avoid subjects or issues that are overworked or that may involve you emotionally. Abortion, gun control, capital punishment, and the legal drinking age are a few topics that may be on your teacher's "avoid" list. These topics are difficult for writers to narrow without their getting involved in larger, emotional issues.

Exploring your library

You can also use your school library for finding a topic. Several of the library tools for locating material on given topics are also useful for suggesting subjects you might like to pursue. For subjects at the most general level, use your library's classification system for its central catalog. There are two major cataloging systems: the Dewey decimal classification system, based on numbers; and the Library of Congress system, based on a combination of letters and numbers. If your library uses the Dewey decimal system, you will find ten major subject headings.

000–099	General Works
100–199	Philosophy
200–299	Religion
300–399	Social Sciences
400–499	Language
500–599	Natural Sciences
600–699	Technology and Applied Sciences
700–799	Fine Arts
800–899	Literature
900–999	History and Geography

Each major heading in the Dewey system is subdivided into subject categories: under Natural Sciences it lists 530 for Physics, for example, and under Social Sciences it lists 340 for Law. Further subdivisions within subject categories are indicated by more specific numbers, such as 538.112 and 342.2384.

Many college and university libraries use the Library of Congress system, which divides subjects into twenty major groups.

A	General works
B	Philosophy, Psychology, and Religion
C	General History
D	Foreign History
E–F	American History
G	Geography and Anthropology
H	Social Sciences
J	Political Science
K	Law
L	Education
M	Music
N	Fine Arts
P	Language and Literature
Q	Science

R	Medicine
S	Agriculture
T	Technology
U	Military Science
V	Naval Science
Z	Bibliography and Library Science

These categories are further classified by combinations of letters and numbers: for example, PS3823. Once you have identified a major subject that interests you, you can begin browsing the subclassifications—on a classification list in your library, in your library's card catalog or online catalog (see descriptions under "Searching the Library"), on the books on the shelves, or on your library's shelf list, which names all the books in your library by subject classification.

Another useful tool for discovering research topics is the *Library of Congress Subject Headings,* a guide to the headings used by the Library of Congress for classifying books. Still other useful sources are the *Readers' Guide to Periodical Literature* and other periodicals indexes (see the list at "Periodicals"). Again, scan subject listings until something sounds interesting to you.

Once you have decided on a general subject, you can use some of the same tools for narrowing your subject to a manageable size as those you used for discovering your topic in the first place: a prewriting technique, the subject headings in your library's classification system, or your library's card catalog or online catalog and periodicals indexes. If you are considering the broad subject of space stations, for example, by looking in the *Readers' Guide* you can find such subheadings as "equipment" and "industrial use," plus a cross-reference to "space colonies." At this point, you may decide that space colonization is what you are really interested in learning more about, so you shift your focus to the narrower subject. With a preliminary search of this kind, you also get a sense of the amount of published material on your subject. If there are a great many sources, your subject is probably too broad; if you are finding very few, you may have to broaden your subject or shift to a related topic.

Phrasing Your Research Question(s) and Tentative Thesis

As you narrow your topic, begin asking questions you want to answer and that can lead to a focus for your research. If you ask questions about subjects that genuinely interest you, the search for answers will not be tedious. Your preliminary search will present questions, but it will also answer questions. Those that are answered readily are not subjects for research. Continue asking questions suggested by your early reading and for which you can supply only tentative answers. Such questions might include

Is pornography "natural"?
What is the danger of toxic wastes?
How do children acquire values?
Will Social Security be there when I need it?

Such questions have no ready answers but promise answers that might come with further reading and searching.

At this point, try adding encyclopedias to your research tools. While these sources of information are not always acceptable as references in a research paper, they can be extremely useful for providing background information at the beginning of the project. They can tell you what is generally known about a subject, what is not known, what its history is, who its leading figures are, and so on. Encyclopedia articles also usually include bibliographies of sources for further reading. Among the most respected general encyclopedias are

Collier's Encyclopedia
Columbia Encyclopedia
Encyclopedia Americana
The New Encyclopaedia Britannica
The World Book Encyclopedia

From your research questions, formulate a tentative thesis that will lend further focus. A thesis (see "Developing Your Bibliography") states the subject, makes an assertion about the subject, and implies the purpose for writing. The following thesis sentences promise informative papers:

Psychotherapeutic meditation reduces anxiety and neuroses.

The nuclear accident at Chernobyl resulted from incompetence.

These more likely presage persuasive papers:

A national health insurance program that covers everyone would provide better medical care for all citizens.

Hopelessly ill people should have the right to decide whether to live or die.

Both kinds of thesis sentences state the subject and make a point. The way they are phrased indicates whether the writer's purpose is to use reasoning, facts, and authority to *inform* the reader or to *persuade* the reader to new actions or opinions. However, some writers disguise a persuasive purpose under an informative thesis and use information to attempt persuasion. To sharpen your sense of the differences between informative and persuasive purposes, examine the following thesis sentences:

> A controlled diet can reduce the risk of heart attack. [informative]
>
> Left-handed people are an oppressed minority. [persuasive]
>
> Single-sex schools should be permitted to exist because they are beneficial to the students they serve. [persuasive]
>
> "Killer" bees are not as dangerous as is sometimes thought. [informative]
>
> Gambling among teenagers is an epidemic of staggering proportions. [informative or persuasive]

Developing Your Bibliography

One of the keys to competent research is a well-developed working bibliography. A working bibliography, compiled at the beginning of your research and built upon throughout the research process, is a compilation of sources where you are likely to find information on your narrowed topic. The items for your bibliography may come from a number of sources: periodicals indexes, your library's central catalog, computer searches, and so on. Additional valuable sources are all the articles and books you read, because very often their authors provide bibliographies for further reading. Usually these sources are valued by the experts in the field and are gold mines for new researchers.

Many experienced researchers recommend keeping the working bibliography on 3-by-5-inch index cards, one source to each card. Cards allow you flexibility when sorting. For example, after you have compiled them in random order as you discover sources, you can sort them by call number for ease in locating the items in the library, sort them again to set aside those references you have not yet located, again according to your order for using them as you write, and yet again alphabetically for writing your list of works cited, setting aside those you did not actually use in your paper. Throughout your research, you can easily add cards with additional sources and notes. In addition to sorting flexibility, the size of your cards makes them easy to carry in

Call number

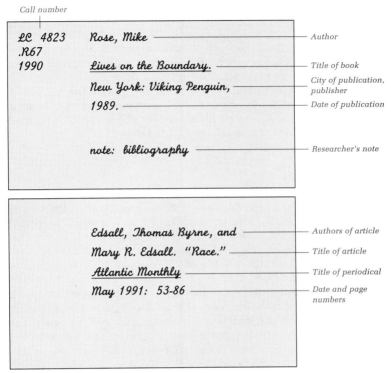

LC 4823   *Rose, Mike* ———————————— Author
.R67
1990   *Lives on the Boundary.* ————————— Title of book
             New York: Viking Penguin, ————— City of publication, publisher
             1989. ———————————————— Date of publication

             note: bibliography ——————————— Researcher's note

             Edsall, Thomas Byrne, and ————— Authors of article
             Mary R. Edsall. "Race." ———————— Title of article
             Atlantic Monthly —————————————— Title of periodical
             May 1991: 53-86 ———————————————— Date and page numbers

FIGURE 3-1   Sample Working Bibliography Cards

your pocket and set down in the library while you are looking for an item.

Figure 3-1 shows sample working bibliography cards for a book and for a journal article. The cards list all the information that will be needed for compiling the list of works cited: author, title, and publishing facts. In addition, they identify the call numbers for ease in locating the items, and the book card has a note reminding the researcher that the book includes a bibliography. It is important that you make these cards accurate and complete; otherwise you may need to locate the item again during the late stages of preparing your paper. (For more details on what information to include on your cards, see "Documenting Your Sources.")

Searching the Library

Your school library will probably be your primary source of information for answering your research questions and supporting your thesis. To complete your research successfully, you should be familiar with the reference room, the library's system for using periodicals, and the central catalog of books. If you need help in using any of the library's tools, ask a librarian. Reference librarians have been specially trained to assist library users in researching a wide range of subjects.

The reference collection

A good place to begin your research is the reference room, the area of your library set aside for reference works. There you will find dictionaries, encyclopedias, periodicals, indexes, biographies, yearbooks, atlases, and gazetteers. It would be worth your while to browse the collection to discover the wealth of sources available to you. The works, you will find, are arranged according to your library's classification system, whether Dewey or Library of Congress (see "Exploring Your Library"). The reference room offers advantages to the beginning college researcher. First, you become acquainted with an important part of your library, including the reference librarian and the collected and stored information. Second, the reference works you find in this part of the library, encyclopedias in particular, can give you a helpful overview of your subject and, often, further sources of information.

Some of the major general encyclopedias have already been named. Here are a number of other general reference tools widely used and covering a variety of subjects:

> *Current Biography*
> *Dictionary of American Biography*
> *Information Please Almanac*
> *Oxford English Dictionary*
> *National Atlas of the United States of America*
> *Statistical Abstract of the United States*
> *Webster's Third New International Dictionary of the English*
>   *Language*
> *Who's Who in America*
> *World Almanac and Book of Facts*

In addition, most encyclopedias publish annuals that review the events of the preceding year.

Beyond general works, each reference collection also has specialized works for major fields of study. For example, there are encyclopedias for art, astronomy, biological sciences, chemistry, computer science, dance, earth sciences, economics, education, film, history, law, literature, mathematics, medicine, music, philosophy, physics, psychology, religion, and social sciences. Most of these fields also have specialized dictionaries. By using specialized reference works you can begin to acquire knowledge of the field, its major issues, and the vocabulary common to its practitioners.

Periodicals

The core of your research will probably be articles in periodicals. If you read articles published in scholarly journals respected in the field you have chosen to research, you will be consulting the experts in that field. Scholars doing primary research publish their findings first in journals, later in books. Because of the longer publishing process, the information in books usually lags at least two years behind the information found in journal articles. It is therefore imperative that you become acquainted with your library's periodicals system.

Articles in periodicals (publications issued at intervals, including magazines, scholarly journals, and newspapers) are listed in indexes. The most common general index is the *Readers' Guide to Periodical Literature,* which lists over 170 periodicals, mostly popular magazines such as *Reader's Digest* and *Sports Illustrated.* Such magazines have limited use in scholarly research, because, among other reasons, their authors rarely cite their sources, though some of the magazines listed in the *Readers' Guide* can be used with confidence, such as *Scientific American,* the *Atlantic,* and the *New York Review of Books.* If you have a question about the respectability of any publication, consult your teacher.

Yet the *Readers' Guide* is a good place to begin your periodicals search. First, it leads you to information written for the general public—information that will be easy for you to read and understand while you are still getting acquainted with your subject. Remember that everything you read does not need to be cited in your paper. A second advantage of the *Readers' Guide* is that most specialized indexes follow the same format, so familiarity with one index will aid you in using another. The following example of an entry from the *Business Periodicals Index,* arranged much like the *Readers' Guide,* can help you use an index appropriate to the subject you are researching.

As Figure 3-2 illustrates, indexes are arranged by subject (shown in bold type at the left margins). Broad subjects often have subdivisions, here indicated by centered bold type, and further subsubdivisions,

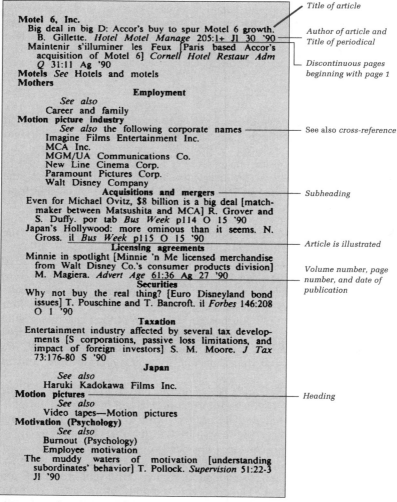

FIGURE 3-2   Excerpt from *Business Periodicals Index* (Vol. 33, No. 4, p. 225. Copyright © 1990 by the H. W. Wilson Company. Material reproduced with permission of the publisher.)

marked by centered italic type. Each entry gives the title of the article, the author, the title of the periodical, its volume number, the page numbers of the article, and the date. Other features of the article such as illustrations and bibliographies are noted. You also find cross-references to other locations of the information you are looking for, introduced by *See,* and to related entries, by *See also.* At the front of the index there are lists of abbreviations and the journal titles they stand for, so if you do not know what *J Mark Res* means, you can find it listed there as *Journal of Marketing Research.* You may also be interested to find in the list of periodicals indexed that this journal is a publication of the American Marketing Association, located in Chicago.

Most major subject areas have specialized periodicals indexes. Some examples are *Art Index, Education Index, Humanities Index,* and *General Science Index.* In many fields, there are also journal abstracts: serially published summaries of journal articles. Many libraries have reference sheets listing the indexes available for various subjects.

When using a periodicals index, first locate appropriate subject headings by using an older bound volume, because it has more numerous headings than the more current paperbound issues. Use the *See also* cross-references to locate other related subject headings that suit your search. Look also at subheadings for narrower, perhaps more suitable, listings. Then list each relevant article on an index card, beginning with the most recently published articles and working backward as far as appropriate for your topic, copying all the information that appears in that entry (see "Developing Your Bibliography").

Another source of information, particularly for historical or current events, is newspaper indexes. Your library probably carries several newspapers that are respected for their news coverage and editorial commentaries: probably the *New York Times,* the *Wall Street Journal,* the *Christian Science Monitor,* and the *Los Angeles Times.* Your library's copies of the newspapers are undoubtedly on microform: usually microfilm (long rolls of film negatives) and microfiche (cards that contain many pages in reduced form). Both microfilm and microfiche require the use of reading machines; if you are using them for the first time, ask your librarian for assistance.

To locate the articles you've found listings for, copy down all the information for each listing; then use your library's serial holdings list to find out which periodicals you'll be able to find, where they are located, and in what form. Many periodicals are bound and shelved like books, several issues or a whole volume together under a hard cover. Current issues are shelved in a current periodicals section; still other periodicals may be available only in microform.

The central catalog

All the books shelved in your school library are listed in the central catalog; also included are nonprint items such as videotapes and sound recordings. At one time, all library catalogs listed books on 3-by-5-inch cards shelved in drawer after drawer and referred to as the "card catalog." Card catalogs list items in three ways: by author, by title, and by subject. Some libraries divide the three lists into two catalogs: author-title and subject.

Figure 3-3 shows a card from a subject catalog. The top line of the card names the subject; it is one of the subjects listed near the bottom of the card. (A title card would have the title on the top line, and an author card would begin with the author line.) This card is from a library that uses the Library of Congress classification system (see "Exploring Your Library"), and the QP call number indicates that the book is shelved in the area of the library designated for physiology. In addition to the full title and the name of the publisher, the card gives the date of publication (allowing you to question whether the information is too old for your purpose), and other descriptive data.

Many libraries have replaced their card catalogs with online catalogs. Instead of drawers and cabinets, these libraries have computer terminals that give library users access to listings of all their holdings. To locate items by author, title, and subject, follow the instructions beside the terminal. Entering the "subject" command and a short subject heading, you would receive a listing of all the library's holdings on that subject (or as many as can be held on a screen; another

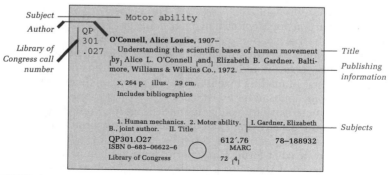

FIGURE 3-3   Sample of a Catalog Card (Courtesy of the Library of Congress)

```
Screen 001 of 001  Record 0021 of 0024 SCS                    Catalog SCS
LOCATION:    BF21 .W56
AUTHOR:      Wolman, Benjamin B        ed.
TITLE:       Scientific psychology; principles and approaches. Ernest Nagel:
             consulting ed.
PUBLISHER:   New York, Basic Books [c.1965]
DESCRIPTN:   xv, 620 p. 25 cm.
BIBLIOG:     Includes bibliographical references.
SUBJECT:     Psychology--Addresses, essays, lectures.
----Type  DS  to Display availability Status  /  RE  to Recall index
SCS=)PRINT ON
PRINTER ON?
SCS=)DS
BAR-CODE-ID      AREA/FLOOR      COPY  DUE--DATE-TIME   HOLDS  RESERVE-ID
30102000073153   CIRC-4th        01   *ON SHELVES       000
30102000073161   CIRC-4th        02   *ON SHELVES       000
SCS=)PRINT OFF
```

FIGURE 3-4   Online Catalog Entry

command would bring up the next screen). When you select a particular title, the screen displays the same information that appears on a 3-by-5-inch catalog card, including the call number. Entering another command, you can learn the status of the book—whether it is on the shelves, checked out, on reserve, and so on. In addition, terminals equipped with printers can give you a printout of the entries you have called up on the screen. If your library has an online system, you need to learn how to use it. It is not difficult, and using it can be much quicker than searching through a card catalog. Figure 3-4 shows an example of an online system's printout describing a book and its availability status.

Government publications

Another useful source of information is government documents and publications, though in using them you should remember that they represent an official point of view. Probably the biggest problem with government publications is their massive number. You can avoid some of the frustration of trying to locate the right document by using the *Monthly Catalog of United States Government Publications* (published monthly by the Government Printing Office) and *Public Affairs Information Service Bulletin* (published semimonthly). If your library does not carry the publications that interest you, you can order them from the Superintendent of Documents, G.P.O., Washington, DC 20402, at nominal cost or free of charge.

Computer searches

Your library probably has two kinds of computer searches: CD-ROM and online. With *CD-ROM,* your library has the database on compact disk (CD) and probably will not charge you for accessing it. Common CD-ROM databases are *Periodicals Abstracts,* indexing 450 popular and scholarly journals from the United States, Canada, and England in all subject areas; *Government Publications Index,* indexing the *Monthly Catalog of United States Government Publications; General Periodicals Index,* indexing 1100 magazines and journals; and ERIC (Education Resources Information Center), the largest education database. There are many more; find out what is available at your library.

Online searches access huge databases at a central location; the database does not reside at your library; rather your library is connected to the database through a few special terminals. Usually you need to work with a librarian to determine appropriate search terms. There is usually a charge, depending on the length of the search, but the cost is well worth it: you gain access to millions of items, from which the program culls a listing of relevant titles based on your combination of search terms.

Taking Notes on Your Reading

The notes you take while reading will be your source of information as you write your research paper, so make them accurate and thorough. Actively read for answers to your research questions, making notes on relevant material, perhaps providing definitions of key terms, examples of important concepts or events, analogies to things your reader may be familiar with, apt quotations from respected authorities on the subject, an account of how a plan would work, and so on. These are the same types of information you use for writing shorter papers; the difference is that in your research paper some of the information comes from other people.

Index cards

Index cards are useful for note taking for the same reason they are handy for compiling your working bibliography: flexibility. Cards bearing single ideas can be collected and classified by key word and type of note as you do your research, held together in a packet or with a rubber band, and thus easily transported. When you begin organizing your paper, you can arrange your cards according to your outline. Drafting, then, becomes an orderly process of turning over note cards as you use them instead of tearing through a notebook trying to find the appropriate note.

Some students, rather than using 3-by-5-inch cards, find the 4-by-6-inch preferable, because there is more space for each note. Some students like to use several colors of cards: organizing their notes with a different color for each type of note (quotation, summary, and so on) or for each key-word heading (explained below). Some researchers like the flexibility and convenience of a 4-by-6-inch notepad, the advantage being that the pages hold together during note taking and can be separated later for sorting and organizing.

To simplify sorting later, put only one item of information on each card, and in a top corner label the card with a key-word heading signifying its content, as illustrated in Figure 3-5. In the other upper corner write the author's name, to correspond to the bibliography card, and the page number. If you have more than one item by an author, number the items—*Rose 1, Rose 2,* and so forth—and mark the bibliography cards with the same numbers. To avoid last-minute trips back to the library, be sure you include the page numbers for all notes containing ideas other than your own; you will need to cite page numbers for the information you use in your paper.

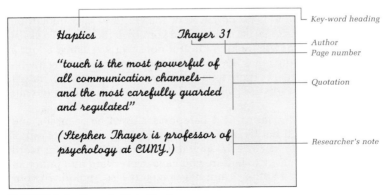

FIGURE 3-5   Sample Note Card

Other note-taking systems

Some articles or sections of books will be so important for writing your paper that you may want more than your notes on their content. In that case, make a *photocopy* so you will have the entire text on hand. Then you can make notes in the margins and highlight particularly relevant sections. As useful as photocopies are, do not consider them alternatives for note cards. Cross-reference them to cards on which you write a heading, the author's name, and observations on how you will use the material. Be sure to reference the photocopied article to a bibliography card.

For books that you plan to use heavily, you can use *self-sticking note sheets* to mark relevant pages. As with photocopied articles, reference your note sheets to corresponding note cards and bibliography cards. Since the pages you mark are likely to cover more than one aspect of your topic, you may well have several note cards for one book page or chapter, each with separate headings.

More and more researchers are using *computers* for recording their notes. To avoid a disarray of notes like those taken randomly on notebook paper, pattern your computer notes after note cards, one note to a page, referenced by a key-word heading, author, and page number. You can print your notes one to a page and arrange them manually as you would note cards. When the time comes to draft your paper, you can move the blocks of notes into a determined order on-screen.

Quotation, paraphrase, and summary

The notes you take will no doubt be of four kinds: exact quotation, paraphrase of the original, summary, and your own thoughts. To assist yourself later in knowing which kind of note you are using, adopt a system for classifying notes that makes sense to you. Enclosing quotations in quotation marks is obvious, and for your own notes you might use brackets; then everything else would be the author's ideas in your words.

Quotations, summaries, and paraphrases must be accurate, and you must be careful not to alter meaning by taking statements out of context. Be sure to enclose in **quotation marks** all word-for-word notes, and double-check to be sure you have every word and punctuation mark right. If an author is quoting someone else, include in your note the name of the person being quoted. When the quotation continues onto a second page of your source, mark on your note where the page break occurs in case you do not use the entire quotation in your paper. While you may wish to record many of your notes as direct quotations, the ideas of other people will fit into your paper better if you write them in your own words.

Rather than relying on direct quotations, learn to paraphrase and summarize material you are reading. A *paraphrase* is a restatement in approximately the same number of words as the original, whereas a *summary* is a shortened version of the original, written in the summarizer's own words. After writing a paraphrase or a summary, review what you have written to be sure it accurately reflects the original—that you have not altered the meaning by your word choice or selection of details.

When you write paraphrases, be careful to use your own words and phrases, not just a rearrangement of the original. Illustrated below is a faulty paraphrase, followed by a better one.

ORIGINAL: Scientific revolutions are forced upon us by the discovery of phenomena that are not comprehensible in terms of the old theories. —Gary Zukav, *The Dancing Wu Li Masters;* New York: Bantam, 1979, p. 192

FAULTY PARAPHRASE: Scientific revolutions, says Gary Zukav, are forced upon us when we discover phenomena that we cannot comprehend in terms of the old theories.

BETTER PARAPHRASE: In *The Dancing Wu Li Masters*, a book about physics for the unscientific person, Gary Zukav observes that revolutions in science occur when old theories can no longer explain new knowledge (192).

The first paraphrase is just a reworking of the original, using much of the same language, and it does not adequately cite the source (see "Documenting Your Sources"). In contrast, the second paraphrase gives evidence that another mind has worked on the sentence and then restated it. It also correctly cites the source, which would also be named in a list of works cited at the end of the paper.

Sometimes, when you are paraphrasing, it is necessary to use particularly apt or technical words exactly as they are used in the original. In that case, enclose the quoted words in **quotation marks.**

In *The Dancing Wu Li Masters*, a book about physics for the unscientific person, Gary Zukav observes that revolutions in science occur when old theories can no longer explain new knowledge. "Old Ideas die hard," he says (192).

You can find a discussion of summaries under Part Four, "Specialized Writing."

Plagiarism

Plagiarism is the use of someone else's words or ideas as if they were one's own. It constitutes dishonesty. An obvious type of plagiarism is the presentation of another student's work under one's own name. Most students recognize this practice as dishonesty and refrain from engaging in it—though, when pressed for time, they may be tempted to take what they see as an easy way of getting their work done. Don't be tempted; your writing assignments are learning experiences, and when you don't do them, you don't learn. You risk serious penalties for plagiarism if you are caught. Look at plagiarism from a long-term perspective: no one wants to build a career on a degree that involves cheating.

In research papers, plagiarism also occurs when students do not take the trouble to learn and practice the conventions of documentation. The rules are simple—though, admittedly, in practice they are more complicated. Conventions of scholarship require that *everything borrowed from another source be cited.* That means not only direct quotations but summaries and paraphrases as well. The sources of words and ideas that are not your own must be named; in addition, quotations must be exact and any text that you borrow must not be altered from its original meaning. Study the section on documentation carefully and refer to it frequently as you draft and revise your paper.

The primary reason usually given for citing sources is to give credit where it is due. This is a valid reason. Whatever you write belongs to you, whether or not you register it with the U.S. Copyright office. If somebody else uses your idea in a piece of writing without citing you as its source, the idea appears to belong to that person. When you write, every idea you do not cite is assumed to be your own. This is the first reason for citing sources. The second is related. Citing the source of an idea answers a reader's question "How do you know this?" And the third reason is related to the second: you back up your knowledge and experience with that of experts, greatly increasing your credibility on the subject. If these reasons are not enough to convince you that documentation is worth the trouble, there is one more reason: careful documentation is expected of scholars and researchers, as well as students who are serious about their college work.

Some kinds of information do not need to be documented. One kind, of course, is your own knowledge, acquired from your own experience, observations, and education. Even so, it is often useful to give the context in which you acquired your knowledge; for example, "In the two years I've worked as a volunteer in Friendly Acres Nursing Home, I have never observed abuse of patients." Another type of information that does not require documentation is common knowledge: historical facts that can be found in any number of reference books (such as "Maya Angelou was born in St. Louis as Marguerite Johnson"), familiar truisms (such as "Writing improves with revision"), and common maxims (such as "Birds of a feather flock together"). The *opinions* of other people are always cited and documented, as well as facts resulting from another person's research. Any time you are in doubt about whether or not to cite a source, cite it.

Organizing Your Notes: Thesis and Outline

As noted earlier, many of the steps involved in doing research occur at the same time. You may begin organizing your notes while you are still reading and taking notes. You formulate a tentative thesis after your preliminary reading but are likely to revise it during your in-depth reading. You will probably see your paper taking shape as you create key-word headings for each of your note cards. The time does come, however, when you need to sit down with your notes and begin to shape an outline.

After you have completed what you perceive to be the greatest part of your reading, try to write a thesis suitable for drafting your paper. By this time, your head is probably full of information about your subject and you should be ready to make a statement about it. Write a sentence that states your subject and makes an assertion, or point, about your subject. Make your statement narrow enough and specific enough that you can develop it adequately in the number of pages assigned for your paper. Here are thesis sentences that state both the subject and the assertion, narrowly and specifically.

> Although some changes have been made in recent years, the amount of medical research with female subjects is still inadequate.
> [Subject: the amount of medical research with female subjects; assertion: it is still inadequate.]

> Regarding the use of time and resources, American and Japanese school systems can learn from one another. [Subject: the use of time and resources in American and Japanese school systems; assertion: the two nations' school systems can learn from one another.]

Your thesis should help you decide how to organize your paper. The paper written using the first of these thesis sentences would describe recent changes in medical research, then show how little is still being done, and conclude that present research with women subjects is inadequate. The second sample sentence implies a point by point comparison of American and Japanese school systems on the matter of how they use time and resources. The methods for developing research papers are similar to those for developing informal essays: narration, description, exemplification, cause and effect, classification, comparison and contrast, analogy, definition, and process analysis. For guidance in organizing and outlining your paper, see Part One, "Writing an Essay" (especially pages 14–22) and the sample outline on pages 313–318.

Evaluating your notes and sources

With your research questions in mind, evaluate the quality of your notes. Do they address your questions in some way? Do they give you some means of developing your thesis? Can you detect any gaps in information that you will need to fill with further research? Set aside notes that may have seemed relevant when you made them but that, it is now clear, will not be needed for your paper. Do not regard the time you spent taking these notes as wasted; the information you gained will increase your authority on the subject, providing your written voice with a more knowledgeable tone.

Evaluate the authority of your authors. Have they been cited by other authors? Do the things they say jibe with what others in the field say? In cases of disagreement, do the differences lie in the facts or in the way the facts are interpreted? As you form your own opinions on your subject, you are likely to find that authorities differ with one another and you must choose among your sources which ones to give more weight to. For example, astronomers interpret the evidence for the origins of the universe in various ways. Each opinion contributes knowledge in the field but no one opinion can be deemed the decisive truth until more evidence is available. In choosing your sources, be aware of the issues and disagreements regarding your subject.

Question how your sources use facts. What do they omit? Do you detect any bias in their selection of details? Do they use loaded words? For example, an author may give you facts on AIDS education in the schools, but if she uses phrases like "usurping the authority of the family," you know she has a one-sided perspective on the facts.

After carefully evaluating your notes as they relate to your research questions and the credibility of your sources and, overall, to what you have learned about your subject, take whatever additional notes you need and set aside those you have rejected. Revise your outline and thesis until you arrive at a statement you want to use for writing your draft. Block out a period of time without interruptions—a few hours if you can. Gather all your information—bibliography cards, note cards, thesis, and outline—and prepare to write.

Drafting Your Paper

In the process of your reading, note taking, and organizing, your head becomes full of ideas. You know a great deal more about your subject than when you started. Using your thesis and your outline as guides, begin drafting your paper. Begin wherever you feel confident about what you want to say. That may be with your introduction, if you know how you want to begin. Or begin by writing your thesis and proceeding with your first main point.

Since drafting a research paper is a bigger project than most people can complete in one sitting, plan to do your writing in chunks, covering a section of your outline at a time. Whenever you must interrupt your writing, try to leave it with a beginning of what you intend to say next. When you return to writing, read over at least the last paragraph or so, so that you can maintain your tone and coherence. Don't allow your outline to confine you; use it for what it is, a guide, but if at any time you see a need to diverge from your preliminary plan, do so—making sure, of course, that you do not go off on irrelevancies.

Using your sources

In writing a paper that uses information outside your own knowledge and experience, it is crucial for you to keep in mind that *this is your paper.* Because it goes out under your name, whatever you write is considered yours unless you state otherwise. Citing sources is therefore one of the most important things for you to do (see "Documenting Your Sources").

Also, because this work is yours, loosely stringing together a series of quotations is not going to be adequate. You have your own thesis, your own outline, your own purpose for writing, your own opinions; your quoted, paraphrased, and summarized material just supports what you have to say. You need to give your own shape and stamp to the material. Remember also that paraphrases and summaries are preferable to direct quotations, the reason being that paraphrases and summaries are written in your own words and therefore make it easier to maintain your own style and purpose. To retain continuity in your written voice, use quotations sparingly. If it is necessary to quote several lines, set them off in a block, indenting the entire quotation ten spaces, keeping it double-spaced, and omitting quotation marks.

Cite your sources as you use them, making the parenthetical notation discussed under "Documenting Your Sources." On separate paper, or at the end of your document if you are using a word processor, add a bibliographical entry to your reference list for each source you cite in your paper. People who put off making these notations often overlook references that require citations.

Introduction, conclusion, and title

There are no special rules for writing *introductions* to research papers. As in shorter essays, you can use anecdotes, questions, definitions, statistics, statements of problems, and so on—whatever is appropriate for setting the tone for your paper, establishing your authority, and announcing your subject (see "Introductions and conclusions," in Part One, "Writing an Essay"). As stated earlier in the chapter, you should strike an objective tone in your research paper, very often avoiding the use of the pronouns *I* and *you* and also avoiding contractions, colloquialisms, and other features of everyday speech. Requirements for level of formality vary somewhat according to situations, so be sure you know what is expected in your research paper. An appropriate tone plus a familiarity with the facts and vocabulary associated with the subject establishes your authority to write your paper. If you write a good introduction, there should be no doubt in your reader's mind about what your subject is and what your perspective on that subject is.

As with your shorter essays, you need to conclude your research paper with something that sounds like an end: a summary of your main points, a restatement of your thesis, a recommendation for action or further study, a statement about the implications of your report, a final persuasive appeal, and so on. A *conclusion* should not just rehash what you have already said; anything said at the end of your paper should draw together, conclude, what you have presented in the paper. If in your introduction you have asked a question, answer it here. If you narrated a relevant incident or presented a problem, resolve it here (see "Introductions and Conclusions," in Part One, "Writing an Essay").

Introductions and conclusions should be short as compared to the rest of the paper—in most cases no more than a paragraph. If your introduction runs more than two-thirds of a page, it is probably too long; a conclusion longer than half a page could probably be shortened as well.

Sooner or later, your paper must have a **title.** Your title, like all titles, should both describe and stimulate interest in your topic. If you still do not have a title when you start drafting, don't worry about it: something will probably come to you later. If nothing has come to you by the time you are ready to type or print your final draft, talk it over with a friend; between the two of you, you are likely to discover something.

Coherence and clarity

Because of its relatively greater size, the research paper can present some problems in coherence and clarity that do not arise in shorter papers. Unless you use an outline as a guide for drafting, you may set off on tangents unrelated to your thesis, forget how you were using terms and begin using them differently, thoughtlessly repeat statements and details, and even lose your sense of direction. In addition to letting an outline be your guide, work in sections—solid chunks of your paper—and for blocks of time. After a break, rereading paragraphs you wrote last helps you make connections to new paragraphs.

Coherence means that your paragraphs are internally unified, developing a single aspect of your subject, and that all your paragraphs connect to one another and relate to your thesis. You can achieve these connections by repeating key words (expressed in your thesis and topic sentences) and related synonyms and pronouns, with transitional words and phrases, and by stating old, or familiar, information before making new assertions. (See also "Coherence," in Part One, "Writing an Essay," and **Transitions.**)

Clarity means that you adequately explain everything that needs explaining, define whatever words your reader may not understand or read the way you intend them, write sentences that are not unnecessarily complicated, and use words that are not unnecessarily technical or obscure. Clarity means having everything right—your thesis, your organization, the development of your ideas, your grammar and mechanics, *everything*—so that nothing stands in the way of your reader's grasping your meaning.

Documenting Your Sources

In scholarly research, sources of information are always documented. But methods of documentation differ according to discipline. In the humanities, MLA (Modern Language Association) is common; in the social sciences, APA (American Psychological Association); in history, the *Chicago Manual of Style.* Each of the physical sciences has its own documentation method. The methods described here are MLA and APA; when you write research papers in other disciplines, you will need to learn what documentary style to follow.

Both MLA and APA have parenthetical styles of citing sources. Instead of footnotes or endnotes, they name the source in a parenthetical note that follows the borrowed information. These parenthetical references correspond to items fully cited at the end of the paper. Before examining these formats in greater detail, remember that *everything you borrow must be documented,* whether you paraphrase, summarize, or directly quote. The discussions that follow, then, apply to all instances of borrowed information.

Documenting with MLA (Modern Language Association)

As a parenthetical system of documentation, MLA calls for citations at the end of the reference rather than footnotes or endnotes. In most cases, all you need do is conclude borrowed information with a parenthetical page number before the sentence period or, if you have not named the author(s), include the name(s) with the page number in your parentheses.

Michael Ruse observes that humans are the "most

interesting" of all organisms biologists might study

(63). [page number cited; no page abbreviation.]

Humans are interesting subjects of biological study

(Ruse 63). [author's last name and page number]

At the end of the document, on a separate page entitled "Works Cited," list all your parenthetical references alphabetically by authors' last names. Double-space the entire list, both within and between entries. What follows are examples of some of the most common types of source citations in papers using MLA style. Observe the examples in close detail, noting spacing, punctuation, abbreviations, capitalization, indentation, underlining, as well as content. (See also the sample student paper beginning on page 293.)

Books

BOOK BY A SINGLE AUTHOR

Ruse, Michael. <u>Philosophy of Biology Today</u>. Albany:

State U of New York P, 1988.

TWO OR MORE WORKS BY THE SAME AUTHOR

Ruse, Michael. <u>Philosophy of Biology Today</u>.

Albany: State U of New York P. 1988.

---. <u>The Philosophy of Biology</u>. London: Hutchinson

U Library, 1973.

BOOK BY TWO OR MORE AUTHORS

Mitsch, William J., and James G. Gosselink.

<u>Wetlands</u>. New York: Van Nostrand, 1986.

EDITED BOOK

Fishman, Joshua A., Charles A. Ferguson, and

Jyotirindra Das Gupta, eds. <u>Language Problems</u>

<u>of Developing Nations</u>. New York: Wiley, 1968.

WORK IN AN ANTHOLOGY

Passin, Herbert.   "Writer and Journalist in the
Transitional Society."   <u>Language Problems of
Developing Nations</u>.   Ed. Joshua A. Fishman,
Charles A. Ferguson, and Jyotirindra Das Gupta.
New York: Wiley, 1968.   442-57.

TRANSLATION

Nemirovitch-Dantchenko, Vladimir.   <u>My Life in the
Russian Theatre</u>.   Trans. John Cournos.   1936.
New York: Theatre Arts, 1968.   [Note: The book was
originally published in 1936 by another publisher.]

ARTICLE IN A REFERENCE BOOK

Hartl, Daniel L.   "Heredity."   <u>World Book Encyclope-
dia</u>.   1989 ed.   [Note: If the article is un-signed,
alphabetize the item under the article title.]

PAMPHLET

Cohen, Pauline.   <u>How to Help the Alcoholic</u>.   Public
Affairs Pamphlet No. 452.   New York: Public
Affairs, 1970.

GOVERNMENT PUBLICATIONS

United States.   Bureau of Land Management.   State of
Arizona.   <u>Wilderness Status Map</u>.   Washington:
GPO, 1991.

Articles

ARTICLE FROM A MAGAZINE

Wiley, J. P., Jr.   "Time Is Running Out for Forest
Birds."   <u>Smithsonian</u> Feb. 1990: 28+.   [Note: The
+ means that the article did not appear on continuous
pages in the issue.]

ARTICLE FROM A SCHOLARLY JOURNAL WITH CONTINUOUS PAGINATION

Kennedy, Liam. "Farm Succession in Modern Ireland:

Elements of a Theory of Inheritance." Economic

History Review 54 (1991): 477-99.

ARTICLE FROM A SCHOLARLY JOURNAL, EACH ISSUE PAGED SEPARATELY

Jensen, Rick K. "Service Screens Delinquent Youths

for Placement in Treatment Programs."

Corrections Today 53.5 (1991): 172-78.

UNSIGNED ARTICLE FROM A NEWSPAPER

"Tokyo Single Life: A Dormitory." New York Times 17

Jan. 1991: C7.

LETTER TO AN EDITOR

Pearson, Hugh. Letter. Wall Street Journal 12 July

1991: A11.

INFORMATION SERVICE

Coombe, Christine A. "A Global Perspective in the

Foreign Language Classroom." ERIC, 1990. ED

326 066.

INTERVIEW

Williams, Catherine. Personal interview. 5 Nov.

1992.

Documenting with APA
(American Psychological Association)

Like MLA, APA is a parenthetical system of documentation that calls
for reference notes in the text rather than as footnotes or endnotes.
APA citations usually include authors' names in the text, followed by
publication dates in parentheses. Page numbers follow direct quotations. When an author has not already been cited, the name and
publication date (plus page numbers for direct quotations) appear at
the end of the sentence and before the period.

Michael Ruse (1988) observes that humans are the
"most interesting" of all organisms biologists might
study (p. 63). [direct quotation; note the use of *p.*]

Humans are interesting subjects of biological study
(Ruse, 1988). [The author has not been previously named in
the text; note the comma before the date.]

At the end of the document, name all your sources alphabetically by
authors' last names in a double-spaced list labeled "References." What
follows are examples of some of the most common types of source
citations in papers using APA style. Observe the examples in close
detail, noting spacing, punctuation, abbreviations, capitalization, indentation, underlining, as well as content. (See also the sample pages
from a student paper beginning on page 309.)

Books

BOOK BY A SINGLE AUTHOR

Ruse, M. (1988). <u>Philosophy of biology today</u>.
    Albany: State University of New York Press.

TWO OR MORE WORKS BY THE SAME AUTHOR

Ruse, M. (1973). <u>The philosophy of biology</u>.
    London: Hutchinson University Library.

Ruse, M. (1988). <u>Philosophy of biology today</u>.
    Albany: State University of New York Press.

   [Note: References are arranged by year of publication.]

BOOK BY TWO OR MORE AUTHORS

Mitsch, W. J., & Gosselink, J. G. (1986). <u>Wetlands</u>.
    New York: Van Nostrand.

EDITED BOOK

Fishman, J. A., Ferguson, C. A., & Das Gupta, J.
    (Eds.). (1968). <u>Language problems of
    developing nations</u>. New York: Wiley.

WORK IN AN ANTHOLOGY

Passin, H. (1968). Writer and journalist in the transitional society. In J. A. Fishman, C. A. Ferguson, & J. Das Gupta (Eds.), <u>Language problems of developing nations</u> (pp. 442-457). New York: Wiley.

TRANSLATION

Nemirovitch-Dantchenko, V. (1968). <u>My life in the Russian theatre</u> (J. Cournos, Trans.). New York: Theatre Arts. (Original work published 1936.)

ARTICLE IN A REFERENCE BOOK

Hartl, D. L. (1989). Heredity. In <u>World book encyclopedia</u>.

PAMPHLET

Cohen, P. (1970). <u>How to help the alcoholic</u> (Public Affairs Pamphlet No. 452). New York: Public Affairs.

GOVERNMENT PUBLICATIONS

United States Bureau of Land Management, State of Arizona. (1991). <u>Wilderness status map</u>. Washington, DC: U.S. Government Printing Office.

Articles

ARTICLE FROM A MAGAZINE

Wiley, J. P., Jr. (1990, February). Time is running out for forest birds. <u>Smithsonian</u>, pp. 28+.

ARTICLE FROM A SCHOLARLY JOURNAL WITH CONTINUOUS PAGINATION

Kennedy, L. (1991). Farm succession in modern Ireland: Elements of a theory of inheritance. <u>Economic History Review</u>, <u>54</u>, 477-499.

ARTICLE FROM A SCHOLARLY JOURNAL, EACH ISSUE PAGED SEPARATELY

Jensen, R. K. (1991). Service screens delinquent

youths for placement in treatment programs.

Corrections Today, 53(5), 172-178.

ARTICLE FROM A NEWSPAPER

Tokyo single life: a dormitory. (1991, January 17).

New York Times, p. C7.

LETTER TO AN EDITOR

Pearson, H. (1991, July 12). Letter. Wall Street

Journal, p. A11.

INFORMATION SERVICE

Coombe, C. A. (1990). A global perspective in the

foreign language classroom. (ERIC Document

Reproduction Service No. ED 326 066).

INTERVIEW

Personal interviews are not cited as references. Include pertinent
information in the text:

(Catherine Williams, personal communication,

Nov. 5, 1992).

Revising Your Paper

By the time you get to the point of revising your research paper, you
may have spent weeks working on it. You may be getting tired of the
whole project and just want to see it ended. Considering that you have
other things going on in your life too, such an attitude is understand-
able. At the same time, the very fact that this paper represents such a
large chunk of your life is the best reason for taking the additional time
to revise it carefully. All too often, student work is downgraded simply
because of too many mistakes (of one kind or another) in the final
draft. Allow time for revision, and then revise your paper carefully.

This section consists of two revision checklists: the first reviews the topics covered in the drafting section, the second contains some reminders on style and accuracy. A third checklist is included in the next section, "Format of Your Final Draft."

REVISION CHECKLIST ON CONTENT

1. *Thesis.* Now that you have written your paper, does your thesis still accurately signal your subject and the position you are taking on it? If not, reword it. Reread pages 260–262 if necessary.

2. *Support.* With your outline in hand, examine your main supporting points. Have you dealt with all the major issues or facets of your subject? Are there any paragraphs or sections that drift off the subject and would be better eliminated? Does the organization of your points still seem logical to you, or would your points be clearer if you did some reorganizing?

3. *Paragraph development.* Is each paragraph or section developed as fully as necessary? Have you defined terms that may be unfamiliar to your audience? Have you included details to explain and exemplify your topics? Do your paragraphs each center on a single aspect of your subject?

4. *Integration of sources.* Have you fully integrated all borrowed information into your text? If your assignment requires you to announce your sources as a way of leading into quotations, summaries, or paraphrases, be sure you have used phrases such as "According to Michael Ruse in *Philosophy of Biology Today* . . ." and "Michael Ruse observes that. . . ." Whether or not such lead-ins are required of you, all your borrowed information must be integrated. Consider borrowed material as support for your points, not as substitutions for your own ideas. If your paper appears to be a series of loosely strung-together quotations and summaries, you still need to do some serious thinking about what you need to say and then say it, using quotations and summaries only to back you up.

   Make sure too that you have marked the end of each piece of borrowed information with an appropriate citation, as described in the "Documenting Your Sources" section. This is critical; well-researched and otherwise carefully written

REVISION CHECKLIST ON CONTENT *(continued)*

papers have failed because all sources used have not been cited.

5. *Introduction and conclusion.* Take a look at your introduction and conclusion together. Because they are separated by several pages (and probably several days in the writing process), they may appear to be going in different directions. Make sure they read as if they both are parts of the same paper. While your conclusion may state your point more completely and more finally than does your introduction, they should both make the same point. Reread the section on introductions and conclusions if you need to.

Further, question whether your introduction and conclusion accurately reflect your finished paper. Because you may have written it while you were still "cold," your introduction especially may be a little stiff and slightly off the topic. You may be able to delete parts of it or to add something—an apt illustration or statistic, for example.

After revising the content of your paper according to this checklist, you will probably have a much stronger paper. However, despite the hours you have already devoted to revision, you still have work ahead of you. While you revise according to the following style checklist, you are likely to continue revising content as well.

REVISION CHECKLIST ON STYLE

1. *Tone.* Read your paper for tone. Have you been objective throughout, avoiding inappropriate references to first person *(I)* and your beliefs and preferences, as well as any inappropriate references to the reader *(you)?* Have you avoided casual, everyday language (contractions, colloquialisms, slang, and so on), relying instead on usage that is appropriate for publication? Have you used with confidence the terms integral to a discussion of your subject? Have you written with assurance throughout, as one who knows the subject well?

2. *Coherence.* Have you related all parts of your paper to their surrounding parts and to your thesis? If one part is related to another by cause and effect, have you shown that causal

relationship (perhaps by phrases such as "A result of this action was . . ." or "This simple act had a number of unfortunate repercussions"). One section may exemplify another, compare one thing to another, present an analogy to explain another, and so on. Make sure these relationships are clear.

Since you have already revised, if necessary, your thesis and organization (the primary coherence devices), you can go back now to see if you have used them as fully as you might have for achieving coherence. Do you repeat the key words of your thesis and topic sentences (as well as any synonyms, related words, and pronouns with clear reference)? Does the first sentence of each paragraph tie into the preceding paragraph in some way (such as "Another example of this circumstance is . . ." and "This decision may be compared to . . .")? In connecting paragraphs with one another, and connecting sentences with one another, do you take advantage of the "old information/new information" principle, recapping what is known before asserting something new (see "Coherence," in Part One, "Writing an Essay")?

3. *"Works Cited" or "References" format.* First make certain you have included all the sources you have cited in your text and that all the sources listed have been cited. Do not include other sources unless your assignment calls for a "works consulted" list too.

Then check the format of every entry. See that each one conforms in all particulars to the documentation style you are using: information, order of items, punctuation, capitalization, spacing, underlining, and abbreviations. Documentary format is similar to spelling or punctuation in that readers expect words to be spelled in certain ways, punctuation marks to mean certain things, and parts of a citation to stand for certain publishing elements. Be consistent with the style you are using.

Format of Your Final Draft

Unless your instructor tells you otherwise, observe these guidelines when formatting your final draft.

Type or print your paper on good quality 8 1/2-by-11-inch white paper; do not use lightweight or erasable paper. Have a fresh black ribbon in your typewriter or printer. Use only one side of the paper. Margins should be one inch on all sides for MLA style and 1 1/2 inches on all sides for APA style. Do not justify the right margin; leave it uneven. Double-space throughout the entire text, including long quotations and your list of references. Number every page in the upper right corner by simply typing the number plus, for MLA style, your last name or, for APA, a short title.

MLA	APA
Johnson 1	Telekenesis
	3

Type the page number 1/2 inch down from the top of the page for MLA and one inch down for APA.

Title pages are usually not necessary for term papers. Instead, at the top left corner of your first page, on separate double-spaced lines, type your name, the name of your instructor, the course number, and the date. If your assignment calls for a title page, your instructor will tell you what elements to include. Your instructor will also tell you if you need to include any other items, such as an outline, an abstract (see Part Four, "Specialized Writing"), or a table of contents. Begin your "Works Cited" or "References" on the page following the last page of text and continue numbering consecutively.

If, when you proofread, you need to make corrections in your typed copy, draw a straight line through the error and insert the correction in the space above it (never in the margins), either typed or written in ink. Strikeovers are never acceptable, but you may use correcting liquid or tape to cover and type over an error. If you find extensive errors, retype the page.

Before typing your final draft, apply the first item of the following checklist: Check your grammar. While typing, refer often to the sample student paper at the end of the chapter, using it as a guide for style and format.

REVISION CHECKLIST ON FORMAT AND USAGE

1. *Grammar.* You may need to go over your draft several times, concentrating each time on different potential problems. On one trip through, check for unclear **pronouns,** making certain that each pronoun stands for an identifiable noun.

Avoid masculine pronouns *(he, him)* when referring to
antecedents of either sex or unidentified sex; recast the
sentence to plural, use *he or she*, or avoid the pronoun
altogether.

Check the consistency and tense of your **verbs.** References to
the work of other writers are usually introduced with
present tense verbs: "As Ruse *points out,* classification is
necessary if we are to make sense of our world." Past tense
verbs refer to completed activities: "Ruse *delivered* a
shortened version of his book as a memorial address at York
University."

Unless your teacher permits them, avoid **contractions** (such
as *won't* for *will not* and *shouldn't* for *should not*) and the
pronouns *I* and *you*. Check for all grammar and punctuation
problems that commonly occur in your writing. (Refer to
alphabetical entries as necessary.)

2. *Format.* There is little room for creativity in the format of
research papers. Apply the guidelines described in the
section on format and follow all your instructor's specifications. Double-check your list of works cited (or references) to
be certain you have been consistent in following the MLA
(or APA) documentary style.

3. *Appearance.* Look at your finished paper with a critical eye.
Does it look good? Do your margins look right? Is your type
clear and black? Are the pages free of smudges and creases?
Redo pages that do not look good. Does any page have more
than two or three corrections? Retype or reprint that page. If
you were on the job, you would want to submit a product
that represented you as a careful worker; your teacher
expects that kind of care.

The End

Read your paper over one more time—yes, *one more time*—to make
sure you have no typing errors. If you do find any, make the corrections as noted already; your paper won't look as neat with a penned-in
correction, but it will read better. Then follow your teacher's instructions for fastening the pages of your paper. Some people want only a
paperclip in the upper lefthand corner, some prefer a staple, and some

advise a binder of some type. If your teacher has not specified a fastener, use a paperclip. Fastening the paperclip is truly the end. Your research paper is completed.

Sample Student Research Papers (MLA and APA)

The following paper is printed here as a guide on format and style for a paper using MLA documentation. Do not think of it as a model paper, because instructors' guidelines differ and this paper was written for an assignment different from yours. Nor should you regard the paper as perfect. Like many papers, it has a few imperfections, which you and your classmates may be able to discuss. Marginal annotations point out pertinent features of the paper. Following the full MLA-style paper are a few pages of the same paper reformatted according to APA style, and a sample outline. Again, use these samples only as guides, not as models.

Wendy Liane (Lankas) Baumann

Professor Virginia Leih

English 163

May 12, 1992

Nonverbal Communication in Gender Contexts

  A firm handshake, a loving hug, a brief pause, a soft whisper, a pinstriped suit, a red dress. These are all components of nonverbal communication, specifically kinesics, paralanguage, proxemics, and artifacts. Nonverbal communication is communication without words, usually displayed unconsciously. It is often overlooked as a means of communicating, yet its influence and implied meanings are relevant in gender contexts, because males and females differ in the ways they choose to nonverbally act.

  <u>Kinesics</u> involves eye contact, facial expression, or gestures. Definite gender distinctions are prevalent within kinesics by the way men and women present themselves, position their bodies, and court one another. In general, males are trained to present themselves as strong and controlling, while women tend to exhibit the qualities of meekness and submission. Displaying dominance by staring, pointing, touching, and interrupting others helps men establish their superiority. Contrastingly, editors Barrie Thorne and Nancy

Author's last name and page number

Double-spacing throughout

Centered title

Introduction announces subject of paper

Thesis

Topic sentence to orient reader

Baumann 3

Henley discovered that women lean toward an
inferior role by smiling more, lowering and
averting their eyes, refraining from speaking,
cuddling to the touch, and allowing themselves
to be interrupted (197). Mark L. Hickson III
and Don W. Stacks suggest that "women may be
more sensitive to kinetic behavior" because
they have been "taught to be aware of it"
(139).

Page number citation

Direct quotation with number citation

   Differing gender facial expression in
nonverbal communication is believed to be
taught early on. "Facial expression is a
result of training from childhood and is also
a type of sex stereotyping" (Hickson and
Stacks 139). For example, boys try not to cry
because they have learned it is not considered
masculine and tough, whereas girls are taught
to smile because they look prettier and more
feminine when they do. Women are also likely
to exhibit more facial expression, in general,
than men.

Authors named in parenthetical citation

   When sitting, men and women position
their bodies differently. Barbara Bate claims
that males have a tendency to "expand to fill
their social space" (60), along with crossing
their arms behind their heads. In contrast,
females hold their limbs closer to their
bodies and remain more composed. Bate also

Paraphrase

Baumann 3

stated, "Women cross their legs from either
ankle to ankle or knee to knee," whereas "men
cross their legs from ankle to knee" (60).

One major area of interpersonal communication between males and females is courting.
The nonverbal communication shown during
courting is just as pertinent as the verbal
communication. When analyzing gestures in
courting, Dr. David Givens says, "We don't
even have to learn what the 'right' signals
are; they are innate" (qtd. in Wilder 63).
This may be true, as evidenced in all the
unconscious actions men and women display.
Rachel Wilder, a contributing editor of
<u>Science Digest</u>, gives an example of these
actions, citing the way both sexes unconsciously raise their shoulders when they are
attracted to each other (64). Bate reinforces
the idea that women display submissive roles
by "tilting their head" when a man is present,
"to appear shorter than him" (60).

Variations in relaxation between males
and females are noticeable in uncomfortable
situations. Mark L. Knapp found that males
possess a less relaxed body around intensely
disliked males, since they are sensed as a
possible threat (101). Yet this male behavior
is not true in the presence of a disliked

Quotation from a
secondary source

Summary

Baumann 4

female. Knapp revealed that females "lean
sideways more intensely when around unfavorable males and females" alike (101). The
kinetic differences between men and women are
evident. Observing the gender contrasts
within kinesics enables people to understand
why others differ in their kinetic behavior
and promotes a conscious awareness of others'
nonverbal actions.

Summary including direct quotation

The second part of nonverbal communication, known as <u>haptics</u>, or touch, is one of
the most common forms of nonverbal communication. Stephen Thayer, a professor of psychology at City University of New York, states
that "touch is the most powerful of all
communication channels--and the most carefully
guarded and regulated" (31).

Authority of source

Men and women differ in their touching
manner and frequency. This may be attributed
to early experiences in life. Mothers tend to
touch their children more than fathers do, and
female babies are touched more frequently than
male babies. "Fathers use touch more for
play, while mothers use it more for soothing
and grooming" (Thayer 32). Throughout life,
women, on the average, are touched more than
men owing to cultural and societal norms.

People demonstrate haptics for a variety

of reasons; and when to touch others is a
matter of preference. People touch to show
encouragement, love, comfort, and concern.
One may offer a handshake to a new acquain-
tance, place an encouraging hand on the
shoulder of a distraught friend, or enthusias-
tically hug a missed relative. Rudolph F.
Verderber, a professor at the University of
Cincinnati, and Kathleen S. Verderber, a
professor at Northern Kentucky University,
suggest that the reasons people touch one
another range from "impersonal and random to
intimate and purposeful" (119).

Touch is necessary to enable people to
feel a sense of worth and belonging in life.
Tactile deprivation occurs when a person is
not held or touched often, and this deprivation can lead to negative effects. Hickson
and Stacks claim that people become distrust-
ful and acquire lower self-esteem because of
the absence of human touch in their life (75).
Touch avoidance can occur when people want to
avoid being touched, or want to avoid touching
others. Males and females exhibit distinct
clashes in touch avoidance. Joseph A. DeVito,
a professor of nonverbal communication,
comments:

> Although men have low touch

Baumann 6

avoidance scores for opposite-sex
touching, they have high touch
avoidance scores for same-sex
touching. Women, on the other hand,
have high touch avoidance scores for
opposite-sex touching but low touch
avoidance scores for same-sex
touching. (140)

Quotation of over four lines is indented 10 spaces from left margin

These gender differences relate to the early
influences of touch both sexes encounter.

DeVito also identifies the five major,
popular classifications of touching functions:
functional-professional, social-polite,
friendship-warmth, love and intimacy, and
sexual arousal (136-37). In functional-
professional touching, the touch does something for the person. For example, a doctor
takes the heartbeat of his patient. The
social-polite function creates a connection
between two people, like shaking hands.
Telling people they are liked through the use
of touch is the friendship-warmth function.
Through hugging and kissing, the love and
intimacy function is communicated. Finally,
the sexual arousal function is similar to the
love and intimacy function, yet DeVito states
that this final touching function also in

Baumann 7

cludes fondling, petting, and sexual
intercourse (137).

The third aspect of nonverbal communication, called paralanguage, or vocalics,
concerns the cues of pitch, rate, loudness,
and pausing that convey nonverbal messages.
Mary Ritchie Key, a professor of nonverbal
communication at the University of California,
claims, "Of the few thousand articulatory
possibilities that a human being has, only a
relatively few sounds are actually used in
language" (41). This section concentrates on
the vocal sounds of nonverbal messages used in
verbal communication.

The first paralingual aspect of pitch is
range. Pitch can vary from extremely high to
extremely low. Paralinguistic and linguistic
pitch differ, as Key distinguishes: "While the
former is part of the grammar of language, the
latter is a component of the expressive system
of a language" (48). Hickson and Stacks
concluded, when comparing gender aspects of
pitch, that it is generally true that men talk
with a deep voice and boastful speech, whereas
women tend to have a high pitch that varies
over a wide range (156).

The rate, or regularity, of vocalics is

Baumann 8

how quickly one speaks, which may include an
increase or decrease of loudness known as
stress. People may increase the rate of their
voices owing to excitement or nervousness. In
contrast, people may also decrease the regularity of their voices owing to depression or
boredom. Hickson and Stacks once again reveal
that men tend to exhibit an aggressive and
blunt speech rate, while women use a smooth
speech rate which is often open and
self-revealing (155).

Loudness in paralanguage refers to not
only volume but also the intensity of a voice.   *Common knowledge*
Loudness, at times, can be effective in
communication; yet at other times loudness can
be annoying and cause interference in a
communication setting. Males are apt to use
dominating and loud speech more than women do.
Females often possess a gentle and emotional
speech.

Pausing, an aspect of paralanguage,
refers to silence in conversations. It is an
essential part of nonverbal communication
because it can allow several actions to occur.
During silence, both communicators are allotted time to collect their thoughts and think
of what they will contribute to the conversation next. A pause can be effective in making

Baumann 9

a point or it can let a person know when someone is finished speaking. Humans need pauses in conversations to allow other nonverbal communication to happen. According to Key, making tape recordings of conversations shows how much silence can occur: "The playback reveals long periods of silence that are filled with continuing gestures and facial expressions or other body movement" (117). Interruption in conversations, which causes the speaker to pause involuntarily, is also relevant in nonverbal communication. It has been agreed that men interrupt other speakers more than women do; accordingly, women pause more than men.

Proxemics is the fourth aspect to explore in nonverbal communication. It involves a comparison of how people perceive and use informal and personal space. Proxemics is also known as spatial communication or territoriality. DeVito and colleague Michael L. Hecht, a professor at Arizona State University, are coauthors of The Nonverbal Communication Reader, in which they describe how people must balance affiliative needs and privacy needs involving the use of space (181). Affiliative needs require human contact with others, rather than isolation. Yet privacy needs

Baumann 10

require that people have quality time alone,
as well as surrounding space. "And so people
must balance their conflicting needs for
affiliation and privacy . . . through controlling . . . territories and personal space"
(181).

Ellipsis dots to indicate omission in quoted text

Four distance zones exist within proxemics, defined by DeVito as intimate distance,
personal distance, social distance, and public
distance (111-12). Each distance has a close
and a far phase. The first zone of intimate
distance "ranges from actual touching, in its
close phase, to maintaining a distance of 6 to
8 inches, in its far phase" (111). Great
detail is visible within this distance; and a
whisper communicates effectively. The second
zone of personal distance "ranges from 1.5 to
2.5 feet in its close phase to 2.5 to 4 feet
in its far phase" (111). This distance allows
people to touch one another with a grasp or
hug by extending their arms. Social distance
ranges "from 4 to 7 feet in its close phase to
7 to 12 feet in its far phases" (111). Business transactions have a more formal tone when
conducted at the social distance; eye contact
is highly important for effective communication.

The final zone, which "ranges from 12 to

Baumann 11

15 feet in its close phase to 25 feet and over in its far phase" is known as public distance (DeVito 112). This distance enables people to be defensive if the situation calls for it. An interesting fact from the far phase of public distance, noted by DeVito and Hecht, is that "[t]hirty feet is the distance that is automatically set around important public figures" (192).

Brackets to indicate change from capital T in the original

Two theories about space, according to DeVito, are the "protection theory" and the "equilibrium theory." The protection theory claims that the space around someone serves as a form of protection. "When one is being threatened, one's body-buffer zone expands; when we feel secure and safe, our body-buffer zone shrinks" (128). As an example, if a person were sitting on a bus and the stranger next to him or her began a conversation, the person would expand his or her body-buffer zone accordingly, to avoid feeling threatened. Conversely, if a woman's fiancé were sitting next to her on the bus, she would tend to relax her body-buffer zone, because she is comfortable with him.

The equilibrium theory claims that intimacy and distance balance one another, depending on whether people are intimate with each other or not. DeVito establishes that "the higher the intimacy, the closer the distance; the lower the intimacy the greater the distance" (128). An example of this theory would be that a girl would tend to move closer toward her mother in the pew at church if an unfamiliar man came and sat next to her. In general, men do not feel as threatened as women when experiencing close proxemics. This probably results from early role definitions, when men are taught to be the dominant and stronger sex while women are taught to be more passive and gentle.

The final aspect of nonverbal communication, called <u>artifacts</u>, involves a variety of items. Artifacts are the objects people wear or possess that make statements about who they are; other people interpret, perceive, and draw conclusions based on the artifacts other people choose to display.

Cranial, facial, and body hair styles are artifacts which yield concrete conclusions. "In 1976, Kelvin Peterson and James Curran found that short-haired men were rated as more intelligent, moral, masculine, mature, wise, and attractive than long-haired men" (Hickson and Stacks 103). Regarding facial hair, Hickson and Stacks found that college students

perceive men with beards as having higher
status and power in life, as opposed to
clean-shaven men (103).

The amount of hair, the texture, length,
style, and color can be changed to produce and
evoke varied messages. Hickson and Stacks
found that most people feel "Long hair con-
notes an artistic, aesthetic, romantic, and
casual mode of life. . . . Very short hair
represents the energetic, precise, athletic,
and youthful type" (106). In females, Hickson
and Stacks also noted that fashion experts
feel a brunette is more of an "authoritative
figure," while a blonde is considered more of
a "popularity figure" (106). "Hair length for
women does not carry the same amount of
information that it does for a man" (DeVito
86).

Clothing is another valid facet in the
study of artifacts. "Clothes do communicate,
however accurate or inaccurate you may believe
that communication to be" (Verderber and
Verderber 119). People tend to forget that
what they wear gives others clues as to how
they should perceive the wearer's attitudes
and behaviors. For example, a teenage boy
wearing a ripped tank top along with cut-off
jeans is likely to elicit a rather different

response than a teenage boy dressed in a
Sunday church suit. A woman in a jumpsuit
sitting next to a woman in an evening gown
would not be regarded in the same manner
either.

In business, the attire people choose to
wear greatly influences the perceptions others
attach to them. John T. Molloy, who has
extensively researched wardrobe engineering,
suggested what he felt business people should
wear to work to be considered successful.
Hickson and Stacks reviewed Molloy's studies,
which recommended that men wear solid, dark
suits which represent authority and credibility; pinstripes are also acceptable. Women
were encouraged to wear a skirted suit with a
blouse, preferably in navy blue, charcoal
gray, or beige (111-12).

Color in clothing is one of the most
important characteristics of artifacts,
because color can create moods and reveal
clues about the personality type of the
wearer. While research seems not to have
dealt with gender differences in relation to
color preferences, the message of color
depends greatly on the individual. "Outgoing
people, for example, do seem to wear brighter
colors than do introverts" (DeVito 87).

Baumann 15

Conversely, DeVito reports that conservative people seem to adopt darker and more muted colors than liberals (87). Warm colors--reds, oranges, and yellows--tend to exhibit vitality. Yet DeVito concludes that little research has confirmed that color preferences are connected to personality, because "color preferences are influenced by a variety of factors--our early exposure to color, our past experiences with colors, our occupation, and our sense of style, to name just a few--as well as our personality" (87).

Nonverbal communication--more precisely *Conclusion* kinesics, haptics, paralanguage, proxemics, and artifacts--is an ever-present aspect of social interchange. Conscious awareness of the impact of such communication and of the differences in gender tendencies is useful when we try to understand the underlying meanings in human discourse.

Baumann 16

Works Cited

Bate, Barbara. <u>Communication and the Sexes</u>.   *Book by one author*
New York: Harper, 1988.

DeVito, Joseph A. <u>The Nonverbal Communication</u>
<u>Workbook</u>. Chicago: Waveland, 1989.

DeVito, Joseph A., and Michael L. Hecht. <u>The</u>   *Book by two authors*
<u>Nonverbal Communication Reader</u>. Chicago:
Waveland, 1990.

Hickson, Mark L., III, and Don W. Stacks. <u>NVC</u>
<u>Nonverbal Communication Studies and</u>
<u>Applications</u>. Dubuque: Brown, 1989.

Key, Mary Ritchie. <u>Paralanguage and Kinesics</u>.
Metuchen: Scarecrow, 1975.

Knapp, Mark L. <u>Nonverbal Communication in</u>
<u>Human Interaction</u>. New York: Holt, 1972.

Thayer, Stephen. "Close Encounters."
<u>Psychology Today</u> March 1988: 31-36.

Thorne, Barrie, and Nancy Henley, eds.   *Editors*
<u>Language and Sex: Difference and</u>
<u>Dominance</u>. Rowley: Newbury, 1975.

Verderber, Rudolph F., and Kathleen S.
Verderber. <u>Inter-Act: Using</u>
<u>Interpersonal Communication Skills</u>.
Belmont: Wadsworth, 1992.

Wilder, Rachel. "Love Signals." <u>Science</u>   *Article in a monthly*
<u>Digest</u> June 1984: 63-65.   *magazine*

Nonverbal Communication in Gender Contexts

Wendy Liane (Lankas) Baumann

St. Cloud State University

April 15, 1993

Centered title; separate title page is counted but not numbered

Running Head: NONVERBAL COMMUNICATION

*Running head and
page number*

Nonverbal Communication in Gender Contexts

Title centered

A firm handshake, a loving hug, a brief
pause, a soft whisper, a pinstriped suit, a
red dress. These are all components of
nonverbal communication, specifically
kinesics, paralanguage, proxemics, and artifacts. Nonverbal communication is communication without words, usually displayed
unconsciously. It is often overlooked as a
means of communicating, yet its influence and
implied meanings are relevant in gender
contexts, because males and females differ in
the ways they choose to nonverbally act.

    <u>Kinesics</u> involves eye contact, facial
expression, or gestures. Definite gender
distinctions are prevalent within kinesics by
the way men and women present themselves,
position their bodies, and court one another.
In general, males are trained to present
themselves as strong and controlling, while
women tend to exhibit the qualities of meekness and submission. Displaying dominance by
staring, pointing, touching, and interrupting
others helps men establish their superiority.
Contrastingly, editors Barrie Thorne and Nancy
Henley (1975) discovered that women lean
toward an inferior role by smiling more,

*Date of publication
immediately
following editors'
names*

Nonverbal Communication

3

lowering and averting their eyes, refraining from speaking, cuddling to the touch, and allowing themselves to be interrupted. Mark L. Hickson III and Don W. Stacks (1989) suggest that "women may be more sensitive to kinetic behavior" because they have been "taught to be aware of it" (p. 139).

Differing gender facial expression in nonverbal communication is believed to be taught early on. "Facial expression is a result of training from childhood and is also a type of sex stereotyping" (Hickson & Stacks, 1989, p. 139). For example, boys try not to cry because they have learned it is not considered masculine and tough, whereas girls are taught to smile because they look prettier and more feminine when they do. Women are also likely to exhibit more facial expression, in general, than men.

Page number following direct quotation; authors' names appear in text

Authors' names, date, and page number for direct quotation not textually attributed to the authors

Nonverbal Communication

4

References

Bate, B. (1988). <u>Communication and the</u>   *Book by one author*
   <u>sexes</u>. New York: Harper.

DeVito, J. A. (1989). <u>The nonverbal</u>
   <u>communication workbook</u>. Chicago: Waveland.

DeVito, J. A., & Hecht, M. L. (1990). <u>The</u>   *Book by two authors*
   <u>nonverbal communication reader</u>. Chicago:
   Waveland.

Hickson, M. L., III, & Stacks, D. W. (1989).
   <u>NVC nonverbal communication studies and</u>   *Editors*
   <u>applications</u>. Dubuque: Brown.

Key, M. R. (1975). <u>Paralanguage and</u>
   <u>kinesics</u>. Metuchen: Scarecrow.

Knapp, M. L. (1972). <u>Nonverbal communication</u>
   <u>in human interaction</u>. New York: Holt.

Thayer, S. (1988, March). Close encounters.
   <u>Psychology Today</u>, pp. 31-36.   *Article in a monthly*
                                                          magazine
Thorne, B., & Henley, N. (Eds.). (1975).
   <u>Language and sex: difference and dominance</u>.
   Rowley: Newbury.

Verderber, R. F., & Verderber, K. S. (1992).
   <u>Inter-act: Using interpersonal communica-</u>
   <u>tion skills</u>. Belmont: Wadsworth.

Wilder, R. (1984, June). Love signals.
   <u>Science Digest</u>, pp. 63-65.

Outline of sample student paper

Outline

Thesis: Nonverbal communication is often overlooked as a means of communication, yet its influence and implied meanings are relevant in gender contexts.

I. Nonverbal communication includes kinesics, haptics, paralanguage, proxemics, and artifacts.

    A. Nonverbal communication is communicating without words.

        1. Nonverbal communication often happens unconsciously.

        2. Males and females differ in the way they communicate nonverbally.

II. Kinesics involves nonverbal communication by the use of eye contact, facial expression, or gesture.

    A. In general, males are trained to present themselves as strong and controlling, while women tend to exhibit meekness and submission.

        1. Men display dominance by their actions.

        2. Women take on an inferior role through their actions.

    B. Differing gender facial expression in nonverbal communication is believed to be

Sentence outline (Some teachers require an outline at the beginning of the paper. When included, the outline is numbered with lowercase Roman numerals, after the title page.)

taught early on.

    1. Men try to be masculine by not crying.

    2. Women smile to look more feminine.

C. When sitting, men and women position their bodies differently.

    1. Men use more of their social space.

    2. Women remain more composed.

D. One major area of interpersonal communication between males and females is courting.

    1. Men and women exhibit unconscious actions during courting.

    2. Women retain their submissive roles.

E. Variations in states of relaxation between males and females are noticeable in uncomfortable situations.

    1. Men are less relaxed around men they consider a threat.

    2. Females lean sideways when around unfavorable males and females alike.

III. Haptics, or touch, is one of the most common forms of nonverbal communication.

A. Men and women differ in touching manner and frequency.

    1. Women touch, and are touched, more than men.

    2. Mothers touch their children more than fathers do.

B. People demonstrate haptics for a variety of

Baumann iv

reasons, and when to touch others is a
matter of preference.

    1. Sometimes people touch to show love or
       encouragement.

    2. The reasons people touch range from
       impersonal to purposeful.

  C. Tactile deprivation can negatively affect
    anyone.

    1. People learn to distrust and have
       little confidence.

    2. Some learn to exhibit touch avoidance.

IV. Paralanguage, or vocalics, concerns the cues of
pitch, rate, loudness, and pausing to convey
nonverbal messages.

  A. Pitch is the range a voice uses, which can
    vary from extremely high to extremely low.

    1. Men talk with a deep voice and boastful
       speech.

    2. Women tend to have a high pitch, which
       can greatly vary.

  B. Rate, or regularity, is how quickly one
    speaks, which may include an increase or
    decrease of loudness (stress).

    1. Men tend to use aggressive and blunt
       speech.

    2. Women use smooth speech which is open
       and self-revealing.

  C. Loudness refers not only to volume but also

to intensity of a voice.

1. Males lean toward dominating and loud
   speech.

2. Females usually have gentle and emotional speech.

D. Pausing is silence in conversation.

1. Men interrupt others more than do
   women.

2. Women pause more than men.

V. Proxemics is the comparison involving how
people perceive and use informal and personal
space.

A. People must balance affiliative needs and
privacy needs.

1. Affiliative needs require human contact
   with others, rather than isolation.

2. Privacy needs allow people to have time
   alone as well as space surrounding
   them.

B. There are four distance zones within proxemics; each zone includes a close and far
phase.

1. The first is intimate distance.

2. The second is personal distance.

3. The third is social distance.

4. The fourth is public distance.

C. DeVito describes two theories about space:

the "protection theory" and the "equilibrium theory."

    1. The protection theory claims the space
       around someone serves as a form of
       protection.

    2. The equilibrium theory claims that
       intimacy and distance balance one
       another.

VI. Artifacts refers to the objects people wear or
possess that make statements as to who they
are; people perceive and draw conclusions about
others based on the displayed artifacts.

    A. Cranial, facial, and body hair style are
       artifacts which yield concrete conclusions.

       1. Short-haired men are perceived as more
          intelligent, moral, and so on, than
          long-haired men.

       2. Men with beards seem to evoke percep-
          tions of higher power and status.

       3. In females, it has been learned that a
          brunette is more of an "authoritative
          figure"; whereas a blonde is considered
          more of a "popularity figure."

    B. In business, the attire people choose to
       wear greatly influences the perceptions
       others attach to them.

       1. Men who wish to be successful are

encouraged to wear solid, dark suits
which represent authority and credibility; pinstriped suits are also acceptable.

2. Women should opt to wear skirted suits
with blouses, preferably in navy, gray,
or beige.

C. Color is one of the most important characteristics of artifacts, because it can
create moods and reveal insight about the
personality type of the wearer.

1. There is no specific evidence linking
gender differences in relation to color
preferences.

2. Warm colors exhibit vitality.

VII. Nonverbal communication is used differently by
men and women, and the meanings and influence
behind the contrasting nonverbal messages can
reveal a great deal about gender tendencies.

PART FOUR

Specialized Writing

Specialized Writing

Abstracts and Summaries, *321*
Critiques, *323*
Essay Examinations, *324*
Business Letters, *328*
Memorandums, *332*
Application Letters and Resumés, *334*

Abstracts and Summaries

An *abstract* is a condensation of another piece of writing, usually reflecting the form and perspective of the original. An abstract concentrates on content, stating what the original says, not what it does, avoiding words such as "The author states" and "The report shows." Like a summary, it omits specific details, examples, descriptions, and unnecessary details.

A *summary* also presents in condensed form the substance of another piece of writing. It is a necessary part of research writing and is often required for a critique (see "Critiques"). Whether the summary is a separate piece in itself or is part of a longer piece of writing, it usually begins with an overall summary statement followed by essential supportive points. The abstract, in contrast, gives the concentrated essence of a larger piece of writing. Whereas an abstract is written from the same perspective as the original, a summary conveys the perspective of the summarizer. Both abstracts and summaries are concise, omitting details, descriptions, illustrations, and sometimes explanations, and avoiding all unnecessary words (see **coordination, subordination,** and **wordiness**).

Writing a summary or an abstract

READ. Before writing a summary or an abstract, read the entire piece and try to understand it. Write a single sentence that expresses the main point. Go back into the piece to see if you are right, and revise your sentence as necessary.

UNDERLINE. Now read the piece again, underlining major points and connecting phrases. Omit all unnecessary details.

WRITE. Begin your summary with the sentence you wrote expressing the main point and then, following your underlining as a guide and using your own words, add as much supportive material as necessary for conveying the substance of the piece. When writing an abstract, follow the order of the original as you condense: begin with the author's first major point, move on to the second, and so on, finishing with the last major point of the original. For either summary or abstract, do not lift phrases and sentences from the original, and do not simply recast the original into different word order.

REVISE. Make certain that your summary or abstract is accurate and true to the original. Read your summary or abstract aloud to see if all parts connect smoothly. Listen for unnecessary words and phrases. Correct errors, and write a clean draft.

SAMPLE SUMMARY AND ABSTRACT

ORIGINAL

The origins of the hypothetical language called Indo-European—believed to be the progenitor of many modern languages, including English, French, German, Finnish, Hungarian, Hebrew, and Arabic—are assumed to be in central or southeastern Europe. This common ancestor of many of the languages spoken and written today, says the hypothesis, was spoken by people living in the Later Stone Age. Identifying the location of Indo-European involved a type of detective work. Linguistic studies have shown that the languages deriving from the protolanguage have similar words for features of a temperate climate without access to the sea. These languages have words, for example, for snow, winter, and spring; for dog, horse, cow, and bear but not for camel, lion, elephant, or tiger; for trees such as beech, oak, and pine but not for palm or banyan; and there is no word for ocean. The language could not have been located, therefore, in Greece, Britain, India, or Africa. Furthermore, because the Indo-European family of languages has words for the honeybee and its products (*honey* and *mead*) and because the bee is not common in Asia, the inference is that the language could not have originated in Asia. The weight of evidence therefore favors a central European location.

SUMMARY

Like many other modern European languages, English is said to derive from a hypothetical language called Indo-European, which linguistic evidence places in central Europe during the Later Stone Age. [The original paragraph is reduced to a single sentence that omits examples.]

ABSTRACT

The original location of Indo-European, a hypothetical language said to be the ancestor of English and many other European languages, has a putative location. Linguists looking at words common to the derived languages hypothesize that, in the Later Stone Age, a people in a central European location spoke this language. [The abstract attempts to maintain the order of the original statements while condensing them and omitting examples.]

Critiques

A critique is an analysis of and a commentary on another piece of writing. In writing a critique, you evaluate both technique and content but generally avoid expressing personal agreement or disagreement. You generally use summary ("Abstracts and Summaries") and references to the original in support of your points. Therefore you also might need to use a method of documenting the sources you cite in your critique. To write a critique, you need to *read, analyze, evaluate,* and *write.*

Writing a critique

READ. Read the piece actively, making no notes but seeking the writer's point, purpose, and attitude toward the subject. Then write a brief reaction.

ANALYZE. Read the piece again, more thoroughly, looking closely at evidence in support of the writer's point, the reasonableness of the position, the logic of any arguments. Question whether the writer is informed about the subject, appears to understand the audience, and is clear about the purpose for writing. Analyze technique: organization of the piece, clarity of details, control and variety of sentence structure, word choice (**diction**), and consistency and appropriateness of tone. Take notes. If necessary for an informed analysis, read related materials.

EVALUATE. Now ask yourself: How good is it? How true is it? Is the author right? Where do I disagree with the writer? Where do I agree? Your judgment may be either positive or negative or even a combination. But you must support your judgments with evidence from the piece, although you may also use evidence from related sources if it helps you make your point. Write your reaction to the piece in a single sentence; then make notes or an outline about how you intend to support your reaction.

WRITE. A critique, like other essays, has an introduction that presents the subject, states the point (or thesis), and includes something to stimulate the interest of an audience. It also names the writer and title of the piece being analyzed. Following your introduction, support your points with summary, **paraphrase,** and limited **quotations** from the original, as well as your own reasoning and other evidence. References to the original should be followed by parenthetical page numbers.

```
Palmer takes an optimistic view of ecology, comparing
the earth to "a fertile hen's egg" that is changing
rapidly but is on its way to becoming something new
and perhaps better (88).
```

At the end of your critique (or at the beginning if your assignment calls for it there), identify the publishing information for the piece of writing you are critiquing.

```
Palmer, Thomas.  "The Case for Human Beings."  Atlan-
     tic Monthly Jan. 1992: 83-88.
```

For more information on documenting sources, see "Documenting Your Sources" in Part Three.

Throughout your writing, adopt a tone that is serious and respectful. Avoid sarcasm, anger, and pathos. In your conclusion, make your final statements. Then revise carefully, making certain your analysis has adequately supported your evaluation. Check the **tense** of your verbs to make sure that you use present tense to refer to what the other writer says and past tense to refer to your own reading or experience. See also Part One, "Writing an Essay."

Essay Examinations

Essay examinations are a specialized type of writing designed to show teachers how much students know about a given subject. Performing well on an exam, then, depends on knowing the material.

Preparing for the essay exam

Cramming for an essay exam will work only if you have kept up with your reading and note taking throughout the term. Students who are experienced at preparing for college essay exams advise that you do your assigned readings when you receive them and review your class notes frequently. For particularly difficult material, they recommend summarizing both your reading and your notes. Here is some of their advice:

TIPS FOR TAKING NOTES ON LECTURES

1. Watch the professor. If he or she conspicuously reads from notes, you know that what is said next is worth taking notes on. It invariably turns up on the exam.
2. Take down everything the professor writes on the blackboard.
3. Make a note that applies the concepts of the lecture to something you know. It's easier to remember a personal application.
4. At the end of the day, review and summarize your lecture notes, phrasing them in your own words. Likewise, review and summarize your highlighted readings. Then at test time you won't have pages of highlights to review, and reading your own words will make recalling information easier.
5. When you review and rephrase, take time to classify your notes, grouping information into categories that make sense to you.
6. Look for concepts, not individual pieces of information. However, if you don't know what to expect from the teacher, you will probably have to note just about everything.

TIPS FOR TAKING NOTES ON READING

1. Highlight important material with a colored highlighter.
2. Use underlines to further accent highlighted material.
3. Use circles to call attention to important words.
4. Use asterisks to point out information to be memorized.
5. Use question marks to indicate material you want to ask the teacher about.
6. Write up page summaries—brief notations on the content of each page.
7. Combine lecture and reading notes on a single summary page.

Close to exam time, review your notes and summaries. Study your assigned readings, picking up points that your teacher covered in class. To aid your review, use one of the methods of invention described on pages 8–13 in Part One, "Prewriting and Invention." The classical probes or the journalist's questions might be especially helpful. Apply the questions to your subject: *what is it? how is it like other things? who are the important figures? where did it happen?* and so on. Aim for a broad understanding of the subject, but also try to file away a number of important details; the most useful way to cram is to drill yourself on details. To aid your broad understanding, write some questions that you could expect on the exam and then work out answers to them.

And during exam period make sure you get plenty of sleep—and food. A rested and alert mind is better able to meet the challenge of showing your knowledge of the subject in response to a difficult question. Then go to class confident that, even though you may not know all the material, you know enough to answer most of the questions.

Writing an essay exam

Don't panic. Take time to read the exam carefully and learn what is required. If you have several questions to answer, budget your time according to the percentage of points allotted to each—spend half of your time on a 50 percent question, for example. Allow some time for planning, most of it for writing, and some for revising and editing. Here are some tips for managing the writing process.

PREWRITE. Read each question carefully, letting key words tell you what you need to do. If the question asks for causes and effects, for example, a list of examples will not do the job. If it asks for a list, several paragraphs on one item will not do. Study the following key words and observe how each word requires a different strategy for answering an essay question.

KEY WORDS IN ESSAY EXAMS	
ANALYZE	Separate the subject into its parts and examine each part, relating each to the whole and each to the others.
COMPARE	Show similarities.
CONTRAST	Show differences.
DEFINE	Give the meaning, keeping in mind the class of the thing and how it differs from other things in its class.
DESCRIBE	Give physical and factual characteristics.
DISCUSS	Give a complete and detailed answer by examining, analyzing, defining, and doing anything else appropriate.
ENUMERATE	List concisely the points required.

EVALUATE	Make a judgment, either pro or con, and explain your decision.
EXPLAIN	State the how and why, clarifying and interpreting the material.
ILLUSTRATE	Explain or clarify by means of examples or diagrams.
OUTLINE	In a concise and systematic form, give main ideas and important supporting material.
SUMMARIZE	Give the material in a condensed form.

If you draw a blank while reading the question, try stimulating your thoughts with the same invention questions you used for studying (classical probes or journalist's questions, for example, see pages 8–13). Jot down ideas as they come to you. Even though you think you will remember your good ideas, they will probably slip away. Make a list of topics you want to cover. But work quickly. Spend about 10 percent of your time prewriting, or planning.

WRITE. When you're ready to start writing, use your prewriting list as a guide. Make your first sentence a rephrasing of the question: "Explain several ways in which science and transportation are related" becomes "Science and transportation are related in several ways." This sentence then serves as your thesis. Write an organized essay, the method of organization determined by the key words of the question, and include specific details wherever appropriate. Don't let yourself get off the topic, and make sure all your paragraphs are related to and support your thesis. Save about 10 percent of your time for revising and editing.

REVISE. Writing an essay exam is necessarily a quick process. But you will be amazed at how much you can improve your essay in only a few minutes. There are mainly two tasks you must do in revision—one relates to the big picture and the other to the little picture—and they are both important.

1. Make sure that all your paragraphs relate to your thesis and that your essay ends with the same point you began with. If one of your paragraphs is widely off the topic, you may have to scrap it; *X* it out and write "omit" in the margin. But a paragraph may be salvageable—if you add a topic sentence that relates the paragraph to your thesis or if you rewrite your thesis to encompass the

paragraph. If your ending makes a point different from your thesis, adjust either the end or the thesis. It is extremely important that all parts of your essay be related. Don't skip this step in your revision.

2. Check for errors and make corrections. Look for the kinds of errors you commonly make, because you probably have some in this essay. Cross out the error and make the correction neatly above it or in the margin. Don't write over the error, because your correction will probably be illegible. Editing for errors is extremely important. It can make the difference of a full letter grade or more.

One final point

For writing essay exams, use a pen, not a pencil. Penciled writing may seem easier to erase and revise, but it usually ends up smudged. Even under the best of conditions, penciled writing is harder on the reader's eyes; ink is brighter and clearer.

Business Letters

In addition to their essential function in commerce, business letters serve as job applications (see "Application Letters and Resumés"), inquiries, complaints, and so on. A business letter resembles an essay (see Part One, "Writing an Essay") in that the first paragraph introduces the subject and states the point or purpose, the middle paragraphs develop the subject, and the final paragraph concludes it. But a business letter is generally more concise than an essay, usually consisting of only one page if possible. While both essays and letters are written for a given audience, the audience of each letter is addressed directly. Tone in the letter, as in the essay, depends on the purpose, audience, and occasion, but in most cases the attitude represented must be objective, respectful, and courteous. A business letter should be clear and direct, not stiffly formal, nor should it express strong emotions. As a written record and evidence of the quality of the writer's work, the letter should be accurate in both content and form.

Appearance

Type the letter on white 8 1/2-by-11-inch paper. If you are not using letterhead stationery, begin the return address two inches from the top of the page, or at whatever depth is necessary to center your letter vertically. Set your margins for 1 inch to 1 1/2 inches, depending on the size of your letter; do not justify (square) your right margin. Typing on only one side of the page, single-space your letter, double-spacing between paragraphs and separate elements. The most common formats for business letters are *full block* and *modified block*. In the full-block style, every line begins at the left margin. In modified block, the return address, the date, and the complimentary close begin at the center of the page; all other lines begin at the left margin.

Parts of the letter

Although business letters can differ widely in appearance, they usually have similar parts. Each of the following elements is illustrated in the sample letters in Figures 4-1 and 4-3.

HEADING.   If you are not using letterhead stationery, begin your letter with your return address and the date. With letterhead stationery, begin with the date below the last printed line. Do not abbreviate words such as *street* and the name of the month; write out your state name in full or use the U.S. Postal Service **ZIP code** abbreviation. Include the ZIP code number after the state name or abbreviation.

INSIDE ADDRESS.   Write the name and address of the recipient of the letter, known as the inside address, below the date two to four spaces (or more) depending on the length of your letter. Again, use postal ZIP code abbreviations or write the state name in full. Include the ZIP code number.

SALUTATION.   Two spaces below the inside address, salute your reader by name: *Dear Ms. Caxton* or *Dear Lynn Caxton*. If you do not know the name of the person who will be reading your letter, you can address the company, department, or position: *Dear Ajax Foods, Dear Parts Department, Dear Personnel Manager*. Avoid the outdated and sexist *Dear Sir, Dear Madam*, or *Gentlemen*. Another option is to replace the salutation with a *subject line:*

```
SUBJECT: Recommendation for Linda Woo
```

Some writers omit both salutation and subject line and begin the body of the letter four spaces below the inside address. In this case, the complimentary close is also omitted, and the letter ends with the writer's signature.

BODY.   Two spaces below the salutation or subject line, identify your subject and purpose for writing. In the case of a letter of application, state the position you are applying for and how you heard about the

St. Cloud State University
St. Cloud, Minnesota 56301
Department of English

January 16, 19--

Professor Charles Johnson
The University of Minnesota
207 Lind Hall
207 Church Street SE
Minneapolis, MN 55455

Dear Professor Johnson:

I understand that Max Fredericks is applying for admission to the University of Minnesota Graduate School. I highly recommend him to you.

Max has been enrolled in two of my classes, and I am absolutely confident that he can perform at the level you expect of your graduate students.

He is one of the most responsible students I have had the experience to know, being regular in attendance and punctual with assignments. Never satisfied to skim the surface of knowledge of a subject, he is pursuing his interest in rhetoric to learn as much as he can before achieving a graduate degree. And the quality of his work is beyond the ordinary. You will approve, I think, of his scholarship and his ability to convey in writing the results of his study.

I hope to have further association with Max myself, but I commend him to you for the value that both he and the University of Minnesota Graduate School can gain from his affiliation with you.

Sincerely,

Amelia Drew

Amelia Drew
Associate Professor

FIGURE 4-1   Sample Business Letter, Full Block Style

opening. Then, in as many paragraphs as necessary, give details to support your point: your qualifications for the job you are applying for, or the problems with the merchandise you are complaining about, or the exemplary qualities of the person you are recommending, and so on. In your conclusion, state what action you anticipate: a job interview, replacement of the faulty merchandise, a positive review for the person you are recommending.

COMPLIMENTARY CLOSE.   Two spaces below the end of your letter, type a polite closing: *Sincerely, Sincerely yours,* or (less formal) *Best regards.* Four spaces down, type your name in full, optionally followed on the next line by a title: *Manager, Bradley University Student,* or *Sophomore.* Above your typed name, sign your letter, using your full name unless you are on a first-name basis with the recipient.

OTHER PARTS.   Other elements may follow below the closing. A person who types a letter for the sender may include initials such as these, *DJK:lss,* meaning that *DJK* composed the letter and *lss* typed it. If your letter is a cover letter accompanying enclosed materials, an *enclosure line* may follow: *Enclosure: Resumé; Enclosures (3);* or *Enc.* If you are sending a copy of the letter to someone other than the addressee, add a *copy notation: cc: Linda Woo.* All of these supplementary items should begin at the left margin.

   If your letter must run to a second page, begin typing at the left margin, one inch down, with a heading that comprises the recipient's name, the page number, and the date.

```
Lynn Caxton
Page 2
November 12, 19--
```

Skip two to four spaces and continue the letter.

Envelope

Fold your letter horizontally in thirds to fit in a full-size business envelope. Type your name and return address in the upper left corner of the envelope and the recipient's name and address in the center of the envelope. The U.S. Postal Service has requested that you use all capital letters, no punctuation in the address, and common address abbreviations, plus the ZIP code—all nine digits if you know them:

```
LYNN  CAXTON   PERSONNEL  MANAGER

AJAX  FOODS  CORPORATION

2238  W  26TH  ST

MILWAUKEE  WI  53202-0342
```

Memorandums

The memorandum is a means of communication within an organization. Like business letters, memos usually deal with only one subject and are written in an objective style. The level of formality depends on the audience and the occasion; your tone is more formal in reports and proposals to superiors and announcements and instructions to subordinates, perhaps less formal for requests and confirmations to peers. However, in writing your memos keep in mind the hidden audience—the file. Memos are records that remain accessible in the files perhaps for years.

Memos have many similarities to essays (see Part One, "Writing an Essay"). The first paragraph introduces the main idea and gives necessary background information (for example, "As we agreed in our meeting yesterday"). The middle paragraphs give details in support of the main point, some of which might be primarily for the record but may be included also as reminders to the reader. The last paragraph concludes the memo, stating expected action or reply, any recommendations, or whatever else is appropriate.

Memo format varies from organization to organization, and it is best to follow the format of your company. Headings almost always have these components: the name of the company, the word *Memorandum* or *Memo,* the name and position of the person receiving the memo, the name and position of the person sending it, the subject (written as a **title**), and the date. If you are sending a copy of the memo to someone other than the person named in the heading, include a copy line (*cc:* person's name) below the text of the memo. Your signature might be in the form of initials or your full name and might be either at the end of the memo or following your name in the heading. See Figure 4-2 for a sample memorandum.

City of SPRINGFIELD

MEMORANDUM

November 9, 19--

TO: Carl Smithson, City Manager

FROM: Jeanine Barritt, Research Consultant   *jb*

SUBJECT: Progress on Research for TIF Projects

Municipalities that want to raise money for eliminating blighted areas can often use tax increment financing (TIF). In forming a TIF district, cities are required by law to hold a public meeting to inform property owners of the effects on their property taxes. My research will appraise the buildings in proposed project areas within the city and determine whether the city must take steps to educate the public beyond the required public meeting. I will also survey owners' opinions about TIF districts.

Work Completed
To date, I have selected 15 TIF project areas in the State—5 within this city and the other 10 in cities of comparable size. I have prepared a preliminary survey to distribute to all property owners within each TIF project area.

Work To Be Done
I will set up a data base for storing the results of the survey. I will also advertise at local universities for an intern to assist me in appraising the buildings in the project areas and in collecting and analyzing data. As part of the intern's training, I will arrange a one-day session with an engineering firm to acquaint him or her with appraisal procedures.

Conclusions
The research will start on schedule if all things fall into place.

cc: Alex Baxter, City Engineer

FIGURE 4-2 Sample Memorandum

Application Letters and Resumés

For job applications, letters of application accompany *resumés*. A letter of application fulfills six tasks:

INTRODUCTION
1. Identifies the job you are applying for,
2. Tells how you learned about the job,

BODY
3. Summarizes and highlights your qualifications for the job,
4. Tells why you want to work for the company,
5. Refers the prospective employer to your resumé, and

CONCLUSION
6. Requests an interview.

This letter is essentially a sales letter, establishing you as a potential employee who will fit the employer's needs. Establish a businesslike yet friendly tone, and be concise. Proofread carefully; errors will be seen as evidence of careless work habits. Figure 4-3 shows a sample letter of application. See also "Business Letters."

A *resumé* is a job-application tool that summarizes a selection of details about your academic and employment background. The usual parts are your name, address, and telephone number; career goals; education; employment experience; and special honors, awards, volunteer work, and any special interests. The resumé should be accurate, specific, attractive, positive, and brief. Unless you have had an extensive professional career, limit your resumé to a single page. Concentrate on the positive aspects of your career, keeping the negatives to yourself unless you are asked about them. But be accurate; *never* lie about your history (think of having to account for your fictions later if you are employed). And give specific names, dates, and places. If you have received honors and awards, name them; but don't brag (don't describe yourself as "talented" or "intelligent," for example). Your resumé should be attractive; as a representation of you, it should have *absolutely no* typing, spelling, or other errors. It should be typed or printed on good quality paper, with enough white space between items to avoid an overcrowded look.

There is no single style or format for a resumé. As you design yours, think of your prospective employer, who may be reading several hundred resumés reporting similar qualifications. What will that employer be looking for? First, that the information is easy to locate, such as previous employment or volunteer work. This implies neatness

1533 College Avenue
San Francisco, CA 94132
March 26, 19--

Shirley Wyklen, Personnel Director
Roberts Inc.
400 E. Sixth Street
Oak Lake, IL 60630

Dear Shirley Wyklen:

Your advertisement in the San Francisco State University Placement office
describes the kind of position I have been preparing for. The vacancy notice
describes a position of executive development leading to one of buyer for your
department store. I believe that my academic and employment background,
coupled with my experience with the Oak Lake area (having grown up in
Markham), qualifies me for the position.

As stated in the enclosed resumé, I will be receiving my B.S. in Marketing in
May, having taken courses in consumer behavior, marketing management,
marketing research, international marketing, and business cycles and
forecasting--among others. Throughout my college career, I have worked in
retail sales and promotions, doing inventory control and at times dealing with
sales representatives. As a result, I have become quite comfortable with the
retail business. My collegiate awards have included selection to represent my
university at the National Marketing Research Forum this year and service on
the College of Business Executive Council for three years.

I will be in Illinois for a week at the end of the month (March 25-29) and would
be available for an interview at your convenience. You can reach me at
415/255-0123 most afternoons from 2:00 to 4:00 P.S.T.

Sincerely,

Maria Denys Lieberman

Maria Denys Lieberman

enclosure: resumé

FIGURE 4-3   Letter of Application, Modified Block Style

and order. Second, that your qualifications fit the job. This implies that you have done some homework about what kind of work the job entails. Third, that the person your resumé represents (you!) is upbeat, confident, intelligent, careful—in other words, an asset to the firm. See Figure 4-4 for a sample resumé.

Maria Denys Lieberman

College Address
1533 College Avenue
San Francisco, CA 94132
415/255-0123

Permanent Address
3842 W. 149th Street
Markham, IL 60426
312/366-4567

Professional Objective: Interested in an executive development program with a large department store that would lead to a position as a buyer.

Education

San Francisco State University, B.S. in Marketing. Expected May 199-
Major courses: Consumer Behavior, Marketing Management, Marketing Research, International Marketing, Business Cycles and Forecasting
G.P.A. 3.75   Dean's list all four years

Employment Experience

Retail sales/purchasing. 199- -- Present
Brooke Stationery and Books
Iona, CA 94300
Inventory control, retail display and purchasing, retail sales and promotions

Media specialist. 198- -- Present
Theater Department, San Francisco State University
Coordination of motion pictures, slides and other instructional aids for film studies courses

Honors and Awards

Delta Sigma Pi (International Business Fraternity) 198- -- Present
President, Senior vice president
College of Business Executive Council, 198- -- Present
Selected to represent San Francisco State University in National Marketing Research Forum, 199-

Community Activities

Laubach Literacy tutor, 198- -- Present
Counselor at summer camp for children with disabilities

References

Furnished upon request from Center for Career Planning and Placement, San Francisco State University, San Francisco, CA 92132

FIGURE 4-4   Sample Resumé

Index

a, an, the, 37, 55–57, 230
Abbreviations, 37–38
Absolute phrases, 38–39, 172
　participles in, 163–164
Abstract words/concrete words, 39
Abstracts, 267, 290, 321–322
　compared with summaries, 321–
　　322
　sample of, 322
accept, except, 39
Active verbs. *See* Voice
Active voice. *See* Voice
Addresses
　abbreviations in, 38
　in business letters, 328–332
　commas in, 72–73
　numbers in, 154
　ZIP codes in, 247–248 (checklist)
ad hominem, 107
Adjective clauses, 39, 81, 194, 220.
　See also Restrictive and
　nonrestrictive elements
Adjective phrases, 40, 170–172. *See*
　also Dangling modifiers;
　Misplaced modifiers
　infinitive, 126–127
　participial, 161–162
　prepositional, 179
Adjectives, 40–42, 144
　adverbs distinguished from, 40
　and agreement of pronouns, 46
　and agreement of verbs, 48–49
　classes of, 40
　comparative and superlative
　　forms of, 41–42 (checklist)
　coordinate, 40–41, 71–72
　cumulative, 40–41, 75

descriptive, order of, 41
　indefinite, 46, 48–49, 95, 114,
　　122–124 (checklists), 186–187
　infinitives as, 127
　participles as, 162
　and parts of speech, 166
　placement of, 40, 41
　possessive, 176–177
　prepositional phrases as, 179
　and pronoun reference, 181
　proper, 40, 186
　as subject complements, 217–218
Adverb clauses, 42, 80, 220
　with commas, 70, 75
　subordinating conjunctions to
　　introduce, 86–87 (checklist)
Adverb phrases, 42, 75
　infinitive, 126, 171–172
　prepositional, 179
Adverbs, 42–44, 145
　adjectives distinguished from, 43
　comparative and superlative
　　forms of, 43 (checklist)
　functions of, 42 (checklist)
　intensifiers as, 128–129
　and *-ly* endings, 43
　as misplaced modifiers, 138–139
　as parts of speech, 166
　prepositional phrases as, 179
　subordinate clauses as, 42, 221
　transitional (conjunctive), 43–44
advice, advise, 44
affect, effect, 44
aggravate, 44
Agreement of pronouns and
　　antecedents, 44–46, 212. *See*
　　also Nonsexist language;

Agreement of pronouns and
   antecedents, (*continued*)
   Pronouns
   when collective nouns are
      antecedents, 45
   compound antecedents, 45
   when generic nouns are ante-
      cedents, 45–46
   when indefinite pronouns are
      antecedents, 46
Agreement of subjects and verbs, 30,
      46–50. *See also* Verbs
   collective nouns and, 48
   compound subjects and, 48
   indefinite pronouns and, 48–49,
      123
   intervening words and, 49
   inverted order and, 49
   linking verbs and, 49
   mass nouns and count nouns and,
      47–48
   noun phrases and, 151
   nouns of plural form and singular
      meaning and, 50
ain't, 50, 89
Aircraft, italics for names of, 131
Allport, Gordon W., 19
all ready, already, 50
all right, 51
all together, altogether, 50
allude, refer, elude, 50
allusion, illusion, 50–51
alot, a lot, 51
already, 51
alright, all right, 51
altogether, 50
American Psychological Association
      (APA) style, 256, 280, 283–286,
      290–291
   format for, 283–286
   sample student paper in, portion,
      309–312
a.m., p.m., 37
among, between, 51
amount, number, 51
an, 37, 55–57
Analogy

   for developing paragraphs and
      essays, 18–19
   as fallacy in logic, 106–107
and/or, 51, 213
ante-, anti-, 51, 179
Antecedents, 44–46, 52, 183, 194
Anthologies, documenting items
      from, 282, 285
anxious, eager, 52
*any body, anybody; any one,
      anyone,* 52
anyplace, anywhere, 52
anyway, anyways, 52
APA. *See* American Psychological
      Association
Apostrophes, 53–55
   for contractions, 54
   misuse of, 54, 175, 176–178. *See
      also it's, its; who's, whose*
   for possessive case of nouns, 53
      (checklist), 63, 85, 116, 124,
      152, 176–179
   special uses of, 54–55
Application letters and resumés,
      328–332, 334–336. *See also*
      Business letter
   accuracy in, 334
   appearance of, 334
   sample application letter, 335
   sample resumé, 337
   tone of, 334
Appositives, 55, 63–64, 65–66, 87,
      148
Appropriate language. *See* Diction
Articles, 37, 55–57, 95, 229, 246
Article titles
   capitalization of, 229
   documentation of, 282–283, 285–
      286
   quotation marks for, 188, 229–230
as, 57, 65
as, as if, like, 57
Ashen, Frank, 20
assure, ensure, insure, 57–58
as to, 58
at, where, 58
Audience, 4–5, 7, 27

Audience, *(continued)*
  appealing to, 4
  questions about, 4–5
  of research paper, 256–257
Auxiliary (helping) verbs, 59, 117–
    119, 144, 239. *See also* Tenses
    of verbs
awful, awfully, 58
awhile, a while, 58

bad, badly, 58
Bandwagon appeal, 107
Bauman, Wendy Liane (Lankas), 293
be, 59 (checklist), 117–118, 134, 188,
    200, 218, 238, 239, 241
because of, 99
Begging the question, 106
being as, being that, 59
beside, besides, 59
between, 51
between you and me, 60
Bibliography, 261, 262–263
  working, 262–263, 271
Block quotation, 278, 298
"Boxcar" sentences, 82
Brackets, 60, 160, 303
Brainstorming, 8–9, 258
bring, take, 60
Bronowski, Jacob, 20
Business letter, 328–332. *See also*
    Memorandums
  appearance of, 328–329
  envelope for, 331–332
  job application, 324–327
  parts of, 329–331
  sample, full block style, 330
  sample, modified block style, 335
  tone of, 326
Business Periodicals Index, 265–267
    (figure)
but, yet, 60

Calendar items, capitalization of, 62
Call numbers, 259–260, 263, 268–
    269
can, may, 61

can't hardly, can't scarcely, 61, 99
can't help but, 61
Capitalization, 61–63 (checklist)
  and abbreviations, 37–38
  in APA documentation, 284–286
  in compound words, 84
  in MLA documentation, 281–283
  proper nouns and proper
      adjectives, 40, 61, 152, 186
Card catalogs, 259–260, 262, 268–
    269
Cases, 63–66
  with *and* or *or,* 65
  of appositives, 65–66
  after *as* or *than,* 65
  of interrogative pronouns, 66
  nominative, 63, 65
  objective, 60, 64, 80
  and parenthetical elements, 66
  of personal and relative pronouns,
      63 (checklist), 194
  possessive, 52, 64, 116, 124, 152,
      176–179
  in relative clauses, 66, 194
  of subject complements, 65, 80
Cause and effect
  connecting terms used in, 17, 231
  for developing paragraphs and
      essays, 16–17
center around, 66
Central catalog, 259–260, 262, 268–
    269 (figures)
  card, 260, 268–269
  online, 260, 269 (figure)
Chronological organization, 15, 19–
    20
  connecting terms used in, 15, 20,
      232
Citing sources. *See* Documenting
    sources
Clarity, 279–280
  commas for, 73
Classical probes, 11
Classification
  connecting terms used in, 17
  for developing paragraphs and
      essays, 17

Clauses, 67. *See also* Adjective
  clauses; Adverb clauses;
  Independent clauses; Noun
  clauses; Sentences; Subordinate
  clauses
  commas with, 70, 75–76, 77–79
  elliptical, 91–92, 221
  as misplaced modifiers, 139
Clichés, 67–68
Clustering, 9
Coherence and transitions, 24–25,
    230–232, 279–280, 288–289
  with consistent subjects, 25
  key connecting terms, 15–20, 24
  in revision checklist, 27
  thesis as primary coherence
    device, 24
Collective nouns, 68
  and pronoun-antecedent agree-
    ment, 45
  and subject-verb agreement, 48
Colloquial (informal) diction, 68, 95,
    114, 149, 288 (checklist)
Colons, 68–69
  in business letters, 68, 329–331
  with explanatory elements, 68
  to link related numbers, 68
  misuses, 68–69, 200
  with nonrestrictive elements, 148
Comma splices, 77–79 (checklist),
    84, 198, 231–232. *See also*
    Fused sentences
Commas, 69–73. *See also* Commas,
    unnecessary
  with addresses and dates, 72–73
  for clarity, 73
  and comma splices, 77–79
  with compound sentences, 70, 83
  with coordinate adjectives, 40–41,
    71–72
  with introductory sentence
    elements, 70
  with nonrestrictive and paren-
    thetical elements, 71, 148–149,
    160–161, 196–197, 231
  and parentheses, 76, 160

  with quotations, 72, 188–191
  in series, 71
Commas, unnecessary, 73–76, 83
Common knowledge, 255, 275, 300
Common nouns, 79, 122. *See also*
    Proper nouns
Community of scholars, 251–252
Comparative forms. *See* Adjectives;
    Adverbs
Comparison
  connecting terms used in, 18, 231
  for developing paragraphs and
    essays, 18
Complaint, letter of. *See* Business
    letters
complement, compliment, 80
Complements, 80. *See also* Linking
    verbs; Object complements;
    Subject complements
  and case, 63–64
Complex sentences, 67, 80–81, 203–
    204. *See also* Subordinate
    clauses
Complimentary close, 331
compose, 85
Compound antecedents, 45, 81
Compound-complex sentences, 67,
    81, 204
Compound predicates (verbs), 74,
    82–83, 246
Compound sentences, 67, 83–84,
    203, 204. *See also* Sentence
    variety
  commas in, 70
  and comma splices, 77–79
  semicolons in, 199
Compound verbs. *See* Compound
    predicates
Compound words, 84–85
comprise, compose, 85
Computer searches, 270
Conciseness. *See* Wordiness
Conclusions, 23–24, 26
  in business correspondence, 331,
    332, 334
  length of, 279

Conclusions, *(continued)*
  in research papers, 278–279, 288, 307
Concrete words, 39
Concursiveness, 254
Conjunctions, 85–87
  coordinating, 76, 78, 83, 85–86
    (checklist), 89, 143, 231–232
  correlative, 86
  in mixed constructions, 87, 143
  subordinating, 86–87 (checklist),
    143, 221–222
  transitional adverbs distinguished
    from, 231–232
Conjunctive adverbs. *See* Transitional adverbs
Connectors, 16–20, 87. *See also*
    Conjunctions; Prepositions;
    Transitional adverbs
Connotation, 88. *See also* Diction
conscience, conscious, 88
consensus of opinion, 88
consequently, subsequently, 88
continual, continuous, 88
Contractions, 88–89
  apostrophes for, 54
  it's as, 54, 89, 132, 177–178
  and research papers, 256, 288, 291
  who's as, 54, 89, 177–178
Contrast
  paragraphs and essays developed
    by, 18
  transitions to signal, 231
Coordinate adjectives, 40–41, 71–72
Coordinating conjunctions, 76, 78,
    83, 85–86 (checklist), 89, 143,
    231–232. *See also* Coordination; Parallelism
  with commas, 70, 71, 74, 78
  in compound antecedents, 81
  in compound predicates, 82–83
  in compound sentences, 78, 83
  in mixed constructions, 87, 143
  transitional adverbs distinguished
    from, 231
Coordination, 83, 85–86, 89–90,
    230–232. *See also* Compound

antecedents; Compound-
    complex sentences; Compound
    predicates; Compound
    sentences; Conjunctions
  coordinate adjectives, 40–41, 71–
    72
  with commas, 70, 71–72, 74
  overuse of, 90, 222
  with semicolons, 199–200
  unequal coordination, 83
Corrections
  on essay examinations, 327–328
  on final draft, 30–31, 290
Correlative conjunctions, 86, 90. *See
    also* Parallelism
Correspondence, 328–332
Count nouns, 47, 56, 90 (checklist).
    See also Mass nouns; Plurals
couple of, 91
Cover letters, 328–332, 334–336
Credibility of writer. *See* Writer's
    credibility
criteria, criterion, 91
Criticism, 27. *See also* Critiques
Critiques, 323–324
  and analyzing writing, 323
  documenting sources in, 323–324
  and evaluating quality of writing,
    323
  tense of verbs in, 324
  tone of, 324
Cumulative adjectives, 40–41, 75.
    See also Coordinate adjectives

-d and *-ed* endings, 130, 192, 237–
    239
Dangling modifiers, 30, 91–93, 127,
    161. *See also* Misplaced
    modifiers
Dash, 93, 148, 197
data, 93. *See also* Facts; Information
Databases, 270
Dates, 154
  commas in, 72–73
Days of the week, 62

Declarative sentences, 204
Definite articles. *See* Articles
Definitions
    for developing paragraphs and
        essays, 19
    dictionary, 96–98
    italics with, 19, 132
Demonstrative adjectives, 94
Demonstrative pronouns, 94
Denotation, 88. *See also* Diction
Dependent clauses. *See* Subordinate
    clauses
Description
    connecting terms used in, 16
    for developing paragraphs and
        essays, 15–16
Details, 23, 25, 26
    in abstracts and summaries, 321
    in essay examinations, 325–327
Determiners, 55–57, 95
Development of paragraphs and
        essays, 14–20
    with analogy, 18–19
    with cause and effect, 16–17
    with classification, 17
    with comparison and contrast, 18
    with definition, 19
    with description, 15–16
    with exemplification, 16
    with narration, 15
    with process analysis, 19–20
Dewey decimal classification, 259,
    264
Diction, 27, 95–96, 288. *See also*
        Abstract words/concrete words;
        Connotation/denotation;
        Figures of speech; Wordiness
    and clichés, 67–68
    and colloquialisms, 68, 95, 288
    and euphemisms, 95, 103
    and idioms, 120–121
    in informal usage, 68, 95, 213–
        214, 255, 288
    and jargon, 95, 132
    and level of formality, 5–6, 256,
        288

    and nonsexist language, 45–46,
        95, 149–150, 183, 291. *See also*
        Gender
    and nonstandard usage, 95, 97,
        150
    and slang, 6, 95, 213–214, 288
    and vocabulary, 5, 255–256, 288
Dictionaries, 96–98
    as research tools, 264–265
different from, different than, 98
differ from, differ with, 98
Direct objects, 98, 155–156, 200–
    202, 238, 243
disinterested, 98
Division of words, 120
do
    in contractions, 99
    for emphasis, 240
    as helping verb, 117–118, 240
    as irregular verb, 130
    in negation, 240
    in questions, 187–188, 240
Documenting sources, 274, 278,
    280–286, 287–288, 294
    APA style for, 256, 280, 283–286,
        290–291, 309–312
    and credibility of researcher, 255–
        256, 274, 276–277, 288
    in critiques, 323–324
    MLA style for, 256, 280–283, 290–
        308
    parenthetical styles of, 280–281,
        283–284
don't, doesn't, 99
Double comparatives, 41–44
Double negatives, 99, 147
Double superlatives, 41–44
Drafting, 23–25. *See also* Drafts;
        Prewriting; Revision
    coherence in, 24–25, 279–280
    conclusions, 23–24, 278–279
    and development, 14–20
    essay examinations, 327–328
    introductions, 23–24, 278–279
    organization in, 20–21
    outlines for, 22

Drafting, *(continued)*
  of research paper, 277–280
  and thesis, 13–14, 23–24
  and writing process, 8
Drafts. *See also* Drafting; Revision
  editing, 30 (checklist)
  and peer review, 27
  proofreading, 31 (checklist)
  revising, 25–27 (checklist), 286–
    291 (checklists)
due to, because of, 99

e, adding suffixes to words ending
    in, 216
eager, 52
-ed endings, 192, 215
Edited American English, 217
Editing, 30 (checklist), 290–291
    (checklist), 328
Editor, crediting book prepared by,
    281, 284
effect, affect, 44
Either/or fallacy, 106
elicit, illicit, 100
Ellipses, 100, 168, 302
Elliptical constructions, 91–92, 220
  dangling, 91–92
Ellison, Ralph, 15
elude, 50
*emigrate from, immigrate to,
    migrate,* 100
Emphasis, 101–102, 207
  dashes for, 93
  italics for, 132
  in organization, 21
  with parallelism, 158
  with repetition, 101, 195
  with sentence variety, 205–206
  subordination for, 101, 221–222
  unintentional, 196
Empty phrases, 244
Encyclopedias, 261, 265
  documenting as source material,
    282, 285
End punctuation. *See* Exclamation
  point; Period; Question mark

ensure, 57–58
enthused, 102
Envelope, for business correspon-
    dence, 331–332
-er and *-est* endings, 41–42, 43, 215–
    216
especially, specially, 102
Essay examinations, 324–328
    (checklists)
  invention questions for study and
    prewriting, 325–327
  key words in, 326–327
  and summarizing reading and
    lecture notes, 324–325
  and taking notes on lectures, 325
  and taking notes on reading, 325
Essays
  coherence in, 24–25
  development of, 14–20
  drafting, 23–25
  editing, 30 (checklist)
  organization of, 20–21
  outlining, 22
  prewriting, 8–13
  proofreading, 31 (checklist)
  revising, 25–27 (checklist)
  theses of, 13–14
Essay titles, 230
et al., etc., 38, 102–103
Etymology, 98
Euphemism, 95, 103
Evaluation of sources, 276–277, 296,
    323
every day, everyday, 103
every one, everyone, 103
Evidence
  facts and opinions as, 7, 104–105,
    277
  primary, 253–254
  secondary, 253–254
ex-, 178
Examples, 16, 104, 327
Exemplification
  for developing paragraphs and
    essays, 16
  connecting terms used in, 16, 231
except, 39

Exclamation points, 103
  avoiding, 101
  in exclamatory sentences, 104,
      206
  in quotations, 190
Exclamatory sentences, 104, 205
  punctuation of, 103
Explaining, 7
Expletives, 104, 126, 129, 223, 229,
    245
explicit, implicit, 104

Facts, 7, 104–106, 276
Fallacies in logic, 7, 105–107
False analogy, 106–107
Farb, Peter, 17
farther, further, 107
Faulty parallelism, 158–159
Faulty predication, 143–144. *See
    also* Shifts
Feedback, 27
fewer, less, 107
Figurative language. *See* Figures of
    speech
Figures. *See* Numbers
Figures of speech, 108
  Metaphors, 108, 137
  Mixed, 108
  Similes, 108, 211
Final consonant, doubling, 215
Final draft
  proofreading, 31
  of research paper, 290–292
  of sample student paper, 31–33
finalize, 108
Finite verbs, 108, 127–128. *See also*
    Verbs
firstly, secondly, thirdly, 108
Footnotes, 280
Foreign words, italics for, 132
Formal outline, 22
  example of, 313–318
Format
  of business correspondence, 328–
      337
  of final drafts, 290–292

former, latter, 108–109
Fractions, 84, 120, 153
Fragments of sentences, 109–111
  acceptable, 111
  appositive as, 55
  clauses as, 67, 109, 185
  and compound predicates, 83
  correcting, 110–111
  identifying, 110
  as incomplete thoughts, 111
  long, 82
  phrases as, 109, 115, 126, 162,
      170, 180, 233
  semicolons as causes of, 199
  verb omissions as causes of, 237
Frank, Francine, 20
Freewriting, 12
Full block format for correspon-
    dence, 329–330 (figure)
fun, 111
further, 107
Fused sentences (run–on sentences),
    112–113. *See also* Comma
    splices
  correcting, 112
  identifying, 112–113
Future perfect progressive, 225
Future perfect tense, 224–228
Future progressive, 225
Future tense, 224–228

Gender, 113–114 (checklist)
  and nonsexist language, 149–150
  and pronouns, 52, 114
Generalizations, 105–106, 114
General to specific organization, 21
General words, 114–115. *See also*
    Abstract words/concrete words
Generic *he,* 45–46, 114, 149–150
Generic nouns, 45–46, 114, 149–150
Geographical area names
  abbreviation of, 38
  capitalization of, 61–62
Gerund phrases, 115, 151, 171. *See
    also* Gerunds; Phrases; Verbal
    phrases

Gerund phrases, *(continued)*
  and dangling modifiers, 91–93
Gerunds, 115–116, 233, 234, 240.
    See also Gerund phrases
get, 116
good and, 116
good, well, 116
Government publications
  APA documentation of, 285
  MLA documentation of, 282
  *Monthly Catalog of United States
    Government Publications,* 269–
    270
  for research, 269
Grammar, 3, 27, 30, 290–291. *See
    also* specific aspects
Grammatical classification of
    sentences, 203–205

half a, a half, a half a, 117
Hamilton, Edith, 12
hanged, hung, 117
hardly, 61
Hasty generalizations, 105–106
have
  as helping verb, 117–118, 239
  as irregular verb, 130
  and perfect tenses, 224–226, 239
he/she, his/her, 117, 149–150
Heading in business letters, 329
Helping verbs (auxiliary verbs), 59,
    117–119, 144, 163, 239. *See
    also* Tenses of verbs
herself, 184, 192–193
himself, 184, 192–193
his/her, 117, 213
hisself, 119, 192–193
Historical evidence, 104–105
Holidays, capitalization of, 62
Homonyms, 31, 119, 214
hopefully, 120
Hours and minutes, 68, 154
Humor, 24
hung, 117
Hyphens
  in compound words, 84–85

to connect spelled-out numbers,
    120. *See also* Numbers
  to divide words, 120

I, capitalization of, 61
idea, ideal, 120
Idioms, 97, 120–121. *See also*
    Diction
i.e., 38
ie or *ei* spelling rule, 217
illicit, 100
illusion, 50–51
  imitation, 12–13
Illustrating points, 16, 21, 27
  in abstracts and summaries, 321
  in essay examinations, 327
immigrate to, 100
impact, 122
Imperative mood, 122, 145, 209,
    235, 237
Imperative sentences, 122, 145, 204
implicit, 104
imply, infer, 122
Incomplete sentences. *See* Frag-
    ments
Indefinite adjectives, 46, 48–49, 95,
    114, 122–124 (checklists), 185–
    186
Indefinite articles, 37, 55–57, 122
Indefinite pronouns, 46, 48–49, 114,
    122–124 (checklists), 187–188
Independent clauses, 67, 124, 198,
    212. *See also* Sentence patterns
  and comma splices, 77–79
  in compound sentences, 83
  and fused sentences, 112–113
  punctuating, 68–69, 70, 74, 199
  in sentences, 202–204
  and sentence types, 80–81, 81–82,
    83–84, 203–204, 211
Index cards
  for note taking, 270–271 (figure)
  for working bibliographies, 262–
    263 (figure)
Indexes
  newspaper, 267

Indexes, (*continued*)
periodical, 260, 262, 265–267 (figure)
specialized, 267
Indicative mood, 122, 124, 145, 235, 237
shifts, 210
Indirect objects, 124, 155–156, 201
Indirect questions, 124–125
punctuating, 125, 187
Indirect quotations, 125–126 (checklist), 190
infer, 122
Infinitive phrases, 126–127, 151, 171, 172, 233. *See also* Infinitives
as dangling modifiers, 91–93
Infinitives, 127–128, 233–234. *See also* Infinitive phrases
sequence of tenses with, 127–128
split, 128, 217
subjects of, 64, 127, 210
verbs followed by, 240 (checklist)
Informal (colloquial) diction, 5–6, 68, 95, 212–213, 256
Information, 104–105. *See also* Facts
for essay development, 7
and research paper, 253–254, 257–258, 277–278
Informative theses, 14, 261–262
Informing as purpose for writing, 6–7, 257–258
Institutions, capitalization of names of, 61–62
insure, 57–58
Integrating source materials, 277–278, 287–288, 296, 310–311
Intensifiers, 128–129. *See also* Adverbs
Intensive pronouns, 184, 192–193
Interjections, 103, 129
as part of speech, 166
Interrogative sentences, 188–189, 204. *See also* Questions
Interrogative words, 9, 129, 188, 204, 258

Interviews
APA format for documentation of, 286
MLA format for documentation of, 283
as primary research, 253
Intransitive verbs, 129, 200–202 (checklist), 238–239. *See also* Linking verbs
Introductions, 23–24, 26
in business correspondence, 328, 332
in critiques, 323
in job application letters, 334
length of, 279
in research papers, 278–279, 288, 293
and theses, 14
Introductory elements, comma after, 70
Invention. *See* Prewriting and invention
Inverted sentence order, 49, 129, 201. *See also* Expletives
irregardless, 130
Irregular verbs, 130–131 (checklist), 224–225 (checklist), 237–238 (checklist). *See also be;* Regular verbs
is when, is where, 142–144
Italics (underlining), 131–132
for emphasis, 101, 132
for foreign words and phrases, 132
for names of vehicles, 131
for titles of works, 131, 229–230
for words, letters, and numbers referred to as words, 19, 132
Items in a series
colons to introduce, 68
commas to separate, 71
unnecessary commas with, 75
it's, its, 54, 64, 89, 132, 177–178

Jackson, George, 17
Jargon, 95, 132. *See also* Wordiness

Journalist's questions, 9, 11, 258
Journals
    in APA documentation, 285–286
    indexes of, 260, 265–267
    in MLA documentation, 283

Keller, Helen, 19
Key words
    for coherence, 16–20, 24, 279
    in essay examinations, 326–327
        (checklist)
    for research note cards, 270–272
kind of, sort of, 133

Languages, capitalization of, 61
"Last Countdown, The" (final draft),
    32–33
"Last Count Down, The" (rough
    draft), 28–29
latter, 108–109
lay, lie, 130 (checklist), 133
leave, let, 134
Leih, Virginia, 293
lend, loan, 134
less, 107
let, 134
Letters, business. *See* Business
    letters
Letters of application, 328–329,
    334–337 (figures)
Letters of the alphabet, italics for,
    132
Lewis, C. S., 18
Library
    card catalog, 260, 268
    cataloging systems, 259–260,
        268
    central catalog, 259–260, 262,
        268–269
    computer searches, 262, 270
    for finding a topic for writing,
        259–260
    government publications in, 269
    microform holdings in, 267
    online catalog, 260, 268–269
        (figure)
    periodicals indexes, 260, 262,
        265–267
    reference collection, 264–
        265
    serial holdings list, 267
    shelf list, 260
Library of Congress classification,
    259–260, 268
*Library of Congress Subject Head-
    ings,* 260
lie, 130 (checklist), 133
like, 57
Linking verbs, 49, 80, 134, 201
    (checklist), 218, 238–240
Listing for prewriting, 8–9
literally, 135
Literature, reviews of, 253, 257
loan, 134
Logical fallacies, 105–107
loose, lose, 135
lots, lots of, 135. *See also a lot*
-ly ending, 43, 216

Magazine articles
    APA documentation of, 285
    MLA documentation of, 282
Magazine titles, italics for, 131
Main clauses. *See* Independent
    clauses
Main verb, 117
man, mankind, 135, 149
Manuscript format, 290–292
Mapping, as prewriting, 9, 10
    (figure)
Mass nouns (noncount nouns), 47–
    48, 56, 135–137. *See also* Count
    nouns
    and subject-verb agreement, 47–
        48
may, 61
maybe, may be, 137
Mechanics, 137. *See also* Abbrevia-
    tions; Capitalization; Hyphens;
    Italics; Numbers

media, 137
Memorandums, 332–333
    sample memorandum, 333
    subject line in, 332–333
    tone of, 332
Metaphors, 108, 137. *See also* Simile
Microforms, 267
might of, 138, 157
migrate, 100
Misplaced modifiers, 30, 138–139.
    See also Dangling modifiers
Misspelled words, common, 139–
    142 (checklist). *See also*
    Homonyms; Spelling
Mixed constructions, 142–144. *See
    also* Shifts
Mixed metaphors, 137
MLA. *See* Modern Language
    Association
Modals, 118, 144, 163, 207–209,
    228, 239
Modern Language Association
    (MLA) style, 256, 280–283,
    290–291
    format for, 280–283
    sample student paper, 292–308
    in "Works Cited," 281–283
Modified block format, 329, 335
    (figure)
Modifiers, 144–145, 165, 196. *See
    also* Adjectives; Adverbs
    dangling, 91–93
    misplaced, 138–139
Money amounts, 153
*Monthly Catalog of United States
    Government Publications,* 269–
    270
Months of the year, capitalization,
    62 (checklist)
Mood of verbs, 145. *See also*
    Imperative mood; Indicative
    mood; Subjunctive mood
    shifts in, 209
moral, morale, 146
Ms., 146
Musical works, titles of
    capitalization of, 61

    italicized, 131, 229
    quotation marks for, 188, 229–230
myself, 184, 192–193

Names
    capitalization of, 61–62 (check-
        list)
    plurals of, 175
    as proper nouns, 152, 186
Narration
    for developing paragraphs and
        essays, 15, 21
    for introductions, 24
    transitions with, 15, 231
Nationalities, capitalization of
    names of, 62
Negative constructions, 146–147
Newspaper articles
    APA documentation of, 286
    indexes of, 267
    MLA documentation of, 283
Nominalizations, 147. *See also*
    Wordiness
Nominative absolutes, 38–39
Nominative case, 63–66, 80
Noncount (mass) nouns, 47–48, 56,
    135–137. *See also* Count nouns
Nonrestrictive elements, 148–149,
    195. *See also* Restrictive and
    nonrestrictive elements
    punctuation of, 55–71, 93
Non sequitur, 107
Nonsexist language, 45–46, 114,
    149–150, 183, 291. *See also*
    Gender
Nonstandard usage, 95, 97, 150. *See
    also* Standard English
"Nonverbal Communication in
    Gender Contexts," 293–318
nor, or, 48, 86 (checklist), 95, 151,
    157
Notes
    on computers, 272
    for essay examinations, 324–326
    from lectures and reading
        (checklist), 325

Notes, *(continued)*
    on index cards, 270–271 (figure)
    organizing, 275–277
    on photocopies, 272
    for research paper, 270–275
    with self-sticking note sheets, 272
Noun clauses, 81, 151, 193, 220–221. *See also* Clauses
    as indirect questions, 125
    introduced by *that,* 221
Noun phrases, 151–152
Nouns, 151–152
    case of, 63
    collective, 48, 68
    count and mass, 47, 56, 90 (checklist), 135–137
    as part of speech, 166
    phrases as, 151
    possessive forms of, 52, 53–54, 64, 85, 116, 124, 152, 176–178, 181–182
    proper, 186
    singular and plural, 172–175, 212
    and subject-verb agreement, 46–50
    subordinate clauses as, 151, 221–222
number (amount), 51
Number, 47, 52, 94, 153, 172–175, 212
    shifts in, 207–208
Numbers, 84, 153–154

Object complements, 80, 155, 201
Objective case, 60, 63–66 (checklist), 80
Objects of prepositions, 156–157. *See also* Case
    and unnecessary commas, 73–74
Objects of verbs, 98, 155–157, 193, 194, 200–201, 238, 241. *See also* Case
of, have, 157
off of, off from, 157
OK, O.K., okay, 157
on, upon, 157

on account of, 157
Opinions
    citing source of, 275
    for development of essays, 7
    evaluating sources of, 276
Options, slashes to separate, 213
or, 48, 65, 86 (checklist), 151, 157
Organization
    chronological, 15
    emphasis, 21
    general to specific, 21
    problem and solution, 21
    question and answer, 20
    of research paper, 275–277
    spatial, 15–16
    specific to general, 21
Organizing research notes, 275–277
Outline, 22, 275–276
    formal, 22
    as guide for drafting, 8, 277, 327
    informal, 22
    sample, 313–318
    sentence, 313–318
Oversimplification, 106
owing to the fact that, 157. *See also* Wordiness

Page format, for final draft, 289–291
Page numbers
    in APA documentation, 283–286
    in MLA list of works cited, 280–283
    on note cards, 271 (figure)
    in parenthetical citations, 280–281, 283–284
    in working bibliographies, 263 (figure)
Pamphlet, documentation of
    in APA style, 285
    in MLA style, 282
Paper, 3. *See also* Essay
Paragraphs, 287, 289, 327
    in business correspondence, 329–332
    and coherence, 24–25, 279–280, 327–328

Paragraphs, (*continued*)
concluding, 24, 278–279, 288, 331, 332
and essay examinations, 327–328
introductory, 23–24, 278–279, 288, 329, 332
methods of developing, 14–20
and revision, 26–27, 287, 288–289, 327–328

Parallelism, 30, 157–158. *See also* Coordination

Paraphrases, 158–160, 273
in critiques, 323–324
documenting, 280, 294–295

Parentheses, 82, 160
and brackets, 60, 160
and APA documentation, 283
and MLA documentation, 280
and other punctuation, 76, 160, 168

Parenthetical documentation, 294
APA style for, 283–284
in critiques, 323–324
MLA style for, 280–281

Parenthetical elements, 160–161. *See also* Nonrestrictive elements
and abbreviations, 38
and case, 66
commas with, 71, 160

Participial phrases, 161, 171, 233
as dangling modifiers, 91–93
as sentence fragments, 162

Participles, 162 (checklist), 233–234 (checklist)
as adjectives, 40
as sentence fragments, 162
as verb parts, 163

Parts of sentences, 164–165. *See also* Sentence patterns; Verbs
modifiers, 144–145, 165
predicates, 165, 178
subjects, 164, 219–220 (checklist)

Parts of speech, 165–166. *See also* individual entries

Passive voice, 166, 241–242. *See also* Voice
and dangling modifiers, 92–93
and shifts, 210–211

Past participles, 118, 162–164 (checklist), 224, 233, 237–240 (checklist), 241

Past perfect tense, 224–228 (checklists), 235
uses of, 226

Past progressive, 225 (checklist), 226, 235, 236

Past tense verbs, 225 (checklist), 227–229 (checklist), 235

Peer review, 27

percent, percentage, 167

Perfect tenses of verbs, 224–228, 234–236

Periodicals indexes, 260, 262, 270

Periods, 167–169, 200
with abbreviations, 38, 167–168
with ellipses, 100, 168, 302
as end punctuation, 167
and parentheses, 168
with quotation marks, 168, 190–191
semicolons compared with, 200
and sentence fragments, 109–111, 169

Person, 169
and agreement of pronouns and antecedents, 44–46
and agreement of subjects and verbs, 46–50
and level of formality, 256, 278
and pronoun forms, 184 (checklist)
shifts in, 169, 208

Personal pronouns, 63 (checklist), 169–170, 184 (checklist), 212

Persuasion, 7, 14, 252, 261–262

Persuasive theses, 14, 261–262

phenomenon, phenomena, 170

Photocopies for research notes, 272

Phrases, 170–172

Phrases, *(continued)*
  absolute, 38–39, 172
  appositive, 55
  commas with, 70, 75
  as dangling modifiers, 91–93, 127,
    161
  as fragments, 109, 115, 126, 162,
    170, 180, 233
  gerund, 115, 171
  infinitive, 126–127, 171–172
  as misplaced modifiers, 139
  noun, 151
  participial, 161–162, 171
  prepositional, 170, 179–180
  as restrictive and nonrestrictive
    elements, 196–197
  verb, 234
  verbal, 233
Place names
  abbreviations of, 38, 247–248
  in business correspondence, 247–
    248, 329, 331–332
  commas in, 72, 248, 331–332
Plagiarism, 172, 274–275
Plans for writing, 20–22. *See also*
  Prewriting
Plays, titles of
  capitalization of, 61
  italics for, 131, 230–231
Plurals, 152, 172–176. *See also*
  Number; Singular
  of compound words, 84
  and proper nouns, 54, 175
plus, 176
Poems, titles of
  capitalization of, 61
  italics for, 131, 230–231
  quotation marks for, 188
  slashes to separate lines of, 214
Possessive adjectives, 63–66
  (checklist), 95, 176–178
  (checklist)
Possessive case, 63–66 (checklist),
  152, 176–178 (checklist)
  with apostrophes, 53 (checklist),
    176

  of compound words, 85
  and gerunds, 116
  and pronoun antecedents, 52
  and pronoun reference, 182
  of pronouns, 54, 63–64 (check-
    list), 89, 124, 176–178
Possessive pronouns, 54, 63–64
  (checklist), 176–178
Post hoc fallacy, 106
precede, proceed, 178
Predicate adjectives, 217
Predicate nouns, 217
Predicates, 164–165, 178
  compound, 82–83
  and faulty predication, 143
  as sentence part, 165, 202, 219
  verbs in, 234
Prefixes, 84, 178. *See also* Suffixes
Prepositional phrases, 156, 170–
  171, 179–180. *See also* Preposi-
    tions
  commas with, 70, 74
  dangling, 91
  as fragments, 170, 180
  misplaced, 139, 179
  as restrictive elements, 196
Prepositions, 180–181 (checklist)
  as idioms, 121, 180
  objects of, 156
  as parts of speech, 166
  in titles, capitalization of, 61
Present participles, 117, 162–164
  (checklist), 224, 233, 238–240
  (checklist)
Present perfect tense, 224–229
  (checklists), 235
Present progressive, 225–227
  (checklist)
Present perfect progressive, 226
Present tense, 224–229 (checklists),
  235–240
  uses of, 226
pretty, 181
Prewriting and invention, 8–13,
  325–327
  brainstorming, 8–9

Prewriting and invention, (*continued*)
  classical probes, 11, 325, 327
  clustering, 9
  and essay examinations, 326–327
  freewriting, 12
  imitation, 12–13
  journalist's questions, 9, 11, 325, 327
  listing, 8–9
  mapping, 9, 10 (figure)
  outlining, 22
Primary evidence, 253
Primary research, 252–254
principal, principle, 181
Problem and solution organization, 21
Process analysis, 19–20
  transitions for, 20, 231
Process of writing essays, 8
proceed, 178
Progressive forms of verbs, 163, 224–227, 240
  shifts in, unintentional, 236
  uses of, 226, 235
Pronoun-antecedent agreement, 44–46, 52. *See also* Agreement of pronouns and antecedents; Nonsexist language; Pronouns
Pronoun case, 63–66, 176–178. *See also* Case
Pronoun reference, 30, 94, 181–183. *See also* Agreement of pronouns and antecedents; Nonsexist language; Pronouns
Pronouns, 183–187
  agreement with antecedents, 44–46, 52
  antecedents of, 52
  case of, 63–66, 176–178
  demonstrative, 94, 186
  indefinite, 46, 48–49, 114, 122–124 (checklist), 186
  interrogative, 66, 129, 185
  and nonsexist language, 149–150
  and parts of speech, 166

  personal, 63 (checklist), 169–170, 184 (checklist), 213
  reference, 30, 182–183
  reflexive, 187, 192
  relative, 66, 109, 184–185, 194 (checklist), 195–197 (checklist), 197–198, 219–221, 243
Proofreading
  application letters and resumés, 334
  for homonyms, 119
  research paper, 291
  tips for, 31 (checklist)
Proper adjectives, 40, 186
Proper nouns, 61–62, 152, 186, 197
Public documents. *See* Government publications
Punctuation, 30, 186. *See also individual marks of punctuation*
Purposes for writing, 6–7
  explaining, 7
  informing, 6–7, 257–258
  persuading, 7, 258
  recording, 6–7
  reporting, 7, 257

Question and answer organization, 20
Question marks, 186–188
  for marking questions in reading, 325
Questions, 188–189, 200, 207
  about audience, 4–5 (checklist), 26
  in classical probes, 11, 26, 325, 327
  as essay organization strategy, 20
  on essay examinations, 326–327
  indirect, 124–125
  interrogative words, 66, 129, 185
  for introductions and conclusions, 23–24
  journalist's, 9–11, 26, 325, 327
  punctuation of, 186–188

Questions, *(continued)*
  research, 251–253, 260–262
  for revision, 26
  tag, 188–189, 223
  for thesis development, 13
    (checklist)
  yes/no, 188
Questions about audience, 4–5
    (checklist)
quotation, quote, 188
Quotation marks, 19, 188–191, 272.
    See also Italics; Quotations
  with other punctuation, 72, 168,
    188, 189–191
  for titles, 189, 229–230
Quotations, 190, 272–273, 280, 287–
    288
  with brackets, 60, 303
  capitalization of, 62
  commas with, 72
  in critiques, 323–324
  documentation of, 280, 283, 294,
    310–311
  with ellipses, 100, 191, 302
  indented block, 278, 298
  indirect, 125–126 (checklist), 188,
    191
  integration of, into text, 277–278,
    287–288, 296
  for introductions, 23
  long or formal, 189, 191
  in note taking, 272–273
  of poetry, 214

Races, capitalization of names of, 62
Radio programs
  italics for titles of, 131
  quotation marks for titles of
    episodes of, 189
raise, rise, 191
Reader. *See* Audience
*Readers' Guide to Periodical
    Literature,* 260, 265
Reading
  for abstracts and summaries, 321

for critiques, 323
for errors, in proofreading, 31
    (checklist)
for essay examinations, 324–328
for revision, 25–26, 286–291
for spelling improvement, 214–
    215
  taking notes on, 270–275
real, really, 191
reason is because, 191
Reciprocal pronouns, 150
Recording as purpose for writing, 6–7
Recursiveness, 254
Redundancies, 191. *See also*
    Wordiness
Reed, Ishmael, 16
Reference. *See* Pronoun reference
Reference collection, 264–265
Reference librarians, 264
"References" list, 284, 289, 312
Reflexive pronouns, 184, 192
Regular verbs, 192, 225 (checklist),
    237–238 (checklist). *See also*
    Irregular verbs
Relative adjectives and adverbs, 192–
    194 (checklist), 219–222
Relative clauses, 66, 109, 183–185,
    193–194, 194 (checklist), 195–
    197 (checklist), 197–198, 220–
    222
Relative pronouns, 66, 109, 148–
    149, 184–185, 193, 194
    (checklist), 195–197 (checklist),
    197–198, 220–222, 243–244
Repetition, 195–197, 243–245
  for coherence, 24, 196, 279
  for emphasis, 101, 196
  ineffective, 30, 196, 244–245
  of key words, 24
Reporting
  as purpose for writing, 7
  research, 253–254, 255
Research
  and audience, 256–257
  and bibliographies of sources,
    261–263

bibliography cards, 262–263 (figure)
and encyclopedias, 261, 265
and evaluating sources, 276–277, 296, 323
in library, 253, 259–260
and note cards, 270–271 (figure)
primary, 252–254
secondary, 252–254
working bibliography for, 262–263 (figure)
Research paper
audience of, 256–257
clarity in, 279–280
coherence in, 279–280
conclusion of, 278–279, 288, 307
documentation in, 274, 278, 280–288, 294
drafting, 277–280
format of, 289–291
informative, 257–258, 261–262
and integration of source materials, 277–278, 287–288, 296, 310–311
introduction of, 278–279, 288, 293
organizing, 275–277
and paraphrase of source materials, 278, 294
persuasive, 258, 261–262
primary evidence in, 253–254
process of, 254, 262
purpose for, 257–258
quotation of source materials in, 278, 294, 295, 298
"References" list in, 284–286, 289, 312
revising, 286–289 (checklists)
rhetoric of, 255–258
secondary evidence in, 253–254
summary of source materials in, 278, 295, 296
thesis of, 260–262, 275–277, 287, 293
title of, 279, 290, 293, 309
topic of, 256, 257–260

"Works Cited," list of, 263, 281–283, 289, 308
Research questions, 251–252
and evaluating your sources, 276–277
and thesis, 260–262
and taking notes, 270
and searching the library, 264
Research thesis, 260–262, 275–277, 287, 293
Restrictive and nonrestrictive elements, 196, 197–198, 228. *See also* Nonrestrictive elements
punctuation of, 55, 47–75
Resumés, 334–337. *See also* Application letters and resumés
Reviews of related literature, 253, 257
Revision, 25–30 (checklist). *See also individual aspects of writing*
applying a checklist, 26–27
on essay examinations, 327–328
invention questions for, 26
peer review, 27
reading like your reader, 25
of research paper, 286–289 (checklists)
sample student papers, 28–29, 292–312
Rhetoric, 3. *See also* Audience; Purpose; Subject of discourse; Writer's role
of research reports, 255–258
Rhetorical classification of sentences, 205–206
rise, raise, 191
Role of writer. *See* Writer's role
Running head, 309–310
Run-on sentences, 197. *See* Fused sentences

-*s* as ending
for plural nouns, 54, 172–175

-*s* as ending, *(continued)*
  for plurals of numbers, 175
  for third-person singular present
    tense verbs, 47, 169, 175–176,
    212, 225, 236
Salutation in business letters, 329
Sample student research paper, 292–
  312
Sanger, Margaret, 15–16
scarcely, 198
Seasons, 61–62
Secondary evidence, 253
Secondary research, 252–254
secondly, 108
Semicolons, 198–199
  in compound sentences, 77, 83–
    84
  misused, 69, 198–199
  and quotation marks, 190
Sentence faults. *See specific fault*
Sentence fragments. *See* Fragments
Sentence outline, sample, 313–318
Sentence patterns, 199–201
  (checklist)
Sentence summary, 321
Sentences, 201–203
  capitalization of first word of, 61
  complex, 67, 80–81, 203–205
  compound, 83–84, 203
  compound-complex, 81, 204
  declarative, 204
  exclamatory, 104, 205
  fragments of. *See* Fragments (of
    sentences)
  fused, 112–113
  grammatical types of, 203–204
  imperative, 122, 145, 204
  interrogative, 188, 204
  patterns of, 202–204
  punctuation of, 103, 167, 169,
    187–188
  rhetorical types of, 204–205
  simple, 203, 212
  types of, 203–205
  variety of, 205–206
Sentence types, 203–205

Sentence variety, 205–206. *See also*
  Sentences
Sequence of tense, 227–228
  (checklist)
  with infinitives, 127–128
Series punctuation, 71
set, sit, 207
Sexist language. *See* Nonsexist
  language
shall, will, 207–208
Shifts, 207–211. *See also* Mixed
  constructions
  in mood, 210, 237
  in number, 208–209, 237
  in person, 169, 208, 237
  in progressive form, 236
  in tense, 209–210, 236
  in voice and subject, 210–211, 237
Ship names, italics for, 131
Short story titles, 189, 230
should of, 157, 211
Simile, 108, 211
simple, simplistic, 211
Simple sentences, 204, 211
since, 211
Singular, 152, 212 (checklist). *See
  also* Mass nouns; Number;
  Plural
  and subject-verb agreement, 46–
    50
  and pronoun-antecedent agree-
    ment, 44–46
sit, set, 206
Slang, 6, 95, 212–213, 288
Slash, 213
*some body, somebody; some one,
  someone,* 213
someplace, somewhere, 213
some time, sometime, sometimes,
  213
sort of, 133
Source materials. *See also* Research;
  Research paper
  bibliographies of, 261, 262–263
  and common knowledge, 255,
    275, 300

in critiques, 323–324
documentation of, 280–286, 293–308, 310–311
encyclopedias as, 261, 265
evaluation of, 276–277, 296, 323
integrating into research paper, 277–278, 287–288, 296, 310–311
primary evidence as, 253–254
secondary evidence as, 253–254
Spacecraft, italicizing names of, 131
Spatial organization, 15–16, 20
key connecting words for, 16
Specialized dictionaries, 265
Specialized encyclopedias, 265
Specialized indexes, 267
specially, 102
Specific to general organization, 21
Specific words, 114–115
Spell checkers, 31, 119, 214
Spelling, 30, 214–217
of compound words, 84–85
of contractions, 54, 88–89
and computer spell-checkers, 31, 214
dictionary as an aid to, 96–97
homonyms, 31, 119
improvement through reading, 215–216
misspelled words, common, 139–142 (checklist)
plurals, 34–35, 172–176
of possessive nouns, 53–54
with prefixes, 84, 179
rules for, 215–217
with suffixes, 84, 215–217, 223
Split infinitives, 128, 217
Standard English, 217
States and countries, abbreviations of, 38, 247–248 (checklist)
Statistics, 24, 105
Story titles, quotation marks for, 189
Student writing, samples of, 28–29, 32–33
outline of, 313–318
research paper, 292–312

Subject complements, 80, 134–135, 217–218
and pronoun case, 63–65
and subject-verb agreement, 49
Subjective (nominative) case. *See* Case
Subject line
in business letter, 329
in memorandum, 332–333
Subject of discourse, 6–7, 23, 27
in research papers, 257, 260–262, 275–276, 278, 287
in business correspondence, 329–332
Subject of infinitive, 64, 127, 211
Subject of sentence, 165, 201–203, 218–219 (checklist)
and case, 63–64
in clauses, 67, 124
compound, 48
and dangling modifiers, 91–93
and faulty predication, 143
implied, 205
and sentence patterns, 200–202 (checklist)
separated from verb by comma, 74
and shifts with voice, 210–211
verb agreement with, 46–50. *See also* Agreement of subjects and verbs
Subject-verb agreement. *See* Agreement of subjects and verbs
Subjunctive mood, 145, 219
Subordinate (dependent) clauses, 219–221
adjective, 39, 81, 194, 220
adverb, 42, 80, 220
in complex sentences, 80–81, 203–204
in compound-complex sentences, 81, 204
elliptical, 91, 220
noun, 81, 151, 194, 220–221
punctuating, 70–71, 74–76, 197–198

Subordinate clauses, *(continued)*
  relative, 66, 109, 184–185, 193–198
  as restrictive and nonrestrictive
    elements, 196–197
  and subordinating conjunctions,
    86–87 (checklist)
Subordinating conjunctions, 86–87
    (checklist), 143, 220–221
  and subordinate clauses, 220–222
Subordination, 221–222. *See also*
    Clauses; Phrases
  excessive, 222
  for sentence variety, 205–206
subsequently, 88
such as, 57
Suffixes, 215–217, 222
Summaries, 321–322
  compared with abstracts, 321–322
  and conciseness, 321
  in critiques, 323
  documentation of, 280
  and essay examinations, 324–327
  in research papers, 272–274, 278
  sample, 322
  sentence expressing main point in,
    321
Superlative forms
  of adjectives, 41–42
  of adverbs, 43
supposed to, used to, 222–223
sure, surely, 223
Swift, Jonathan, 21
Syllables, 96, 120
Synonyms
  and coherence, 279
  and dictionaries, 97

Tag questions, 188–189, 223
take, 60
Television programs
  italics for titles of, 131
  quotation marks for titles of
    episodes of, 189
Tenses of verbs, 224–228 (checklist),
    235, 291

  past perfect tense, uses of, 226
  present tense, uses of, 226, 291,
    324
  progressive forms, use of, 163, 226
  with quoted material, 291, 324
  shifts in, 208, 236
  sequence of, 227–228 (checklist)
  summary of, 224–225 (checklist)
Testimony, 104–105
than, then, 65, 229
that, omitted, 196, 222
that, which, 228
  commas preceding, 76
the, 37, 55–57, 229
their, there, they're, 229
theirselves, themselves, 192–193,
    229
Theme, 3. *See also* Essay
then, 228
there, 229
Thesis, 13–14
  assertion in, 13
  and coherence, 24
  informative, 14, 261–262
  and essay development, 13, 228
  and essay examinations, 327–328
  persuasive, 14, 261–262
  placement of, 14, 23, 293
  questions leading from topic to,
    13 (checklist)
  in research paper, 260–262, 287,
    293
  subject of, 13
  tentative research, 260–262
thirdly, 108
this, ambiguous use of, 183
till, until, 229
Time
  as a method of organization, 15,
    19–20
  transitions to signal, 15, 20, 231
Time of day, 68, 154
Title on library catalog cards, 268–
    269
Title, writer's, 27, 229, 279, 290,
    293, 309

Titles of works
  in APA documentation, 283–286
  articles in, 189, 230
  capitalization, 61, 229
  and critiques, 323–324
  italics, 131, 230
  and library catalog cards, 268–269
  in MLA documentation, 280–283
  in periodicals indexes, 266–267
  and pronoun reference, 183
  quotation marks for, 189, 229–230
  and working bibliography cards,
    262–263
to, too, two, 230
Tone. *See also* Voice of Writer
  in application letters, 334
  in business letters, 328
  in critiques, 324
  in introductions and conclusions,
    23–24
  in memorandums, 332
  in research papers, 258, 278, 288
  and shifts in, 24
Topic sentence, 24, 327
Topics (subjects) for writing
  discovering, 8–13
  overworked, 258
  research, 252, 257, 258–260
  and thesis, 13
toward, towards, 230
Trade names, capitalization of, 62
Trains, italics for names of, 131
Transitional adverbs (conjunctive
    adverbs), 230–232 (checklist)
  for coherence, 15–20, 25, 279–280
  coordinating conjunctions,
    compared with, 78, 231
  with semicolons, 199
Transitional words and phrases, 15–
    20, 279. *See also* Transitional
    adverbs
Transitive verbs, 232, 238–239
Translations, documenting
  in APA style, 285
  in MLA style, 282
try and, try to, 232

two, 230
type, 133

Uncountable nouns. *See* Mass nouns
Underlining. *See* Italics
Understood subject, 204
uninterested, 98–99
unique, 232
Unnecessary commas, 73–76, 83
until, 232
upon, 157
U.S., 38
Usage, 3, 27, 98, 288, 290–291
  (checklist). *See also specific
    items*
used to, 222–223
us or *we,* 64

Variety in sentences, 205–206. *See
    also* Sentences
Verbal phrases, 233. *See also*
    Verbals
  as dangling modifiers, 91–93
  as fragments, 233
  gerund, 91–92, 115, 171
  and implied subjects, 92–93
  infinitive, 91–93, 126–127, 171–
    172
  participial, 91–92, 161–162, 171
Verbals, 233–234 (checklist). *See
    also* Gerunds; Infinitives;
    Participles
  as direct objects, 234, 240
Verb phrases, 234
Verbs, 234–241 (checklists)
  and agreement with subjects, 46–
    50
  in clauses, 67
  and compound predicates, 82
  form and meaning in, 235–236
  and fragments, 109, 237
  helping (auxiliary), 59, 117–119,
    144, 240

Verbs, *(continued)*
    infinitives and gerunds following, 240
    linking, 49, 134, 200 (checklist), 218, 238–240
    modals, 144, 163, 228, 239
    mood of, 145, 210
    and parts of speech, 166
    in predicates, 165, 178, 234
    regular and irregular, 213 (checklist), 238 (checklist)
    shifts in forms of, 209–211, 236–237
    tenses of, 225–229 (checklists), 235
    transitive and intransitive, 129, 232, 238–239
    voice of, 163, 241–242
Verb tenses. *See* Tenses of verbs
very, 240–241
Vocabulary. *See* Diction
Voice (active or passive), 163, 241–242
    appropriate use of, 242
    converting passive to active and active to passive, 241 (checklist)
    and dangling modifiers, 92–93
    and mixed constructions, 241
    shifts in, 210–211, 237
Voice of writer, 5–6, 255–256, 278

and expletives, 247
and inflated sentence structure, 147, 244 (checklist)
and passive voice, 246
and repetition, unintentional, 30, 196, 244–245
Word omissions, 56, 196, 222, 246
Word processor
    and note taking, 272
    and proofreading, 31
    and writing a research paper, 278
Words. *See also* Diction; Wordiness
    accurate and unambiguous, 27
    in proofreading, 31
    used as terms, 132
Working bibliography, 262–263
"Works Cited" list, 263, 281–283, 289, 308
"Works Consulted" list, 289
would of, 156, 246
Writer's credibility, 5–6, 26
    and application letters, 334–335
    and business correspondence, 328, 334
    and research papers, 255–256, 274, 276–278, 288, 291
Writer's role, 5–6, 255–256, 278
Writing process. *See* Drafting; Editing; Prewriting; Process of writing; Proofreading; Revision
Wrong or missing preposition. *See* Prepositions

way, ways, 242
well, 116
when, where, 143–144, 193
which, who, that, 242–243
who, whom, 243
who's, whose, 54, 64, 89, 243
will, shall, 206–207
Word choice. *See* Diction
Word divisions, 120
Wordiness, 30, 243–246
    with empty words and phrases, 192, 244 (checklist)

y, adding suffixes to words ending in, 216–217
Years, plural of, 54–55, 153–154
yet, 60
Young, Deneen, 28, 32
your, you're, 247
yourself, 192

ZIP code, 247–248 (checklist), 329–332

ESL Index

This index lists items of grammar and usage of particular interest to second-language speakers and writers. Please refer also to the main index beginning on page 338 and to the entries marked with the ▼ icon in "The Alphabetical Reference Guide."

Adjectives
  adverbs distinguished from, 40
  comparative and superlative
    forms of, 41–42 (checklist)
  coordinate, 40–41, 71–72
  cumulative, 40–41, 75
  demonstrative, 94
  descriptive in series, 41
  double comparative and superla-
    tive, 41–42
  forms of, 40
  placement of, 40, 41
  possessive, 63–66 (checklist), 95,
    176–178 (checklist)
Adverb clauses, 42, 80, 220
  with commas, 70, 75
  subordinating conjunctions to
    introduce, 86–87 (checklist)
Adverbs
  adjectives distinguished from, 43
  comparative and superlative
    forms of, 43 (checklist)
  functions of, 42 (checklist)
  transitional (conjunctive), 43–44
Agreement of pronouns and
    antecedents, 44–46, 212. *See*
    also Nonsexist language;
    Pronouns
  when collective nouns are
    antecedents, 45

compound antecedents, 45
  when generic nouns are anteced-
    ents, 45–46
  when indefinite pronouns are
    antecedents, 46
Agreement of subjects and verbs, 30,
    46–50
  with collective nouns, 48
  with compound subjects, 48
  with indefinite pronouns, 48–49,
    123
  with inverted sentence order, 49
  with intervening words, 49
  with linking verbs, 49
  mass nouns and count nouns, 47–
    48
  and noun phrases, 151
  with nouns of plural form and
    singular meaning, 50
Apostrophes, 53–55
  for contractions, 54
  misuse of, 175, 177–178. *See also*
    it's, its; who's, whose
  for possessive case of nouns, 53
    (checklist), 63, 85, 116, 124,
    152, 176–179
  special uses of, 54–55
Articles, 37, 55–57, 95, 230, 247
  summary of usage, 56–57

be
to ask questions, 188
forms of, 59 (checklist)
as helping verb, 59, 117–118, 239
as irregular verb, 59, 237–238
as linking verb, 134, 200, 218, 238
with passive voice, 241

Clauses
independent, 67, 124, 198, 211
relative, 193–195
subordinate, 67, 219–221
Commas, 69–73
in compound sentences, 70, 77–79, 83
with introductory sentence elements, 70
with nonrestrictive and parenthetical elements, 71, 148–149, 160–161, 196–197, 231
in series, 71
Commas, unnecessary, 73–76, 83
Comma splices, 77–79 (checklist), 84, 199, 232–233. *See also* Fused Sentences
Complex sentences, 80–81, 203–204
Compound sentences, 83–84, 203
commas in, 70, 77–79
semicolons, 77–79, 199
Conjunctive adverbs. *See* Transitional adverbs
Coordinating conjunctions, 76, 85–86 (checklist)
mixed constructions with, 87, 143
transitional adverbs distinguished from, 231
Count nouns and mass (noncount) nouns
articles with, 56, 90 (checklist)
compared, 135–137
and subject-verb agreement, 47–48

Dangling modifiers, 91–93
Demonstrative pronouns and

adjectives *(this, that, these, those),* 94
Diction, 95–96. *See also* Abstract words/concrete words; Connotation/denotation; Figures of speech; Wordiness
and clichés, 67–68
and colloquialisms, 68, 95, 288
and euphemisms, 95, 103
and idioms, 120–121
and informal usage, 68, 95, 212–213, 255, 288
and jargon, 95, 132
and level of formality, 5–6, 256, 288
nonsexist language, 45–46, 95, 149–150, 183, 291
nonstandard usage, 95, 97, 150
slang, 6, 95, 213–214, 288
vocabulary, 5, 255–256, 288
Direct objects, 155–156
do
in contractions, 99
for emphasis, 239
as helping verb, 117–118, 239
as irregular verb, 130
in negation, 239
in questions, 187–188, 239
Double comparatives and superlatives, 41–44

Endings of words
-d and *-ed,* 130, 193, 215, 236–237
-e, adding suffixes to words ending in, 216
-s. See -s as ending
Expletives *(it, there),* 104, 126, 129, 223, 229, 245

Fragments (of sentences), 109–111
acceptable, 111
appositives as, 55
clauses as, 67, 109, 184
and compound predicates, 83

correcting, 110–111
identifying, 110
incomplete thoughts, 111
long, 82
phrases as, 109, 115, 126, 162,
170, 180, 233
semicolons as cause of, 199
verb omissions as cause of, 237
Fused sentences (run–on sentences),
112–113. *See also* Comma
splices
Future perfect progressive, 225
Future perfect tense, 224–228
Future progressive, 225
Future tense, 224–228

Gerunds, 115–116, 233, 234, 240
as direct objects, vs. infinitives,
234
verbs followed by, 240
get, 116

have
as helping verb, 117–118, 239
as irregular verb, 130
and perfect tenses, 224–225, 239
Helping verbs (auxiliary verbs), 59,
117–119, 144, 163, 239. *See
also* Tenses of verbs

Idioms, 97, 120–121. *See also*
Diction
Independent clauses, 67, 124, 199,
211. *See also* Sentence patterns
and comma splices, 77–79
in compound sentences, 83
and fused sentences, 112–113
punctuating, 68–69, 70, 74, 199
sentence types, 80–82, 83–84,
203–204, 211
Indirect questions, 124–125
punctuating, 125, 187

Indirect quotations, 125–126
(checklist), 191
Infinitives, 127–128, 234–235
as direct objects, vs. gerunds, 235
sequence of tenses with, 127–128
split, 128, 218
subjects of, 64, 127, 210
verbs followed by, 241 (checklist)
Irregular verbs, 130–131 (checklist),
225 (checklist), 238 (checklist).
See also be; do; have; Regular
verbs
it's, its, 54, 64, 89, 132, 177–178

Mass nouns. *See* Count nouns and
mass (noncount) nouns
Misplaced modifiers, 30, 138–139.
See also Dangling modifiers
Mixed constructions, 87, 142–144.
See also Shifts
active and passive voice, 241–242
coordinating and subordinating
conjunctions, 87
Modals, 118, 144, 163, 206–208,
228, 239
Mood of verbs, 145
shifts in, 209

Negative constructions, 146–147
Noncount (mass) nouns. *See* Count
nouns and mass (noncount)
nouns
Nonrestrictive elements, 148–149,
195
punctuation of, 55, 71, 93
not vs. no, 146–147
Noun phrases, 152
Nouns, 151–152
with adjectives, 40–42
plurals of, 152, 172–175. *See also*
Plurals
types of, 152
Number, 47, 52, 94, 153, 172–175,
212
shifts in, 207–208

Parallelism, 30, 157–158. *See also* Coordination
Participles, 162 (checklist), 233–234 (checklist)
  as adjectives, 40
  dangling, 91–93, 161
  present vs. past, 164
  as sentence fragments, 162
  as verb parts, 163
Passive voice, 163, 241–242
  and mixed constructions, 241, 242
  shifts in, 210–211, 237
Past perfect tense, 224–228 (checklists), 235
  uses of, 226
Past progressive, 225 (checklist), 226, 235, 236
Past tense verbs, 225 (checklist), 227–228 (checklist), 235
Perfect tenses of verbs, 224–228, 234–235
Plurals, 152, 172–176. *See also* Number; Singular
  of compound words, 84
  and proper nouns, 54, 175
Possessive case, 63–66 (checklist), 176
  with apostrophes, 53 (checklist), 176
  of compound words, 85
  and gerunds, 116
  and pronoun antecedents, 52
  and pronoun reference, 182
  of pronouns, 54, 63–64 (checklist), 89, 124, 176–178
Prepositions, 180–181 (checklist)
  as idioms, 121, 181
  objects of, 156
  as parts of speech, 166
  phrase modifying the right word, 179
Present participles, 117, 162–164 (checklist), 224, 233, 237–239 (checklist)
Present tense, 224–228 (checklists), 234–239

  in indirect quotations, 125–126
  uses of, 226
Pronoun reference, 30, 94, 182–183

Questions, 188–189, 200, 207
  indirect, 124–125
  interrogative words, 66, 129, 185, 187
  tag, 187–188, 223
  yes/no, 188
Quotations, 191, 272–273, 280, 287–288
  commas with, 72
  indirect, 125–126 (checklist), 188, 191

Reference. *See* Pronoun reference
Relative clauses, 66, 184–185, 193–197 (checklist), 220–222, 243–244
  double object in, 194

-s as ending
  for plural nouns, 54, 172–175
  for plurals of numbers, 175
  for third-person singular present tense verbs, 47, 169, 174–175, 212, 224, 236
Sentences, 200–202
  complex, 67, 80–81, 203–205
  compound, 83–84, 204
  compound-complex, 81, 204
  interrogative, 188, 204
  negative, 146–147
  punctuation of, 103, 167, 169, 186–187
  simple, 203, 211
  subject-verb agreement in. *See* Agreement of subjects and verbs

Shifts, 207. *See also* Mixed constructions
in mood, 209, 237
in number, 207–208, 237
in person, 169, 207, 237
in progressive form, 236
in tense, 208–209, 236
in voice and subject, 209–210, 237
Singular, 152, 212 (checklist). *See also* Mass nouns; Number; Plural
and subject-verb agreement, 46–50
and pronoun-antecedent agreement, 44–46
Spelling, 30, 214–217
of compound words, 84–85
of contractions, 54, 88–89
and computer spell-checkers, 31, 214
dictionary as an aid to, 96–97
homonyms, 31, 119
improvement through reading, 214–216
misspelled words, common 139–142 (checklist)
plurals, 34–35, 172–176
of possessive nouns, 53–54
with prefixes, 84, 178
rules for, 215–217
with suffixes, 84, 215–217, 222
Subject of sentence, 218–219 (checklist)
and dangling modifiers, 91–93
and faulty predication, 143
and shifts with voice, 209–210
verb agreement with, 46–50
Subordinating conjunctions, 86–87 (checklist)
in mixed constructions, 143
and subordinate clauses, 219–221

Subordination, 221–222
excessive, 222
in mixed constructions, 143
for sentence variety, 205–206

Tenses of verbs, 225–229 (checklist), 235, 291. *See also individual tenses*
sequence of, 227–228 (checklist)
shifts in, 208, 236
summary of, 225–226 (checklist)
there, beginning sentences with, 104, 229
Transitional adverbs (conjunctive adverbs), 231–233 (checklist)
coordinating conjunctions compared with, 78, 231
with semicolons, 231

Verbs, 234–241 (checklists)
agreement with subject, 46–50
form and meaning, 235–236
helping (auxiliary), 59, 117–119, 144, 239
infinitives and gerunds following, 240
linking, 49, 134, 200 (checklist), 218, 238–239
modals, 144, 163, 228, 239
in predicates, 165, 178, 234
regular and irregular, 212 (checklist), 238–239 (checklist)
shifts in forms of, 208–210, 236–237
tenses of, 225–228 (checklists), 235
transitive and intransitive, 129, 232, 238–239
voice of, 163, 241–242

Correction Symbols

ab	abbreviation error	⊙	period needed
ad	adjective/adverb error	?	question mark needed
agr	agreement error	!	exclamation point error
ap	apostrophe error	,	comma error
awk	awkward construction	;	semicolon error
ca	case error	:	colon error
cap	use capital letter	" "	quotation marks error
cit	error in source citation	--	dash error
coh	coherence needed	( )	parentheses error
coord	coordination error	[ ]	brackets error
cs	comma splice	. . .	ellipsis error
d	diction, word choice	/	slash error
dev	needs development	*rep*	needless repetition
dm	dangling modifier	*shift*	shift error
emph	needs emphasis	*sl*	avoid slang
frag	sentence fragment	*sp*	spelling error
fs	fused sentence	*subord*	subordination error
hyph	hyphenation error	*sxt*	use nonsexist language
ital	italic/underlining error	*t*	tense error
lc	use lower case letter	*trans*	transition needed
mx	mixed construction	*us*	usage error
mm	misplaced modifier	*vb*	verb error
num	number use error	*vb agr*	verb agreement error
¶	new paragraph	*var*	variety needed
no ¶	no new paragraph	*w*	wordy
//	faulty parallelism	*ww*	wrong word
pl	plural error	*x*	obvious error
pred	faulty predication	^	insert
pn agr	pronoun agreement error	∿	transpose
pn ref	pronoun reference error	ꝗ	delete
p	punctuation error	??	unclear or illegible